S0-BNW-457

FLORIDA STATE
UNIVERSITY LIBRARIES

JUN 21 1996

TALLAHASSEE, FLORIDA

FDR
and
HARRY

FDR
and
HARRY

Unparalleled Lives

Robert Underhill

PRAEGER

Westport, Connecticut
London

Library of Congress Cataloging-in-Publication Data

Underhill, Robert.
    FDR and Harry : unparalleled lives / Robert Underhill.
      p. cm.
    Includes bibliographical references and index.
    ISBN 0–275–95420–X (alk. paper)
    1. Roosevelt, Franklin D. (Franklin Delano), 1882–1945.
2. Truman, Harry S., 1884–1972. 3. Presidents—United States—
Biography. 4. United States—Politics and government—1933–1945.
5. United States—Politics and government—1945–1953. I. Title.
E807.U53   1996
973.917′0922—dc20   95–40284
   [B]

British Library Cataloguing in Publication Data is available.

Copyright © 1996 by Robert Underhill

All rights reserved. No portion of this book may be
reproduced, by any process or technique, without the
express written consent of the publisher.

Library of Congress Catalog Card Number: 95–40284
ISBN: 0–275–95420–X

First published in 1996

Praeger Publishers, 88 Post Road West, Westport, CT 06881
An imprint of Greenwood Publishing Group, Inc.

Printed in the United States of America

The paper used in this book complies with the
Permanent Paper Standard issued by the National
Information Standards Organization (Z39.48–1984).

10 9 8 7 6 5 4 3 2 1

For Sue and Sandy—in lieu of dollars

All the world's a stage,
And all the men and women merely players;
They have their exits and their entrances;
And one man in his time plays many parts,
His acts being seven ages. At first the infant,
Mewling and puking in the nurse's arms.
And then the whining school-boy, with his satchel
And shining morning face, creeping like snail
Unwillingly to school. And then the lover,
Sighing like a furnace, with a woeful ballad
Made to his mistress' eyebrow. Then a soldier,
Full of strange oaths and bearded like the pard,
Jealous in honour, sudden and quick in quarrel,
Forever seeking the bubble reputation
Even in the cannon's mouth. And then the justice,
In fair round belly with good capon lined,
With eyes severe and beard of formal cut,
Full of wise saws and modern instances;
And so he plays his part. The sixth age shifts
Into the lean and slipper'd pantaloon,
With spectacles on nose and pouch on side,
His youthful hose well saved, a world too wide
For his shrunk shank; and his big manly voice,
Turning again toward childish treble, pipes
And whistles in his sound. Last scene of all,
That ends this strange eventful history,
Is second childishness and mere oblivion,
Sans teeth, sans eyes, sans taste, sans everything.

—William Shakespeare, *As You Like It*,
II, vii, 139–66.

FDR Delivering Fireside Chat at the end of the Banking Holiday, March 12, 1933. *Courtesy of the Franklin D. Roosevelt Library.*

President Harry Truman in December on a morning stroll. *Courtesy of the Harry S. Truman Memorial Library.*

Contents

Acknowledgments

The idea for this book was distilled through several decades of teaching even though the actual writing did not begin until three years ago. However, no book is published without assistance, and giving full acknowledgment to all who have helped or encouraged this one would be impossible.

I will always be indebted to several generations of students, undergraduate and graduate, who enlivened my classes with friendly challenges that kept a damper on pedant aloofness. Faculty colleagues at Iowa State University and elsewhere likewise have guided and sometimes tested my assertions.

The Iowa State University Research Foundation assisted in financing an initial trip to Hyde Park, New York. In addition to the staff at the Franklin D. Roosevelt Library there, other archivists have given me their fullest cooperation. I am particularly grateful to the dedicated staff under the direction of Dr. Benedict Zobrist at the Harry S. Truman Library in Independence, Missouri. During frequent and extended study at the Truman Library, Dr. Zobrist, Lenore Bradley, Dennis Bilger, Pauline Testerman, Elizabeth Safly, and others were without fail efficient and helpful in the preparation of this manuscript as well as two former ones for earlier books.

In commenting upon presidential libraries, I should add a personal observation. In this age when it is popular to criticize politicians and government, we ought not forget that for every instance of bad judgment or malfeasance there are thousands of conscientious, hard-working government employees who are no different from the rest of us. Without the paper trail left by such key figures as Morgenthau and Ickes from the Roosevelt years or Acheson and Elsey from the Truman era, intensive primary research would be impossible.

In addition to assistance at the two presidential libraries cited, I am indebted to innumerable persons on the staff of the William R. and Ellen S. Parks Library at Iowa State University. Joan Mueller in particular has been consistently helpful in providing a secure place for study and my materials.

I am indebted also to John D. Eades, Senior Editor, and other editors and staff at Greenwood Publishing Group who have made publication of this book an exciting, cooperative enterprise.

Finally, thanks go to Sue Mills and Sandy Ryan—my daughters—who have waited more or less patiently for the book to emerge. Without their continuing interest and encouragement it could not have been written.

FDR
and
HARRY

PART I

FOUR EARLY AGES

Chapter 1

Entrances

At first the infant,
Mewling and puking in the nurse's arms.
—William Shakespeare, *As You Like It*,
II, vii, 143–44.

On the night of January 30, 1882, in Hyde Park, New York, a proud father wrote in his diary: "At quarter to nine my Sallie had a splendid large baby boy. He weighs 10 lbs., without clothes."

Two years later and 1,300 miles to the west in Lamar, Missouri, another equally proud father celebrated the birth of his first son by planting a tree in the front yard of the small white frame house he recently had purchased for $685. The entire house measured all of 20 feet by 28 feet, only slightly larger than the living room in the Hyde Park home.

Franklin Roosevelt and Harry Truman were born during a decade that introduced to the world other boys destined to play important roles in history. In West Branch, Iowa, a boyish Herbert Hoover went skinny-dipping under the willows down by the railroad bridge, used bent pins and butcher string to catch green sunfish, and picked potato bugs for a penny a hundred. In the year of Franklin Roosevelt's birth, Winston Churchill was an eight-year-old youth having trouble with schoolwork.

In that decade in Georgia—not the American state, but a province marking the southern boundary of the Soviet Union—Josef Dzhugashvili, son of a peasant cobbler, was a pockmarked boy living in a leaky adobe hut and growing up in a land seared by national strife; the world would come to know him as Joseph Stalin.

In central Italy, Benito Mussolini, son of a socialist blacksmith, slept on a sack of corn leaves. He later was sent away to school, where he ate at third-class tables before being expelled at the age of eleven.

Three years before the decade ended, in a small northern Austrian town near the German border, was born a child who turned into a moody, introspective young man with ambitions for becoming an artist. At fifteen he was orphaned, but he would serve in the German army and win the Iron Cross, an unusually high decoration for a mere corporal. Few people could understand his complex personality but, from 1933 until his death in a bunker outside Berlin in 1945, the words and actions of Adolph Hitler shook the world.

Years later history would remember Franklin Roosevelt and Harry Truman in part because of the ways in which they met the world crises created by these diverse leaders.

In America the 1880 decade saw the first centennial of the United States as a nation—a time when the young country was expanding westward. Population was slightly below 50 million—less than one-fifth of what it is today—and the present states of Arizona, New Mexico, the Dakotas, Oklahoma, Utah, Idaho, Washington, Wyoming, and Montana were territories yet to be homesteaded.

The 1880s was an age of moguls—an age that displayed poverty and wealth, unrest and stability—an age when thousands of unemployed workers searched for jobs, bread, and shelter while a few fortunate others built half-million-dollar yachts and sumptuous mansions. Horatio Alger's rags-to-riches writings encouraged entrepreneurs, and mainly because of vast natural resources and unsettled territories there was just enough evidence to advance his thesis.

The Scottish immigrant Andrew Carnegie, Colossus of Pittsburgh, had amassed millions of dollars through manufacturing steel, and Cornelius Vanderbilt had made a fortune in steamboats. Vanderbilt was the first to foresee possibilities for huge railroad combinations, and mainly through those far-reaching enterprises he had garnered ever more financial power. His descendants kept adding to their founder's enormous wealth.

The Vanderbilts lived in a fifty-four-room Renaissance mansion a few miles to the north of where Franklin Roosevelt was born, but despite the wealth started by Cornelius and enlarged by his son W. H. Vanderbilt, Franklin's father would always consider the Vanderbilts as newcomers yet to be accepted in the best levels of society.

Vanderbilts, Carnegies, Morgans, Rockefellers, Astors, Pullmans, Westinghouses, Goulds, and Harrimans, as well as families slightly below them on the economic ladder, held fast to the laissez-faire concept, which they maintained was for the good of the country. If the federal government would only keep its hands off industrialists, financiers, railroad builders, brokers, and investors—all those whose businesses were being allowed to wax and grow to undreamed-of proportions—then others would survive and perhaps prosper.

For many Americans, however, the economic picture was not so rosy. In agricultural regions farmers were shackled by soaring interest rates and exorbitant charges demanded by railroads for taking crops to market. The average income of eleven million out of the twelve million American families was slightly less than $400 a year, and in Eastern cities were slums, sweatshops, crowded tenements, and plenty of unemployed workers. Labor was cheap, and the propertied classes wanted to keep it that way.

In New York State the Delano and Roosevelt families had no firsthand knowledge of such poverty. The first Roosevelt—Claes Martenszen van Roosevelt—came from Holland to New Amsterdam in 1613. On the Delano side, Philippe de la Noy Delano, a Flemish seafarer, settled around New Bedford, Massachusetts, not long afterward.

The descendants of these two progenitors married so consistently with English families in New England that future generations would become ever more English in orientation and outlook. Warren Delano, Sara Delano's father, had taken the sizable fortune he had made in China and returned to the United States where he invested it wisely in coal and other securities. At his death, Sara, who by that time was Franklin's mother, inherited more than a million dollars.[1]

Isaac Roosevelt, Franklin's great-great grandfather, founded a successful sugar refining business, and his son James (born in 1760), after a failed attempt at gentleman farming in Harlem, had been the first of the Roosevelt line to settle on the banks of the Hudson. It was he who established the family estate in Dutchess County, a comfortable distance up the Hudson River from New York City. The elder James died in 1847, leaving a son also named James (1828–1900), and it was this James who became Franklin's father.

The second James Roosevelt, after a short stint at Harvard Law School, had returned to Hyde Park in 1867 and purchased a home called Springwood, where he devoted himself to investments and lived a quiet life of rural dignity. He paid $40,000 for the house and its accompanying 110 acres of "water lots" worked by tenant farmers. The house would be remodeled many times, and the family holdings would grow to 1,300 acres by the time Franklin was born.

James' first wife, Rebecca Howland, died in 1876, and the marriage had produced a son, Rosy, almost the same age as Warren Delano's daughter, Sara. However, it was the widower, not Rosy, who courted and won Sara's hand; their wedding united two of the area's oldest families.

A tall man with mutton chop whiskers, James Roosevelt bred trotting horses and collected a famous herd of Alderney cattle that he continually crossed with Jerseys and Guernseys. He admired British nobility, took numerous trips to health spas in Germany and Austria, hunted grouse in Scotland, and was regarded as a pillar of New York society.

James eschewed politics as not quite befitting a gentleman, but he did fulfill a squire's obligation to the village of Hyde Park, where he was a volunteer fireman, warden and vestryman of his church, a town supervisor, and president of a small railroad. Because of this last-named position, he was entitled to a private railroad car, the "Monon," which he could take to any part of the country. Such was the style and substance of the fifty-two-year-old widower that Sara Delano, then aged twenty-six, married in 1880.

Franklin was the only child the couple would have. His mother later insisted that both she and the baby almost died in childbirth because of an overdose of chloroform.

James Roosevelt wrote that his wife, having lain in labor for more than twenty-four hours, "(poor child) . . . has had a very hard time." Perhaps that "hard time" helped explain the indestructible, lasting bond between this mother and her child. Franklin's well-being became the central object of Sara's life, and she would record nearly every detail of his development. She once described the new arrival:

> [He] . . . was plump, pink, and nice . . . born right here in this house; of course—one never went to hospitals in those days . . . I realize how much more scientific hospital care is, but I am old-fashioned enough to think it's nicer for a baby to be born in his own home. I've passed the door of that sunny, upstairs room many hundreds of times in my long life, and oh! so often I've remembered that there my son first saw the light of day . . . I used to love to bathe and dress him . . . Franklin's early care would, I am afraid, be considered very unscientific, by modern standards. We never had a formula.[2]

The infant had no need of a formula during his first year, for Sara breastfed him throughout that period. Even though a nurse had been hired a few days after the baby arrived, she proved to be unsatisfactory and was dismissed only to be replaced by Helen McRorie, a gentle, experienced Scottish woman whom Franklin called "Mamie" as soon as he learned to talk. Mamie tended her charge for the first nine years of his life.

Everything about Franklin's infancy was planned to make him happy and feel loved. His parents took him with them when they went to visit neighbors, to New York City, or for carriage rides along the Hyde Park roads.

Sara became the most doting of mothers, and reluctant to see her baby grow older, she kept him in dresses and long curls until he was nearly six years old. Only then did she soften enough to allow him to wear miniature sailor suits and to have his hair cut short like other boys his age. On the day those long curls were shorn, Sara swept them up from the floor and put them away for safekeeping.

Even though Franklin would always consider Hyde Park his home, his parents rarely stayed there long. In 1884, for example, when the boy was only two the family went often to New York City, lived most of the year in England, and actually spent only four months of that year at Springwood. Every summer after he was three, the parents took their young son with them to Campobello, a ten-mile-long rockbound island in Canadian waters just off the coast of Maine.

All accounts picture Franklin Roosevelt as a bright, handsome, and happy infant. Constantly in the company of an adoring, watchful mother and surrounded by servants, he entered a boyhood that had few rivals if measured by comforts, travel, security, formal training—all the privileges enjoyed at the time by the few families with wealth and high social position.

About the only way in which the childhoods of Franklin Roosevelt and Harry Truman were similar is that they occurred at the same time.

Truman was a thorough Midwestern creation, and his career can be fully understood only within the context of the geography and history of that region. During this decade of the 1880s there still were pockets of old loyalties, and Truman's parents were among those who could not easily forget former animosities. A measure of the fierce sectionalism aroused by the Civil War had faded, however, and was beginning to be replaced by other attitudes and opinions.

Throughout the Midwest an ever-widening gap had opened between the titans of finance and the average citizen. Voices of protest—voices that within ten years would be identified as Populists'—echoed up and down the Mississippi and Missouri River basins. Harry's parents and grandparents knew firsthand the frustrations and disappointments that stimulated the Populist movement.

In May the Missouri countryside is at its best, and it was in the spring of 1884 that Harry S. Truman was born. His parents, John and Martha Ellen Truman, were living in Lamar, Missouri, a pretty village which lies among the rolling hills of this Midwestern state. In such hamlets life then spread outward from the post office or the grocery store where farmers and town folk gathered to discuss crops, cracker-barrel politics, funerals, and births.

Truman's grandfather on his mother's side was Solomon Young, a man who had driven cattle and wagon trains across Western plains and through mountain passes in the years between 1840 and 1870. In later life he farmed successfully near the small community of Hickman's Mill in Jackson County, Missouri. As an area on the line between free and slave states, the entire locality suffered from the border wars of 1859 and 1860, the Civil War, and depredations of the roving bands of outlaws who came later.

Solomon's daughter, Martha Ellen—destined to become Harry Truman's mother—was eleven and twelve years old when the pillages occurred. She attributed them to Union forces and, understandably, remained a Confederate sympathizer all her life.

Small and vivacious, Martha Ellen Young had in her character the tough-fibered determination found in pioneers—a strong-willed person to whom frankness was a virtue, and evasions were sinful. Good and evil, heaven and hell, salvation and damnation—these were the eternal truths set forth in her Bible and rules enough for proper conduct.

Harry Truman's paternal grandfather, Anderson Shippe Truman, also farmed in Jackson County and seems to have been a mild-mannered man, proud of his Southern heritage. For a time, this grandfather lived with Truman's parents, but he died in 1887 when Harry was only three years old.

Harry's father, John Anderson Truman, was born in Jackson County in 1851 and spent most of his adult life as a farmer and livestock trader although his avocation of Democratic politics kept him almost equally occupied. Indeed, 1884 would prove to be a banner year for John because, in addition to his happiness with the birth of his son, he won a $75 bet on the election of Grover Cleveland over James Blaine. (There is a popular belief that in keeping with local tradition on the day of Truman's birth his father nailed a mule shoe over the door of his small home, but the story has never been substantiated.)

John Truman and Martha Ellen were childhood sweethearts who grew up together on the families' neighboring farms at Grandview. Martha Ellen was thirty-two-years old and had been married for two-and-a-half years when on the afternoon of May 8, 1884, her first son arrived. The boy was born in a bedroom off the parlor—a bedroom so small there was barely space for the bed. The new arrival did not receive much attention except among members of the immediate family and a few close friends and neighbors. The attending doctor was given a fee of $15 but did not bother to register the baby's birth at the county clerk's office until a month afterward.

The couple named their son Harry after Martha Ellen's brother, Harrison, and gave him the simple middle initial S.—an initial which could have been in honor of either grandfather, Solomon Young or Anderson Shippe Truman.[3]

Both by temperament and economic situations, John Truman found it hard to stay in one place for very long. While Harry was still an infant, John moved his family from Lamar to a farm just southeast of the village of Belton in Cass County, and here another boy, Vivian, was born in 1886. A year later the family moved in with Grandfather Solomon Young on his farm at Grandview, twenty-four miles south of Kansas City. As an inducement to his daughter and son-in-law, Solomon sold the couple forty acres from his own farm, and they acquired another eighty nearby. John and Martha Ellen Truman farmed here for three years, and their daughter, Mary Jane, was born on that homestead in 1889.

There is nothing in Truman's history to suggest that his early childhood was anything other than happy; on the contrary, the evidence is that he was born in a modest Midwestern home with loving and attentive parents. While not deprived of life's necessities, he enjoyed few of its luxuries. Moreover, considering the economic circumstances of the time and region, as well as the character of his mother, one can be certain that little Harry was judged by strict standards and seldom if ever pampered.

Chapter 2

School Boys

And then the whining school-boy, with his satchel
And shining morning face, creeping like snail
Unwillingly to school.

> —William Shakespeare, *As You Like It*,
> *II, vii, 146–47.*

FRANKLIN ROOSEVELT

Although Franklin Roosevelt's and Harry Truman's early lives were remarkably different, in one aspect they were similar: each in his own way was a "mama's boy."

Upon Franklin's arrival Sara Roosevelt's goal in life became the proper rearing of her child. Determined to protect her son from abrasions that might come as a result of contact with the roughness of the outside world, she built a shelter around him and patrolled it diligently.

For example, the boy was eight-and-a-half years old before he was allowed to bathe by himself. That happened on one of the rare weekends he was separated from Sara and was permitted to stay at Algonac, the home of his maternal grandparents. That very day Franklin wrote an exultant letter to his father telling of the newly found freedom: "Mama left this morning, and I am to take my bath alone!"[1]

There is no reason to suspect that Sara did not continue to be tub-side supervising her son's bath after he returned home; in fact, the evidence is that she followed the practice until he was sent to preparatory school. It was she who decided what family members the boy could visit, how long he could stay, and how he could spend his limited allowance. She also chose his friends and organized their play schedules.

Yet all evidence points toward Franklin's having had an abundantly happy childhood. There was no competition for attention at home, and as far as we know he was never severely punished. Largely due to his mother's constant protection, distresses and disappointments that sometimes confront growing children passed him by.

James Roosevelt took his son sledding, taught him to skate and to ride a fat Welsh pony named "Debbie," and let him at age six hold the wheel of the big yacht as it sailed off the shores of Campobello. Fifty-four-year-old James did his best to act like a young father, but it was Sara who directed the boy's life. Franklin never grew old enough to go out on a wet day without her reminding him to put on his rubbers.

Sara put her son on a tight schedule: breakfast at eight o'clock, lessons from a private tutor from nine until noon, an hour for play, then lunch followed by more lessons until four. Next came two hours of mother-approved games, supper at six, reading aloud at seven, and into bed by eight.

Franklin was taken to Europe for the first time when he was three, and thereafter he spent a few months of each year abroad. In the course of his boyhood, he had a series of nurses, governesses, and tutors—seven different ones by the time he was fourteen. He seems not to have been a particularly difficult assignment but was not above playing an occasional joke on the one in whose charge he had been placed.

An early victim of his pranks was a German-speaking nurse his parents hired while he was traveling with them in their annual tour of Europe during 1892. One afternoon while this particular nurse was downstairs, ten-year-old Franklin sneaked into her room and poured a generous amount of effervescent powder into the chamber pot under her bed. That night when she used the pot, the powder began its hissing roil, and in great distress the poor nurse rushed down the hall to awaken Sara and tell her of the alarming symptom.

Apparently, Sara and the nurse never figured out what had happened—at least, that was the version FDR promoted in later life. However, his father detected the prank and summoned Franklin into the smoking room for chastisement. Solemnity was difficult to maintain, however, and James laughingly dismissed the offender by saying, "Consider yourself spanked."[2]

The tutors Sara brought to Hyde Park were expected to drill her son in Latin, French, and German, with a smattering of European history, penmanship, and basic arithmetic. Such was the nature of Franklin's education until he was fourteen, at which time his mother enrolled him at Groton, a private school in Massachusetts that had an average roster of 110 boys drawn from families with economic and social status similar to the Roosevelts.

Despite his excellent tutoring at home, the young Roosevelt did not distinguish himself at Groton. His grades averaged only C (D was failing), and although he participated in football, baseball, hockey, golf, and tennis, he excelled in none of those sports. There is no evidence that he got into student mischief worthy of notice; nor is there any single event that might suggest the political career that lay ahead.

The four years of preparatory school, however, may have helped shape his basic attitudes toward social and moral problems. The rector at Groton was Endicott Peabody, a young clergyman who was something of a Christian socialist. Peabody worried about the needy and underprivileged in society, and he may have implanted similar concerns in the mind of young Franklin. The pupil also was mightily impressed with Peabody's skill in reading aloud. The rector read to his students every evening, usually from the Bible, and liked to interpret orally selected passages from great literature.

From Groton, Roosevelt went to Harvard, following the path of other boys in his economic and social class. Although he undertook a varied program of studies at the university, his primary academic interests there were history and government. During his sophomore year he took a one-semester course in public speaking, and throughout the year 1902–1903 he studied public address under George P. Baker, the most famous teacher of speech in the country at the time.

At Harvard, Roosevelt also became interested in journalism, advancing in student ranks from reporter, to editor, to managing editor, and finally to presidency of the *Crimson*, the university's newspaper. His Harvard record was an active one but again only average scholastically.

After graduating from Harvard, he went to Columbia University, where he studied law from 1904 to 1907. Upon gaining admission to the bar of New York State, he left that school without graduating and joined a well-established law firm. Roosevelt termed his three-year practice of law with the firm "more or less casual" and in 1910 opted for active politics.

HARRY TRUMAN

If Franklin Roosevelt's boyhood was princely, Harry Truman's was hardscrabble.

Martha Ellen Truman, Harry's mother, like Sara Roosevelt, was a strong-willed woman. Young or old, Harry strove to please her. As a boy he cheerfully ran her errands, dutifully carried out his daily chores, did his schoolwork to her satisfaction, and combed his little sister's hair—forever seeking his mother's approval. The mother's influence on Harry was profound, and the son never attempted to deny it.

In 1890, when Harry was six years old, his father had amassed enough money to buy a house in Independence, Missouri—a town which then must have seemed quite large to the boy because 6,000 people lived there. The move from the farm at Grandview permitted John Truman, Harry's father, to enlarge his interest in buying and selling mules, but primarily it meant better schooling for the children. Years later, Harry's daughter Margaret asserted that better schooling was the prime reason for the family's move:

Mamma Truman [Martha Ellen] was the moving spirit behind the family decision to set up housekeeping in Independence. They had been living on the Young farm for three or four years, but the country schools in nearby Grandview were decidedly inadequate, compared to those in Independence.[3]

Martha Ellen had attended a Baptist "female academy" near Lexington, Missouri, and had developed a taste for literature and the piano. She taught the basics of the instrument to her young son, and at the age of thirteen he began taking regular music lessons from a teacher in Independence. Those lessons continued twice weekly until Harry was seventeen; in the early years especially he was conscientious in his daily practice.

Harry's general education came mostly from his extensive but unsystematic reading. The town had a small library, and for many years it had no more faithful patron than this quiet, studious little boy dressed not in the common overalls but in knickers and a clean shirt and tie.

He had begun wearing glasses when he was eight. His observant mother had noticed the trouble her son was having in making out objects he should be seeing and the difficulty he had in reading fine print. She took him to an oculist in nearby Kansas City who discovered that the boy's eyeballs were so flat that he was severely shortsighted. The eye doctor warned him about the danger of breaking the glasses and injuring his eyes, so Harry did not try to play ball or join rough games with other boys his age. No matter whether it was natural inclination or compensation for his sight impairment, he developed reading habits that would never leave him.

His favorite reading came from history. At home there was the red-backed four-volume set of biographies edited by Charles F. Horne, *Great Men and Famous Women*.[4] The set is extremely modest in size and detail when compared with modern collections, but the young Harry must have read each of the biographies many times. Their impact on him can be inferred partly by the frequent references he made to episodes and lives contained in the volumes.

Another book always within easy reach in the Truman home was the family Bible. The Bible was relevant to Truman's regular Sunday school lessons; it was the subject of frequent family discussions, and he liked the large type in which such Bibles were printed. On several occasions, he stated that by the time he was thirteen or fourteen years old he had read "our big old family Bible three times through."

The accounts of Truman's formal schooling are meager and consist mainly of scattered recollections given years later by his former teachers and classmates. The high school building in Independence burned to the ground in 1938 and all the early records were lost. It is known that Harry Truman was a punctual, dutiful student who graduated in 1901 when he was seventeen years old. He was one of eleven boys in a class of forty, and although well up in the class standing he did not capture any special academic honors; those went to his tall, lank friend, Charles Ross—a man Truman forty-four years later chose for his press secretary.

It cannot be said that Harry Truman's formal schooling was at all similar to that of Franklin Roosevelt or indeed as complete as that of many other statesmen with whom he would associate. While Truman was studying high school Latin in Independence, Roosevelt, whose entrance to the academy had been delayed two years because of tutoring and overseas traveling, was at Groton pursuing a curriculum that stressed Latin, Greek, English literature, and composition.

For Truman, wide reading and practical experience had to substitute for formal education. His high school teachers encouraged him in his reading, but nevertheless it and the study that accompanied it were largely self-motivated. The extensive reading begun in his youth and maintained throughout his life constituted an indirect but very important preparation for the role he was destined to play. Reading was not merely a pastime, but a source of inspiration and knowledge. Truman maintained it was the one great influence that nourished and sustained his interest in government and public service.

Chapter 3

Young Lovers

And then the lover,
Sighing like a furnace, with a woeful ballad
Made to his mistress' eyebrow.

—William Shakespeare, *As You Like It*,
II, *vii*, *147–49*.

FRANKLIN ROOSEVELT

Shakespeare's confinement of the lover to a young age was not entirely accurate in Franklin Roosevelt's case, for after he discovered the attractions of the opposite sex he was never again unaffected by them. Most assuredly he was not a rake in the pattern of others who have occupied the White House, but the evidence is irrefutable that FDR was not inexperienced with women and, in fact, was unfaithful to his wife throughout most of his adult life.

As an adolescent at Groton he had shown little interest in girls his own age, perhaps because it was a boys' school and there were few girls around. More likely, he was still so tied to his mother's apron strings that he felt it necessary to disparage young females who otherwise might have caught his attention. Knowing it would please Sara, he wrote to her that the ones he met were "pills" or "elephantine."

Franklin went to Harvard in the fall of 1900, where he spent four happy years under a more relaxed environment than any he hitherto had known. He majored in American political history and government, but again was only an average student, getting grades seldom above a B and failing several examinations. While his experiences as an undergraduate never meant as much to him as the ones in prep school, they greatly broadened his outlook. He lived at one of the most elite Gold Coast dormitories, Westmorly, and belonged to numerous organizations and clubs.

At that time he was a lanky, narrow-shouldered lad, a shade over six feet with darkening blond hair parted on the left and eyes rather closely set. At 146 pounds he was too light for football but went out for the freshman team anyway. He did not make the lowest of the scrub teams but did become an oarsman on one of the rowing clubs and also was chosen secretary of the glee club.

The big change came in his social life, which took a dramatic upswing. Formerly his contacts were mostly with older persons—persons to whom he showed impeccable manners and whom he strove hard to please. Now for the first time he was independent enough to move in circles with people his own age.

His mother had encouraged him to keep a diary, and he did that faithfully for three years. Although the entries are noticeably circumspect, perhaps because of Sara's prying eyes, from the diary we learn names of numerous young ladies with whom he teased and flirted. It is clear that while in college he led a very active social life, going often to mixed parties, staying out until three or four in the morning, dining at Boston's swankiest hotels, and drinking enough that he felt "like hell" the next morning.[1]

With his new friends he cheered at football games, danced at numerous balls, and attended concerts in Boston and New York. He kept a trotter and a light runabout for forays into Boston, and there was never a lack of invitations to dinners or parties. Between terms he journeyed to Hyde Park or the family home on Campobello.

One of the girls with whom Franklin had more than a casual relationship was Alice Sohier, a seventeen-year-old belle whose parents had a house at Beverly, an ocean resort fifteen miles northeast of Boston. The two met in the spring of 1902 and continued to see each other throughout that summer and early fall. Franklin escorted Alice to dinners, dances, parties, and attended swimming get-togethers at her home. By this time, he was an expert sailor, and one day he took Alice and her family sailing. His diary entry for July 8, 1902, reads: "We all landed and played tennis. Took the Sohiers, T.P.B. and Swain out for a good long sail to Marblehead in p.m. All dine at Sohiers . . . Alice confides in her Dr."

Often Franklin made entries in a private code, and the last sentence poses a puzzle. The following day's entry adds to the mystery, for it reads: "Worried over Alice all night. . . . Left Beverly at 6:30 A.M. Breeze as far as Thatcher's island. Lay off in five hours. Started engine and got to Portsmouth Harbor at 7."[2]

No one knows what Alice confided to her doctor or if the "Dr" was code for FDR himself. Nor is there any evidence that might explain why he "worried over Alice all night." The only other diary reference to her comes three months later on October 8, when Franklin jotted: "See Alice off on the COMMONWEALTH for Europe."

The *Commonwealth* was a packet running between Boston and New York that connected with Europe-bound ships. The relationship between Franklin and Alice obviously was important enough for him to take time off from a busy college schedule, but he gives no hint as to why Alice's parents sent her to Europe for an extended visit.

Speculations arose later. One was that Alice had a less beautiful sister who was coming out soon, and the parents did not want the younger girl to eclipse the older one's debut. Another involving Franklin more directly was that he had told Alice he wanted to have six children. She was turned off by that prospect because her doctor had warned that her anatomy was not the most suitable for childbearing.

A third possible explanation for Alice's departure is built around the theory that she might have been pregnant and that had been the reason for Franklin's worry. The extended European visit fits the pregnancy thesis, for if an abortion had been decided upon, Europe was the place to do it, away from relatives and a gossipy society.[3]

The fact is, however, that no one knows for sure what really caused the breakup between Franklin and Alice. He saw her only occasionally after her return late the following year, noting then that she was in poor health and had had her appendix removed. Years later he would write to a friend in Boston: "Once upon a time when I was in Cambridge I had serious thoughts of marrying a Boston girl and settling down in the Back Bay to spend the rest of my days . . . it was a narrow escape."[4]

Alice Sohier was not the only girl on Franklin's mind in that fall of 1902; he was growing ever more serious about another young woman, Anna Eleanor Roosevelt. This daughter of Theodore's younger brother Elliott, and, therefore, a distant cousin of Franklin's, was two years younger than he and had played with him in his Hyde Park home when he was only five years old.

Eleanor's mother had died when Eleanor was eight; her father, when she was ten, and thereafter the lonely girl became an orphan dependent on relatives who provided her with places to live but never a home. For more than a decade she was shunted from one private school to another, mostly abroad, but because the extensive Roosevelt families and her own Hall ancestors often traveled in similar circles she and Franklin had been together on several occasions.

In the fall of 1898, when Franklin was still a Groton student, he had been in Eleanor's company often enough to remark to his mother, "Cousin Eleanor has a very good mind."[5] That same year, at a Christmas party held in the home of Eleanor's aunt, Corinne Robinson, he asked the shy, pathetically dressed, fourteen-year-old Eleanor for a dance.

Four years later, when she returned to the United States from Allenswood, a finishing school on the outskirts of London, Eleanor made her debut to New York society at a ball held at the Waldorf-Astoria.

For the next year she was one of several teenage girls, including Uncle Theodore's daughter Alice, with whom Franklin exchanged flirtatious letters. One day during the summer of 1903, while enroute to her grandmother's home, Eleanor and Franklin met on the train. The meeting must have revived his interest in this cousin, for his diary began showing frequent references to Eleanor, E, Nell, or other pet names. The two were together frequently that fall, and in late November he asked her to marry him. She accepted despite personal misgivings as to why the handsome, debonair Franklin had chosen her.

Breaking the engagement news to Sara called for tact and planning because the announcement meant that the mother would have to yield her exclusive hold on her son as well as abandon plans she had made for their life together after he left college. It must not have been totally unexpected, therefore, when Sara pleaded with the couple to keep their engagement secret for at least a year; meanwhile, she would take Franklin on a cruise and the separation would let the two test how they really felt about each other.

Franklin and his fiancée agreed to the conditions, but the stratagem, if that is what is was, did not work. For more than a year Franklin and Eleanor played out the charade of being friendly cousins rather than plighted lovers. Their affections withstood the forced separations, however, and in December of 1904 their engagement was announced to the public.

They were married three months later in a widely reported occasion made notable by their famous name and the appearance of the bride's uncle. The ceremony began with the traditional wedding march and the president of the United States briskly descending the staircase with Eleanor on his arm. When Reverend Peabody, Franklin's former headmaster from Groton recruited for the occasion, asked, "Who giveth this woman?" it was the ebullient Theodore who boomed, "I do!"

The marriage joined two very strong but diverse characters. Notwithstanding the fact that they would become the most highly publicized couple in American history and despite tensions and animosities unknown to the public, the alliance survived for forty-five years. In the span of that time the couple would produce six children, one of whom died in infancy, and would attain unprecedented heights as public servants.

Every marriage has its problems, but this one had three that were especially challenging. First, there were traditions and alliances within the extensive Roosevelt, Delano, and Hall families that had to be kept under consideration at all times. Second, as Franklin's career inched upward his public persona loomed ever more important. Underneath these factors lay an undeniable third, namely, the ever-constant rivalry between Sara and Eleanor for Franklin's time and attention.

Circumstances would sorely test Eleanor's tolerance, and in the early years of marriage she was submissive to a degree which she later came to regard as disgraceful.

During World War I, while FDR was serving as assistant secretary of the Navy, an extramarital affair threatened to destroy his political future. The relationship developed slowly and was more than a youthful indiscretion or mere infatuation.

Frequently, when FDR was in Washington, Eleanor and the five children were at Campobello or with other family or friends. She had come to accept her husband's gregariousness which she recognized was often accompanied by what she thought were harmless flirtations. Moreover, her own public duties were growing rapidly.

In 1914 Eleanor hired Lucy Mercer, a young, attractive society girl whose father had died poor leaving mother and daughter in straitened circumstances. Lucy was efficient and did everything for the Roosevelt family. She was well-bred, intelligent, charming, wonderful with the children, and because of her background a natural for the "extra" woman at dinners and parties.

During the winter and spring of 1917 and 1918, FDR and Eleanor saw little of each other, and it was during this time that his romance with Lucy burst into full bloom. Franklin and Lucy were together so frequently and became so indiscreet about appearances that soon everyone of importance in Washington knew they were sweethearts.

In the middle of the summer, FDR left for Europe and returned in September sick with influenza and pneumonia. His sickness was not the main issue, however, for when Eleanor unpacked his bags she found a hefty packet of Lucy Mercer's revealing letters.

According to one of Eleanor's biographers, the "bottom dropped out"; the evidence confirmed her worst fears: her husband—the man in whom she had anchored all her hopes and who had helped pull her out of her own insecurity—was being unfaithful. Moreover, his partner in infidelity was a person she had considered a friend.[6]

Eleanor confronted her husband and told him she was prepared to grant him his freedom if that was what he really wanted; however, she had gained a stalwart ally in her mother-in-law. Sara was aghast at the prospect of a divorce in the family and made it clear to her son that unless he promised to quit seeing Lucy and to try to repair the damage done to his wife and children she would disinherit him.

Moreover, Eleanor displayed her own steely determination. Franklin had betrayed her trust. She was willing to grant a divorce or if he promised never to see Lucy again she would stand by him and keep up appearances for the sake of his political future. He could make the choice, but never again would she and her legal husband live together as man and wife.

It was a hard bargain, but realizing that a divorce would destroy his political career as well as the effect it would have upon his children, Franklin agreed to the terms. The immediate crisis was averted, and he returned to his political agenda.

FDR's unwavering support of the national leadership of his party led to his vice-presidential nomination on the losing Cox ticket in 1920. Despite that defeat, he attained countrywide exposure as a rising star in the Democratic party. His ambitious career was right on track!

The next year, however, fate dealt him a personal blow—a blow that would have felled a lesser man. A sudden and severe attack of polio at the Roosevelt summer home in Campobello left him apparently a hopeless invalid.

FDR's courage in overcoming this disaster proved to be as great as his ambition, for during the next seven years he fought his way back to health, used his leisure time for study and correspondence, and emerged from his forced retirement no longer just a likeable, wealthy playboy apt to be a political figurehead. Here was a man knowledgeable and deeply committed to his party's principles.

His comeback got its biggest boost at the Democratic National Convention in 1924 when he nominated New York governor Al Smith, a man he named "the happy warrior," for the presidency. Despite Roosevelt's oratorical triumph, his nominee did not win the nomination, but four years later Smith did get the nod, and the following month the Democrats chose FDR to succeed him as governor of the Empire State. Then in 1932, when the depression was at its lowest point, FDR was nominated and won the presidency in his own right.

Even after his polio attack and during his political ascendancy, however, FDR was never free from romantic involvements. In addition to his affair with Lucy Mercer, there were ever-present questions about his attachment to his personal secretary, Missy LeHand. The evidence linking FDR and LeHand romantically is not as direct as that which connected him with Lucy Mercer although his association with LeHand was far more constant.

Shortly after Roosevelt's vice-presidential run in 1920, Marguerite LeHand, whom everyone called "Missy," was hired as an assistant secretary. A very proficient stenographer, she also was an attractive, slender, twenty-one-year-old woman with a fair complexion and unusually beautiful blue eyes.

Missy contributed a decidedly feminine presence and soon became FDR's constant companion. As his personal secretary, she later would move into the White House, where there was no need to explain her presence. She accompanied him on numerous extended vacations, inspection trips, or to Warm Springs, Georgia, for rest, relaxation, and recuperation.

For nearly twenty-five years Missy proved to be a perfect companion for Franklin, monitoring his physical therapy, supplying humor to relieve daily problems and pressures, and sharing his sailing and fishing expeditions, card games, and other recreations.

In FDR's personal life informality was the rule. When Missy was with him on his boat, the *Larooco*, and they were cruising the Florida coast in 1924 she might be seen in her nightgown sitting on his lap chattering merrily away. Nor during his first term as president was it unusual for her to wander the halls of the White House at night clad only in a peignor.

Elliot, FDR's son, insisted that after the polio attack his father was still capable of physical intimacy, but the matter is relatively unimportant. Even if Missy was not FDR's mistress in a sexual sense she certainly became his surrogate wife by giving him warm companionship and moral support.

Eleanor accepted Missy probably because her husband's personal affairs no longer were of concern to her as long as he was discreet and did not cause her further ignominy. An exception occurred in the spring of 1944 when FDR arranged for Missy to visit him at Warm Springs. This time when Eleanor found out about the proposed trip she vetoed it, telling Missy that she, too, wanted to be present but would be busy for the next several weeks.

After that episode Missy LeHand never saw FDR again, and she passed away a few months later without being aware that he had named her as one of the beneficiaries in his will.

Nor did Lucy Mercer ever drop completely out of FDR's life. After the breakup with Franklin, she married Winthrop Rutherfurd, a fifty-six-year-old widower with five children. Winthrop Rutherfurd died in 1941 and, despite promises not to see Lucy, FDR did that numerous times. He arranged to have her present at his first inaugural and saw her whenever she visited her mother in Washington. He also visited her near her estate in Aiken, South Carolina. Moreover, on several occasions when Eleanor was away and her daughter Anna was presiding over the White House, it was arranged for Lucy to attend small, intimate social gatherings.

Six times during 1944, while Eleanor was out of town on wartime jaunts, FDR was driven to Georgetown in order to meet Lucy and bring her to the White House. It would have been much easier and less noticeable for Lucy to come on her own, but for some inexplicable reason FDR preferred to escort her himself.

By 1945 the years and pressures had taken their toll upon him. He had lost weight, his skin was discolored by liver spots, and his eyes were surrounded by dark purple shadows. To family and close friends it was a picture of a dying man.

In the first weeks of April, soon after an exhaustive trip to Yalta, he went to Warm Springs hoping to recuperate. Eleanor remained in Washington carrying out endless wartime duties. Knowing that he needed mental as well as physical relief, FDR's daughter Anna with assistance from other relatives arranged for Lucy Rutherfurd to join him.

Lucy brought with her an artist commissioned to paint a portrait of FDR. On April 12, 1945, Franklin was sitting for this painter and talking to his old friend and lover when suddenly he grasped his head and slumped forward in his chair.

Dr. Howard Bruenn, a cardiologist in the Naval Reserve, was at Warm Springs with the president's entourage at the time. Although Dr. Bruenn arrived on the scene within minutes, FDR was unconscious and covered with cold sweat. His labored breathing turned to gasps, and there was little the doctor could do. At 3:35 P.M. Central War Time, Dr. Bruenn announced that the president was dead.

Franklin Roosevelt had spent the last days of his life not with his wife but with another woman he loved—a woman he might have married if he had followed the inclinations of his heart.

HARRY TRUMAN

Every president has biographers eager to ferret out romantic involvements, but such searchers will be disappointed in Truman's history. Even as a soldier in France, amid the fracturing of loyalties brought on by war and separation, Truman remained absolutely faithful to his girl back home.

He had the same opportunities as most soldiers, but there has never been a scintilla of evidence suggesting then or later that he was ever involved in any way with women outside his immediate family.

Harry Truman admired women, thought most of them deserved special protection, and believed they all were cast in the same mold as the four he knew and loved: his mother, his sister, his wife, and his daughter.

The influence of Truman's mother upon him was an enduring one, and his attitude toward women in general was shaped in part by his love and respect for her. In an interview after he left the presidency, Truman expressed his opinion of any man who did not live up to the teachings of his mother or was not loyal to his wife or family:

> Three things ruin a man if you want to know what I believe. One's power, one's money, and one's women. . . . And a man who is not loyal to his family, to his wife and mother and his sister can be ruined if he has a complex in that direction. If he has the right woman as a partner, he never has any trouble. But if he has the wrong one or if he's mixed up with a bunch of whores, why, then, he's in a hell of a fix. And I can name them to you, the ones that got mixed up that way.[7]

No one can understand Harry Truman's career without taking into consideration the lasting affection he held for his wife. Few presidential couples ever displayed such closeness and total dependence on each other as did the Trumans.

Harry was six years old when he first met Elizabeth Virginia Wallace. Everyone called her "Bess," and so did he, except years later when he would refer to her formally as "Mrs. Truman" or jocularly as "the Boss." With family members or intimate friends, he might call her "the madam" in pretense that she was forever attempting to control his reckless deeds and utterances.

The first meeting of Harry and Bess most likely occurred in Sunday school in Independence. When he wrote his memoirs after leaving the presidency, Truman gave this account:

> We made a number of new acquaintances, and I became interested in one in particular. She had golden curls and has, to this day, the most beautiful blue eyes. We went to Sunday school, public school from the fifth grade through high school, graduated in the same class, and marched down life's road together. For me she still has the blue eyes and golden hair of yesteryear.[8]

Bess Truman was born on February 13, 1885, the daughter of Madge (Gates) Wallace and David Willock Wallace. Stories persist that the Wallaces represented "aristocracy" more than did the Trumans during those days in Independence. Actually, there seems to have been little class distinction among citizens of that Midwestern community although it is likely that Bess' mother did enjoy her status as the daughter of one of the town's leading and richest citizens.

Madge's father, George Porterfield Gates, was the founder of a milling company that made "Queen of the Pantry" flour—a brand famous throughout the South and Midwest. When he died, George Gates' will showed that his fortune amounted to slightly under half a million dollars.

Bess Wallace was eighteen in the summer of 1903 when tragedy struck her family. Her convivial, civic-minded father had begun drinking heavily. The more he drank the more despondent he became, and early one morning he committed suicide.

The suddenness of her husband's death devastated Madge Wallace as well as Bess and her three younger brothers. The shocked widow never recovered from the effects of her husband's suicide and for the rest of her life led a very secluded existence. The stark tragedy also had a lasting impact on Bess, for she likewise grew ever more concerned about privacy.

There was a time when the paths of Harry and Bess seemed to be going in different directions. He was successively a bank clerk in Kansas City and then a farmer; she was conspicuous among the young social set in Independence. Her grandfather owned the first Studebaker in town, and she drove it. She dressed conservatively but wore the richest tweeds and frequently was seen walking two greyhounds—a gift from her affluent grandfather.

One day sometime after Bess had ended her training at a finishing school in Kansas City and was spending more time in Independence, Harry came from the farm to town in order to visit his Aunt Ella Noland. That morning Mrs. Wallace, Bess' mother, had sent over a cake to the Nolands, and Aunt Ella asked her daughter to return the cake plate. Instead Harry insisted he would do it, seized the plate, and rushed out. Two hours later he returned, grinning foolishly, and announced, "Well, I got to see her."[9]

This episode or some event similar to it must have intensified their friendship, for not only did he start seeing Bess more often, he began a correspondence pattern that would last their lifetimes. Exchanging letters became a habit he continued whenever he was at military camps, overseas, or years later in the White House when he and Bess were not together.

The love story between Harry and Bess is told largely through these countless letters. Their daughter Margaret once declared that her father was a "demon letter writer." As Harry progressed in his career, he and his wife were frequently separated, and whenever that happened he wrote her daily.

More important perhaps than the love inherent in the massive exchange is the fact that Harry wrote candidly about whatever he was doing that day. His letters trail his work, first in managing the farm, then trying to make a living from lead and zinc mines, next the oil business, leading an artillery battery overseas, and supervising Jackson County's business following World War I. The letters continue throughout his two terms in the Senate, his brief vice-presidency, and his nearly eight years in the Oval Office.

Although Harry and Bess were considered to be "going steady" sometime during 1913, it was not until shortly before he was shipped overseas in World War I that they announced their engagement. At that time, Bess gave him her picture and inscribed on its back, "Dear Harry, May this photograph bring you safely home again from France—Bess." Harry carried the picture in his mind, heart, and pocket during the weeks of training in Oklahoma and while his battery survived mud and dangers on the Western Front.

Six weeks after he was released from the army, Harry and Bess were married at Trinity Episcopal Church in Independence; he was thirty-five, and she was thirty-four. Following a brief honeymoon, the newlyweds moved into the Gates house, already occupied by the bride's mother, her grandmother, and her younger brother.

Truman's zealous protection of the members of his family would become very well known. At one time early in his presidency this sensitivity pushed him close to an international incident. It happened in January 1946 on the day of his first annual diplomatic dinner—an event to which all the chiefs of missions, their deputies, and their wives were invited, together with their American counterparts, to an evening in the White House.

On the afternoon of this scheduled dinner, Chief of Protocol Stanley Woodward received a phone call and a female voice informed him that Soviet Ambassador Nikolai V. Novikov and his counsellor suddenly had been taken ill; they regretted that they would not be able to dine with the president. Just to be sure the phone message was authentic, the State Department put through a call to Ambassador Novikov in New York, and found him to be cheerful and in good health. The reason for the cancellation was diplomatic rather than physical. The State Department thoughtlessly had invited to the same dinner envoys from the Soviet Union and Lithuania, a small country which, along with Latvia and Estonia, had been swallowed up by the Soviet Union. The United States had continued to recognize the three former states as sovereign nations, however.

The next morning Secretary of State Dean Acheson and Woodward were summoned to the president's office. They were flabbergasted to learn that he was planning to tell the Soviet ambassador to leave the country because he had been "inexcusably rude" to Mrs. Truman!

The dismayed Acheson and Woodward pointed out that such action would be regarded as rash and might have serious consequences abroad even among America's best friends. President Truman remained adamant until Matt Connelly, his appointment secretary, came in and handed him the telephone, announcing, "Mrs. Truman."

After listening for a few moments and saying only, "I'm talking with him now. He agrees with you," President Truman gave the receiver to Acheson, who later recounted his conversation with Mrs. Truman:

I must not, Mrs. Truman said, let the President go through with his plan. I agreed in the objective, but asked for operating instructions. Mrs. Truman thought delay while the President's temper cooled the best procedure. She added that if he went ahead his critics would have a field day. This gave me an idea. While she talked I murmured in horror pretending to be repeating phrases that she never uttered, such as " . . . above himself . . . delusions of grandeur . . . too big for his britches . . ." The President took the receiver from me, "All right, all right," he said. "When you gang up on me I know I'm licked. Let's forget all about it."[10]

A few minutes later, Truman was smiling and seemed in better humor, but he picked up the old-fashioned photograph of Bess as a young lady and handed it to Acheson, saying, "I guess you think I'm an old fool, and I probably am. Look on the back." Most accounts of the incident report that Truman added, "Any s.o.b. who is rude to that girl is in trouble with me."

Other matters were discussed before Acheson and Woodward left a short time later, but as they were doing so the still unmollified president called out to them, "Tell OLD NOVOCAINE we didn't miss him!"

In retrospect this incident seems small and might even evoke grudging admiration for a husband so protective of his wife. It also has its comic overtones, but it shows that on occasion Bess did curb rash actions or words of her peppery husband.

Bess' modesty was anything but a handicap to Harry's career. Though she preserved the common touch, she was ever the lady, poised but with no exalted notions about her status. Standing by her husband's side she represented stability and careful judgement. Her devotion to him and to his well-being was unshakable. Once an old friend asked her what she considered the most memorable aspect of her life, and she replied, "Harry and I have been sweethearts and married for more than forty years—and no matter where I was, when I put out my hand Harry's was there to grasp it."[11]

Bess persistently played down her role, but her influence was ever present. She was the one person who, on occasion, might persuade Harry to ignore an attack or soften a statement. Her natural inclinations, strengthened by her unusually close association with her mother, were toward dignity, conservatism, and restraint—three traits in sharp contrast with the ebullience of her husband.

Throughout their marriage, Bess Truman served as Harry's most valuable listener. It was not simply that he wanted his persuasions to please her; he knew that if he failed to convince her of the soundness of his argument or the propriety of his position, a great many other practical-minded persons would be unmoved.

More than mere posturing to promote the all-American story of a poor country boy who married his childhood sweetheart and went on to become president, Harry Truman's unbroken reliance upon Bess marked an indelible trail of enduring love and devotion.

Chapter 4

Soldiers

Then a soldier,
Full of strange oaths and bearded like the pard,
Jealous in honour, sudden and quick in quarrel,
Forever seeking the bubble reputation
Even in the cannon's mouth.

—William Shakespeare, *As You Like It*,
II, vii, 149–53.

FRANKLIN ROOSEVELT

Today there is general agreement that in 1914 none of the leading statesmen of Europe wanted a major conflict; yet many toyed with the idea of limited or local war. Imperialistic and economic rivalries had been building throughout the latter half of the nineteenth century; the assassination of Archduke Francis Ferdinand (June 28) was the spark that set off the powder keg.

In August of that year, President Woodrow Wilson proclaimed American neutrality, and his message sent to the Senate declared, "The United States must be neutral in fact as well as in name." But it was not to be. Before it ended, the war that nobody wanted drew participants from the farthest corners of the world.

In America, Franklin Roosevelt was serving as assistant secretary of the navy, where his initial work was routine, carrying out whatever duties were assigned him. The young assistant secretary had shown himself to be ambitious, however, and kept broadening the scope of his activities. Soon he was in charge of all civilian personnel, including labor in the navy yards. When it came to navy ceremonials or relations with Congress, FDR was in his element; moreover, he was politician enough to recognize the need to dramatize the navy to the electorate. Josephus Daniels, secretary of the navy, put great trust in his subordinate and tolerated FDR's admission that he was putting his "fingers into about everything, and there's no law against it."[1]

Daniels, an opponent of U.S. involvement in the war, regarded the battles there as a strictly European problem. FDR, on the other hand, believed involvement was inevitable and that it was vital, therefore, for the country to step up its preparedness program. Consequently, without alienating either his indulgent chief or President Wilson, FDR did all he could to promote the navy's buildup.

After President Wilson's declaration of war, Lucy Mercer, Franklin's paramour, enlisted in the navy, and FDR managed to get her assigned to his office. In the fall of 1917, however, it became more difficult to carry on their affair because she had been relieved of her duties, possibly because Secretary Daniels—a firm Christian fundamentalist—had gotten wind of the adulterous relationship.

FDR had convinced himself that the road to the White House first had to cross a battlefield. That path had proved successful for Theodore, who urged his young cousin to get into uniform.

Then in early summer Congress authorized an investigation of naval installations in Europe. Franklin persuaded Daniels to permit him to represent the department, and this trip became the high point of Roosevelt's years as assistant secretary of the navy.

He sailed aboard the U.S.S. *Dyer* on July 19, 1918, and in London he talked to a variety of English politicians as part of the fact-finding mission. One of them was Winston Churchill, who Franklin said "was rude" to him.[2]

FDR and his party then crossed the channel and went to Chateau-Thierry, which had been regained from German defenses only ten days earlier. From Chateau-Thierry he went to Belleau Woods where U.S. Marines had fought with great heroism; signs of the fierce battle still littered the ground.

Next the committee motored west, and on August 6 Franklin, wearing a French helmet and carrying a gas mask, crossed the Meuse in order to see firsthand the villages destroyed earlier by Germans.

From France the party went to Italy for consultations with the government there. Then the group returned to Paris and held a press conference.

After brief excursions to Bordeaux and Brest to tour some of the Allied installations, Roosevelt and several in his party made a side trip to Scotland, where they fished for salmon and drank the famous single malt Scotch whisky. Then came more socializing in London before the group began the trip home during the second week of September.

FDR was on the Atlantic when he fell victim to the influenza epidemic. His flu worsened into double pneumonia, and when the ship docked in New York, Eleanor was there to see her seriously ill husband on a stretcher carried off the ship. Later that night while unpacking his luggage she discovered the incriminating love letters from Lucy Mercer. The affair had continued despite Franklin's promises!

At the war's end, FDR persuaded his boss, Secretary Daniels, to authorize another trip to Europe—this time for the purpose of overseeing naval demobilization—and on this junket, Eleanor went with him.

Delegates from everywhere on earth flocked to Paris in order to pursue their own agendas in the settlement being discussed at Versailles. President Wilson, the most acclaimed attendee, arrived with a retinue of more than twenty academic advisers but without a single member of the U.S. Senate—the body that had responsibility for ratifying whatever treaty might be signed.

FDR played no part whatsoever in treaty deliberations; his role was to "lubricate" negotiations with the French over the sale of naval property. The trip did, however, provide him and Eleanor with extensive opportunities for socializing in London and Paris. For Eleanor, Paris was a dangerous city where women were too wordly and brazenly made up—a place, she wrote to Sara, that makes "you wonder if any are ladies."[3]

FDR's stint as assistant secretary of the navy was marked by the kind of hyperbole and zeal he had shown at Groton and Harvard. Despite two swashbuckling trips overseas, actual accomplishments were meager, and if it had not been for later fame his name would have fallen into the dustbin of history.

His role in World War I most certainly was less than he liked to proclaim. Although often in the public eye, he was there largely because Daniels, his busy chief, had neither the inclination nor the desire for publicity. Nevertheless, Roosevelt brought to his civilian post imagination and unbounded enthusiasm. Moreover, he displayed keen political instincts, gained a reputation as an expediter, and showed a knack for getting along with people—traits that would serve his country well in the years ahead.

HARRY TRUMAN

Shakespeare's description of the soldier's age is more accurate in the case of Harry Truman than it is for that period in Franklin Roosevelt's life. Few "oaths" were "strange" to Truman by the time he began active military duty; he had heard most of them long before. The army environment, moreover, nourished and encouraged their frequent use.

In 1901 young Harry's first full-time job had been timekeeper for a construction crew grading track levels for the Atchison, Topeka, and Santa Fe Railroad. It was no place for the dainty, and he once said that it was while working with this crew that he learned "all the cuss words in the English language—not by ear but by note."[4]

Truman was never "bearded like the pard," but the "sudden and quick" nature with which he was endowed showed itself during his military service in World War I as it would continue to do throughout his life. And as a line officer in the artillery he advanced into "the cannon's mouth" on more than one occasion.

Twenty-one years old when he first joined the Missouri National Guard, he reenlisted for another term in June 1917 and was elected a first lieutenant by the men in his artillery battery. In August of that year the entire National Guard was called into active duty by presidential proclamation.

The 35th Division, composed of former National Guard units from Missouri and Kansas, formed at Camp Doniphan on the Fort Sill Military Reservation near Lawton, Oklahoma. At full strength, the division had 27,865 men and consisted of three brigades: the 69th and 70th Infantry and the 60th Field Artillery. Truman arrived at Camp Doniphan in late September and was assigned to the 129th Field Artillery Regiment.

Having been put in charge of the regimental canteen, a business venture of considerable importance, he at once sought help from a sergeant friend, Eddie Jacobson. The latter knew more about merchandising because he had been a shirt salesman in Kansas City. Jacobson understood the ways of buying low and selling profitably, so he actually ran the canteen while Lieutenant Truman acted as accountant and chief policy maker. They began collecting two dollars from every one of the 1,100 men in the regiment. After six months each man received back not only his two dollars, but Truman and Jacobson declared dividends of $15,000 on the original $22,000 investment.

In March 1918 Truman, along with about 100 other men constituting an advance force, sailed for France on the *George Washington*. Two weeks later the ship docked at Brest. After a short training period, he rejoined the remainder of his regiment at Camp Coetequidan in Brittany, where he was given command of his own combat unit, Battery D, 129th Field Artillery Regiment, 35th Division.

In August the 129th entrained for the Alsatian front—a front that had been relatively quiet since the failure of a major French offensive four years earlier. Once when the regiment was moving toward its assigned battle position, a French commandant invited Truman and a few fellow officers to an extended, multicourse lunch—the type that raised his hackles. "It takes them so long to serve a meal," he complained, "that I'm always hungrier when I get done than I ever was before."[5]

The end of the month found Truman, now a captain, and his men slogging their horse-drawn gun carriages up steep, muddy roads to the edge of a forest area atop a hill not far from the village of Mittlach. On August 29, Battery D began firing at German targets 4.3 miles away. The battery shot off 500 rounds in thirty-six minutes, exactly on schedule, and then prepared to withdraw before Germans could return the fire.

Unfortunately, before Battery D was able to evacuate the area, enemy shells began falling upon them. For a few moments, all was in chaos; horses bolted in every direction, two teams broke away from gun carriages, and a German shell landed so close to Captain Harry it spewed shrapnel on him. The horse he was riding went down, either hit or spooked by shells, and a comrade had to pull him out from under the animal.

The first sergeant added to the panic by yelling, "Run, boys! They've got a bracket on us!" His cry set off a flight despite an infuriated Truman, who kept trying to rally the men back to their duties. He put it wryly later by saying, "A great many of the men on that occasion distinguished themselves as foot racers" and did so "in spite of the loud swearing of the Battery Commander."

Truman's immediate job was to regroup his battery, and in doing that he liberally used the profanity he had learned from Missouri farmhands and army doughboys. Many of the "no-good Irish sons-of-bitches" sheepishly came straggling back. In a more temperate letter to Bess, Harry described the encounter:

I shot my gas barrage at 8:00 P.M. The first sergeant failed to get the horses up in time, and the Hun gave me a good shelling. The sergeant ran away and I had one high old time getting out of that place. I finally did with two guns and went back to my former position, arriving at 4:00 A.M., where the cooks had the best hot meal I've tasted since I arrived in France without exception. The boys called that engagement the Battle of Who Run, because some of them ran when the first

sergeant did and some of them didn't. I made some corporals and
first-class privates out of those who stayed with men and busted the
sergeant.[6]

Shortly after their baptism in combat, Truman and his men were shifted
to the Meuse-Argonne area where they participated in the most decisive
battle of the war. Their battery joined in the opening barrages of the
offensive on the morning of September 26, 1918.
    Months later Captain Truman recalled the experience:

There was more noise than human ears could stand. Men serving the
guns became deaf for weeks afterward. The sky was red from one
end to the other. . . . Daylight came about 6:30. It was a smoky, foggy
morning. We could see our observation balloons beginning to go up
behind us . . . evenly spaced and all ascending together. The guns got
very hot. It was necessary to keep them covered with wet gunny sacks
and to swab after every second or third shot.[7]

Immediately after firing its initial barrages, Battery D followed the 35th
Division Infantry across hilly shell-pocked terrain considered a no-man's-
land. Mud and enemy fire slowed their progress, and Truman alternated
between directing barrages from forward observation posts and advancing
with the men in his battery. Meanwhile, three kilometers north the infantry
was trying to repel a ferocious German counterattack.
    The next morning, while moving toward the town of Cheppy, Truman
and his men witnessed the destruction wrought by their shells the preceding day. The entire area was a disaster, looking as if humans, dirt, rock,
trees, and steel had been plowed up. Wounded American soldiers and
captured Germans kept moving through the ranks and toward the rear.
Nearly all the corpses, scattered here and there, were American; retreating
Germans had carried their own dead away with them.
    At a crossroads near Cheppy, seventeen dead American infantrymen
were lying together, and farther down the road the battery came across a
dozen more laid heel to toe—all shot in the back. Apparently the infantry-
men, with more valor than professional training, had mistakenly charged
past silent pillboxes, assuming they had been vacated or destroyed, only
to be mowed down by enemy machine guns.
    Throughout the 35th Division, casualties were staggering—as high as
50 percent in the infantry. On September 29 the decimated 35th Division
Infantry pulled out and was replaced by fresh 1st Division troops. For
several more days Truman's battery along with other veteran units contin-

ued to give artillery support to the newcomers; then on October 2 he received welcome orders to move back to Seigneulles, a little village near Bar-le-Duc, for rest, resupply, and reassignment.

Battery D saw other action east of Verdun, but the Meuse-Argonne campaign was its major engagement. That battle exacted 129 lives from the regiment although Battery D itself suffered only three wounded men, one of whom died later. To many of the men in the battery it seemed a miracle. One participant, Private Vere Leigh, viewed it as a combination of luck and leadership: "We were just—well, part of it was luck and part of it was good leadership. Some other batteries didn't have that kind of leadership."[8]

The weather in France turned cold in late October. Truman's regiment at the time was near Verdun on somewhat easier duties, firing barrages only when ordered. At the very end of the month a German pilot shot down near them said the war would be over in ten days. The enemy pilot proved remarkably prophetic, for on November 11, 1918, the Great War—one that had taken 10 million lives—ended. The victors were certain it was a triumph for civilization; now it would be up to statesmen to write a peace accord and make the world safe for democracy.

Truman's regiment remained in France until spring before coming home in May 1919. His ties to the military did not end then, however. His military record admittedly was not as extensive as that of other presidents—Washington, Jackson, Grant, and Eisenhower to name a few. Nevertheless, the army left its indelible mark on him as a person and had a profound influence upon his subsequent political career.

Truman came out of uniform battle-hardened by experiences—experiences that gave him self-confidence and the conviction that he had the capacity to lead. Wartime buddies remained lifelong friends, and veterans' organizations formed one of the bulwarks of his political support.

Truman stayed in the Officers Reserve Corps, attending summer camps and rising to the rank of colonel, although the next time he returned to active duty it would be as Commander in Chief.

PART II

THE FIFTH AGE: PRESIDENCIES

Chapter 5

Preludes

And then the justice,
In fair round belly with good capon lined,
With eyes severe and beard of formal cut,
Full of wise saws and modern instances;
And so he plays his part.

—William Shakespeare, *As You Like It,*
II, vii, 153–57.

A broad interpretation could reasonably place the U.S. presidency within Shakespeare's context of man's fifth age—the "justice"—and it was during this segment of their lives that Roosevelt and Truman made their marks on history.

Franklin Roosevelt entered the Oval Office when he was fifty, and Harry Truman became president when he was sixty-one. How did they do it? What were the conditions and challenges each faced? What were their successes and failures? In what ways during their terms of office were the two presidents similar? How did they differ? To answer such questions, a brief account of their activities immediately preceding their respective entries into office is in order.

FRANKLIN ROOSEVELT

In 1905 Franklin and Eleanor Roosevelt had been married for nearly three months before they sailed on the White Star liner *Oceanic* for a delayed honeymoon in Europe. The newlyweds returned in September of that year, and Franklin successfully passed examinations in two courses he had failed earlier at Columbia University's law school. He did not complete his work for an LLB degree but was able to pass the New York bar examinations, and in 1907 he was admitted to the practice of law. Undeniable assets of name and background helped him win a position with a prestigious Wall Street firm where a remunerative future was assured had he chosen to make law his career.

During his first year with the firm, FDR confided to several of his coworkers that his main interest was in politics: he intended to run for an elective office at the earliest opportunity. The initial step would be a seat in the state assembly. After a term or two there he thought he could win appointment as assistant secretary of the navy. Given his class and social background those goals did not seem unrealistic, but he aimed still higher. Following the path of his admired cousin, he intended to become governor of New York. But even that was not enough; he wanted to become president of the United States!

If advanced by most persons such aspirations would be judged fatuous, but one of Roosevelt's listeners, Grenville Clark, recalled the conversation long afterward and said that somehow FDR managed to make what might otherwise be considered empty boasting seem "proper and sincere; and moreover, as he put it, entirely reasonable."[1]

Roosevelt did not care for the drudgery involved in searching out references or helping prepare briefs for senior members of the legal firm that employed him, but he learned fast, and he enjoyed meeting people of the sorts he had not encountered before: frustrated plaintiffs, small-time lawyers, courthouse loungers, county officials, judges, and witnesses, both credible and otherwise. However, it was not the practice of law Franklin had in mind; he set a course toward the practice of politics.

Despite Cousin Theodore's leadership of Republicans, FDR had decided as early as his second year at Harvard that his own future lay with the Democratic party. Only as a Democrat from outside the immediate family of the more famous Theodore could a Roosevelt expect to rise to real political heights.

Franklin's first goal was a seat in the New York State Legislature, and in the early summer of 1910 he expressed his interest to several influential Democrats around his home base at Hyde Park. Slim, rich, and as exuberant as he had been at Harvard a decade earlier, the young man with the famous name and a rich mother—two undeniable assets that strapped Democrats could ill afford to ignore—garnered support from several leaders in Dutchess County.

Consequently, he left the law firm that summer and began to climb the political ladder, expecting to make a run first for the state assembly. However, that spot already had been promised to another Democrat, so he convinced his backers he could win a race for the state senate.

Republicans in the state were badly split—a fact that worked to FDR's great advantage. He portrayed himself as fighting against privilege, graft, and corruption wherever they were to be found.

He waged a very spirited campaign, first hiring a bright red, two-cylinder Maxwell touring car. Along with the car came a driver who knew all the back roads in Dutchess, Putnam, and Columbia counties. Nearly every day for six weeks Roosevelt was in that open red car, American flags mounted on its fenders and speeding along at twenty-two miles per hour, exhorting voters to support him and fellow Democrats.

On the stump, he showed his customary enthusiasm and charm. Backers wanted him to avoid the slightest hint of aristocracy so, accepting their advice, Franklin endeavored to be plain and on common ground with his listeners, beginning each speech with a simple, "My Friends!"

The messages were superficial, but his ability to speak fluently and to spar with the occasional heckler convinced lots of skeptics, and that November the campaigning paid off when he won his first elective office by more than a thousand votes—running far ahead of the state ticket in Dutchess County.

At that time in New York as well as across the nation, a new progressivism was seeping into both parties, and from this movement came programs aimed particularly at middle-class farmers, small businessmen, and professional men. It was logical, therefore, that the pragmatic Roosevelt would concentrate his attention upon rural Republicans in his home state rather than upon urban Democrats from New York City.

Indeed, during his three years in the New York State Senate, Roosevelt had to weather considerable blasts from Tammany Hall regulars. His reluctance to commit himself to wholesale changes in the state's labor laws distressed such reformers as Frances Perkins, an ardent young woman lobbying in behalf of improving wages, hours, and working conditions for women and children.

There were more supporters than critics though and by the summer of 1912 when his first term was nearing its end, Roosevelt had decided to run for reelection. Shortly after making his decision, however, bad luck struck when he contracted typhoid fever and was too ill to do much personal campaigning. Because few Democrats emerged to work for him, his prospects looked dim. Fortunately, however, Dame Fortune suddenly appeared in the guise of Louis McHenry Howe, a correspondent covering Albany for the *New York Herald.*

Howe, a Hoosier by birth, had moved to New York and become well known around the racing and vacation places in the East. He was an unattractive, enigmatic little man who realized his own appearance and background destroyed any personal hopes for a political career. He was smart enough though to recognize potential leadership, and the dashing young Roosevelt looked like a real comer who, if properly presented, could go far.

From 1912 until his death in 1936 Louis Howe worked steadily for FDR, and it would be difficult to explain the latter's career without noting the strategies devised by this shrewd political confidant. It is impossible to learn just when Howe decided that Roosevelt could reach the White House, but soon after entering FDR's employ Howe addressed him, perhaps facetiously, as "Beloved and Revered Future President."[2]

In 1912 Howe took over much of the responsibility for Roosevelt's campaign for reelection to the state senate and personally combed the district while FDR was bedridden. That November when the ballots were counted, Roosevelt again was the victor. He told Eleanor that she and the family should plan to spend another two years in Albany.

FDR's second term in the New York State Senate had just begun when he first met President-elect Woodrow Wilson. The meeting took place in the governor's office in Trenton and was resumed in the afternoon when the two of them boarded a train and talked while enroute to Princeton Junction, a drop-off five miles from Wilson's home in Princeton.

The previous fall Democrat Wilson, who had given up a college presidency in order to become governor of New Jersey, had scored a slender victory over his Republican rival, William Howard Taft, and the Bull Moose candidate, Theodore Roosevelt. On his part, FDR had been reelected by a wider margin than he had achieved in 1910, and as a result of outrunning both the presidential and gubernatorial winners, he could claim he had helped in their victory.

After his initial meeting with Wilson, FDR's career took a sharp turn toward Washington. On the morning Wilson was inaugurated, FDR encountered the new secretary of the navy, Josephus Daniels, in the lobby of the Willard Hotel. Roosevelt congratulated Daniels upon his appointment, and the latter countered by asking Roosevelt if he would like to come to Washington and serve as assistant secretary. FDR chose one of Teddy Roosevelt's favorite words and gave an enthusiastic reply.

How would I like it? I'd like it bully well. . . . All my life I have loved ships and been a student of the Navy. The Assistant Secretary of the Navy is the one place, above all others, I would love to hold.[3]

It was no huge surprise therefore, when on March 13, seven weeks after his thirty-first birthday, Franklin Roosevelt was sworn in as assistant secretary of the navy—the youngest in its history.

He served as assistant secretary for the next seven years and made two official trips overseas in conjunction with the war and demobilization.[4] Thanks to Howe's energetic promotion and his own ambitions, Roosevelt's name had appeared often in the news during the war years, and when in the summer of 1920 the Democrats held their nominating convention in San Francisco, he was there.

The outlook was gloomy, for the party's leader, President Wilson, had suffered a stroke and was barely alive. Moreover, the U.S. Senate had rejected participation in the League of Nations—participation which Wilson had made a major goal. Now Democrats were badly divided on whether to continue their leader's gallant fight for the League of Nations or to concede it as a lost cause. Several major figures in the party refused to run for the country's top office because they saw inevitable defeat.

The convention finally nominated James M. Cox, Progressive governor of Ohio. Cox's stand on the League question was unknown, but he was recognized as being opposed to anti-Wilson city machine bosses. Having chosen Cox to head the ticket, party leaders decided it would make sense to select a strong Wilsonian as their vice-presidential candidate and thus keep within the fold all the League supporters who otherwise might be turned away. Who better than the aspiring politician with the prestigious name of Roosevelt?

Cox and Roosevelt undertook an ambitious campaign; FDR himself made no fewer than 800 speeches, and right up until the end he thought they had a good chance of winning. No one could ever fault FDR for lack of confidence! But he was in a losing race; the Cox-Roosevelt ticket was beaten decisively by Warren G. Harding and his running mate from Vermont, Calvin Coolidge.

Following his defeat at the polls, FDR took a leisurely vacation, going with his brother-in-law, Hall Roosevelt, to the Louisiana marshes where he hunted ducks and was a houseboat guest of the state's conservation commissioner. After returning to Washington for a few weeks to clean out his desk at the Navy Department, he shifted to New York City to begin anew as a lawyer and financier on Wall Street.

FDR was there only a few months before he went up to Campobello to join Eleanor and the "chicks" (all his children had been born by this time). A few days after arriving on the island, however, he was stricken by a disaster of monstrous proportions.

The severity of his polio attack confronted him with the greatest crisis of his life—a crisis that would have destroyed all hopes of a lesser man for a political career. For weeks the disease kept him in bed wracked with fevers and pain. Even after the actual infection had passed, the muscular inflammations and weaknesses were still there. He had to face the fact that he would be paralyzed for life.

The grim story of Roosevelt's valor in handling his crippling illness has been told many times, yet it is worth pointing out again that despite acute pain and the frequent humiliations suffered by a man once extremely proud of his physical appearance, FDR never failed to put a smiling, gallant front on his plight.

He exercised indefatigably, trying to strengthen the unimpaired muscles in his chest and arms. He discovered that exercise in swimming pools benefited him most, for he could swim and even walk a little when aided by the buoyancy of warm water.

In a curious way the tragedy of FDR's polio and its resultant paralysis seemed to bring from him a determination that otherwise might have lain dormant. Refusing to succumb to illness and unwilling to retire from public life, by 1922 FDR was again active in politics, helping rally New York Democrats in support of Alfred E. Smith's run for the governorship.

Two years later Democrats from all forty-eight states flocked to New York City and Madison Square Garden for their national convention. The honor of placing Governor Smith's name in nomination for the presidency went to Franklin Roosevelt.

Heat that summer was intense and, of course, the spacious Garden with its glaring lights was without air-conditioning. The convention was near deadlock over candidates when the sweating delegates saw Franklin Roosevelt rise from his place within the New York delegation and slowly make his way toward the rostrum.

He was the personification of courage, defying pain and paralysis as he hobbled on his crutches slowly and carefully across the stage. He had not yet mastered the technique of seeming to walk while supported by the strong arms of aides. The crowd empathized with the risk in his approach and wondered if he would fall. Arriving at last at the rostrum, FDR put aside the crutches, gripped the lectern firmly, smiled triumphantly into the spotlights, and began speaking in a firm, slow voice.

Advisers earlier had warned him that his own writings for the speech he wanted to deliver were too "fancy," too "literary," but he had accepted a proud title contributed by Governor Smith's strategists—a quotation from William Wordsworth: "This is the *Happy Warrior*; this is he/Whom every man in arms should wish to be."

FDR's speech and particularly its stirring conclusion brought forth an outburst of emotion. Although Smith would lose the subsequent national election, the young Democratic orator who nominated him gained great new stature within the party.

Four years later in 1928 the Democrats had little choice but to renominate Governor Smith, and that move left the gubernatorial candidacy of New York open. The most obvious person was Franklin Roosevelt, now pressed by Smith himself in an endeavor to keep the Empire State within the party's fold.

In the presidential race Smith went down in defeat to Herbert Hoover and the Republicans, but Roosevelt narrowly won the governorship, running ahead of Smith in his home state.

Roosevelt was governor of New York for four years, garnering an overwhelming victory for a second term in 1930. By then two factors—his undeniable political attractiveness as well as the unprecedented hard times sweeping the nation—were pushing him toward the presidency.

The great economic crash came in the fall of 1929, and nowhere was the crisis worse than in the nation's most populous state. As the Depression worsened, Governor Roosevelt was brought into its every aspect—failed businesses, bank closings, joblessness, destitute farmers, and homeless people. As governor he tirelessly traveled the state visiting the hungry, the unemployed, and the homeless, and for the first time in his life he began to understand the cruel realities faced by struggling, impoverished people.

New Yorkers discovered that even in adversity Governor Roosevelt showed an exciting enthusiasm that helped make hardships a little more tolerable. Later it would be apparent that FDR's record as governor of New York was a forecast of his presidencies.

As New York governor he instituted old-age pensions, fought for control of public utilities, established the State Power Authority, created guidelines for reforestation, argued for social security, and set up the first unemployment-relief system in the country.

Franklin Roosevelt did not hesitate to spend money. In 1928 when he became governor, New York had a surplus in its treasury; it had a $100 million deficit when he left that office. But it cost a lot to repair roads and bridges and to rebuild the state's shattered economic system.

Meanwhile, he was surrounding himself with talented and dependable persons—persons who would serve him well for the next seventeen years. Among his early selections in addition to Howe was Samuel I. Rosenman, a young former state legislator who had worked on the legislative bill drafting commission. Then came James A. Farley, formerly secretary of the state Democratic committee. Missy LeHand, more than an ordinary secretary, already was aboard, and soon the dependable Grace Tully joined Governor Roosevelt's official family.

He also selected the redoubtable Frances Perkins as chairman of the State Department of Labor. Henry Morgenthau, Jr., became head of the Agricultural Advisory Commission, and soon after meeting Harry Hopkins, FDR picked him to be chairman of a state-wide emergency relief program, a precursor of many subsequent New Deal agencies.

Roosevelt achieved notable successes during his two terms as governor of New York, but those successes would be overshadowed by accomplishments yet to come. Moreover, performance within the confines of one state was not what he had in mind; to Franklin Roosevelt the governorship of New York was a necessary step up the best path leading to the White House.

HARRY TRUMAN

World War I was a turning point in Harry Truman's life. Those war years provided him with experiences, friendships, and a self-confidence that would play huge parts in his political future.

Not long after his return from France, Truman arranged to sell his farm implements and move into Independence, where he and Bess were married on June 28, 1919. As a result of success with the canteen at Camp Doniphan, Truman and Eddie Jacobson decided to open a haberdashery in downtown Kansas City. At first the store did a remarkable business, not merely with returned veterans but also with passersby who had money to buy fairly expensive shirts, ties, and hats. Soon, however, Truman and his partner were caught in the recession of 1921–1922. They refused to sell out when they could have recaptured their initial investment. Instead they held their shelf stock and watched prices plummet. When they finally closed the store they had lost $25 thousand on a $35 thousand inventory.

The circumstances prompting Truman to become a candidate for county judge (a term applied to administrators who in other sections of the country might be called commissioners) grew from the failure of his haberdashery business, the attraction politics always had held for him, and assurances of support from the Pendergasts, who were the undisputed leaders of the dominant Democrats.

Improvement of Jackson County roads was an issue that helped start Truman on his political career. He had begun to take a deep personal interest in the road system in 1914 when he succeeded his father as a road overseer in the eastern part of the county. In 1922 when he ran and was elected as the Eastern District county judge on the old Jackson County Court, the opening line of his campaign brochure stated: "My Platform—Good Roads." Two years later Truman ran for reelection but was a victim of the Republican tide that engulfed the nation that year. Even in Jackson County, Republicans gained control, and Truman's opponent went into the judgeship as only the second Republican elected Eastern District county judge since the Civil War.[5] It was the only political campaign Harry Truman ever lost.

In 1926 Truman ran again and this time was elected presiding judge of the county court, a position he held until 1934. In that year Boss Tom Pendergast of Kansas City sent his nephew Jim Pendergast to encourage Truman to run for the U.S. Senate.

Truman often had described the nephew as "my war buddy," and because he really had set his eyes upon running for the House of Representatives he professed reluctance at first to accept the Pendergast offer.

> I told them I had no legislative experience, that I thought I was something of an executive and I'd rather wait two years and run for Governor. But they insisted that I owed it to the party to run, that Senator Clark was from the eastern side of the State and that Jackson County was entitled to one of the Senators.[6]

In his first campaign for the Senate, Truman concentrated his efforts in the agricultural midstate counties and on the environs of Kansas City. When he won the primary he was in an advantageous position, for President Franklin Roosevelt and his party were at the height of popularity. Truman unequivocally endorsed FDR's leadership and praised all the national relief programs.

Normally in an off-year election the party in power would expect to lose strength, but that year Democrats counted an unprecedented gain of thirteen seats in the House. In the Senate they increased their margin by ten with the election or reelection of twenty-three Democrats. Truman was among the victors, and on January 3, 1935, wearing a long frock coat, striped pants, and a gardenia boutonniere, he joined eleven other newly elected senators in Washington for the swearing-in ceremonies.

HST began his Senate career with something to live down. He had been narrowly elected with the help of the infamous Pendergast political machine, and as a result he was tagged as "the gentleman from Pendergast." Despite that early epithet his years in the Senate would always hold a special place in his memory; he later called the decade "the happiest ten years of my life."

Senator Truman's first term was marked by his involvement in various transportation issues. He helped write the Transportation Act of 1940, which was aimed at straightening out the financially troubled railroads. He also helped draft the Civil Aeronautics Act, which set up the regulatory structure for the then-infant commercial airlines industry. Returning to the Congress in 1941 after a tough battle within his own party for renomination and reelection, he continued to talk mainly about transportation matters.

It was in the Senate that HST learned how legislation got through Congress, what buttons to push to get things done in government, and how to harness the complex war machine he would eventually command. As the war in Europe widened, American involvement appeared ever more likely. Hitler's string of victories forced a rapid American armament program, and by the end of 1940 President Roosevelt was proclaiming that the United States must become the great "arsenal of democracy."

Problems accompanying armament and mobilization were immense, and the location of a new camp or defense plant often carried with it an odor of the pork barrel. Truman won Senate approval of a special committee aimed at detecting waste and inefficiencies in war production. Soon his vigorous investigating group became known as the Truman Committee.

He had got the idea for the committee during the interval between his 1940 victory at the polls and his return to Washington to begin his second term. During that period he had taken a fact-finding trip (at his own expense) to check out complaints of waste and corruption on government projects. His worst suspicions were confirmed when he went to Fort Leonard Wood, Missouri, then under construction, and found workers loafing and mountains of unused materials piled up. He widened his travel and drove about 30 thousand miles visiting sites and installations in several states, including Maryland, Pennsylvania, Georgia, Oklahoma, Nebraska, Louisiana, and Missouri,

By January 1941, the United States was launched on a crash program to build, equip, and train a two-ocean navy and to arm a million men annually for the next five years. Already defense expenditures had ballooned to more than $25 billion. It was clear to HST that someone should be monitoring the spending of these vast sums, and his knowledge of history led him into seeing a parallel between then and Civil War times, when Congress had established a committee on the conduct of the war.

Through his efforts, at the beginning of March 1941, the Senate Special Committee to Investigate the National Defense Program came into existence. The original Truman Committee consisted of five Democrats and two Republicans, but nine months later, because of its successes and increasing workload, it was expanded to ten members. Under HST's energetic leadership, the committee investigated the nation's defense housing; the production of rubber, aluminum, and magnesium; the rationing of gasoline; the use of dollar-a-year executives; excess profits; and the distribution of government contracts to small business firms.

While the degree of influence exerted by Truman in the making of overall defense policy during the nearly four years he headed this committee is impossible to measure accurately, it is clear that as chairman of the increasingly powerful group he became at least indirectly a participant in policy formulation. His prestige among Senate colleagues soared and undoubtedly served to propel him into the vice presidency.

When July 1944 arrived, bringing with it the Democratic National Convention, there was no question that FDR, then in his twelfth year of office, would be renominated. Certainty over Roosevelt's renomination, however, was tempered by concern over his visible aging and his declining health. Such concerns fueled speculation over whom he would choose as his running mate.

The leading contenders were Vice President Henry Wallace, War Mobilization Director James Byrnes, Supreme Court Justice William Douglas, and Senator Harry Truman. Finally, at the time the convention was getting under way, Roosevelt gave a private letter to National Democratic Chairman Robert Hannegan from Saint Louis and an old friend of Truman's. In the letter FDR acknowledged that he would be glad to run with either Douglas or Truman.

William O. Douglas was anathema to organized labor, so political wheels began churning to get the junior senator from Missouri nominated. Party regulars were told that Truman, not Douglas, was really FDR's first choice. To most persons and to the press at the time, Truman announced that he was not a candidate for the vice presidency, that he preferred to remain in the Senate, and that he was going ahead with his own plans to help secure the nomination for his friend James Byrnes.

It is unlikely that coyness alone prompted Truman's remarks, for most assuredly he had made his own assessment of campaign strategy. He was not yet convinced that he had received FDR's blessing, and he was too politically astute to overlook its necessity. Subsequent to getting further endorsements from Roosevelt and even after locking up the nomination, Truman insisted he had tried to forestall his selection:

> When the 1944 election was approaching mention began to be made about Truman for Vice President. Every effort was made by me to shut it off. I liked my job as a Senator and I wanted to stay with it. . . . I had tried to make it very plain wherever I went that I was not a candidate for Vice President. . . . There were two dozen men at the Chicago Convention of the Democrats in 1940 [*sic*] who would have gladly taken the honor of the Vice Presidential Nomination and have been exceedingly happy with it. I spent a most miserable week in trying to stave off the nomination.[7]

Dramatic events occurring throughout the world in the fall of 1944 made it difficult for either major political party in the United States to arouse public attention over domestic policy. The Republicans faced a particular challenge in trying to unseat Roosevelt because of his tenure and enormous prestige as a wartime leader. The campaign opened late and was unusually brief—a brevity that worked in favor of the Roosevelt-Truman ticket because most voters apparently felt it was no time to swap horses.

The earliest returns on November 7 indicated a fourth Roosevelt sweep, and the sweep became greater as more returns were tabulated. The electoral landslide was 432 to 99; the percentages of the popular vote were 53.4 for Roosevelt and 45.9 for his Republican opponent, Thomas Dewey.

It is not likely that Harry Truman's name on the ticket helped win many votes; however, he had been no liability, and more important, he now was only a blood clot away from the presidency.

Chapter 6

The Hustings

FRANKLIN ROOSEVELT

Section 1 of Article II in the U.S. Constitution begins: "The executive Power shall be vested in a President of the United States." The Constitution does not mention what prompts a person to run for office nor does it describe how presidential campaigns should be conducted, yet campaigning is common coin for presidential aspirants. No matter how lofty his or her goals or what his or her capabilities, a successful politician must first get elected.

Franklin Roosevelt was in his second term as governor of New York and was no longer a novice in the arts of campaigning when the presidential election of 1932 approached. He first had gone on the hustings when he was twenty-eight years old and running for the New York Senate. He had waged a successful campaign for reelection in 1912 and had made an aborted attempt to secure the Democratic nomination for U.S. Senator in 1916. In 1920 he was the vice-presidential candidate on the national ticket with James M. Cox. Four years later, he stumped for Governor Alfred E. Smith as he did again in 1928. That was also the year during which in his own right FDR won the governorship of his native state. For more than a decade he had wooed political powerbrokers and trod through the maze winding toward the White House; in 1932, he was ready to make a direct move.

The move meant battling the fear, panic, distrust, and defeatism that engulfed the nation. The Great Depression, triggered by the stock market

crash three years earlier, had so shattered the country that millions of
Americans were shackled by poverty and despair. Unemployment was
somewhere between 12 and 14 million—close to one-third of the total
workforce—and more than half the nation's farmers as well as a high
percentage of other homeowners were in dire danger of having their
mortgages foreclosed.

By the time the Democratic Convention opened in Chicago, it was
evident that Roosevelt would be the leading contender. A mere majority
was not good enough to win the nomination, however; his backers would
have to round up enough uncommitted delegates to attain the two-thirds
majority demanded by the party's rule. Roosevelt supporters could present
an impressive list of their champion's credentials: he had been a state
senator, an important federal executive as assistant secretary of the navy,
a vice-presidential candidate, and a Democratic loyalist, and he had
initiated vigorous programs of economic and social welfare during his four
years as New York's governor.

Some journalists were not impressed, however. Heywood Broun, a
liberal columnist of the period, called Roosevelt a "corkscrew candidate
of a convoluting convention." Literary critic Edmund Wilson categorized
him as essentially a boy scout with a spirit of cheerful service. Many felt
that he was a playboy with no depth of conviction or intellect. The most
devastating comment came from the influential columnist Walter
Lippmann:

> Sooner or later some of Roosevelt's supporters are going to feel badly
> let down. For it is impossible that he can continue to be such different
> things to such different men. . . . The art of carrying water on both
> shoulders is highly developed in American politics, and Mr.
> Roosevelt has learned it. . . . In the case of Mr. Roosevelt, it is not
> easy to say with certainty whether his left-wing or his right-wing
> supporters are the most deceived. The reason is that Franklin D.
> Roosevelt is a highly impressionable person, without a firm grasp of
> public affairs and without very strong convictions. . . . Franklin D.
> Roosevelt is an amiable man with many philanthropic impulses, but
> he is not the dangerous enemy of anything. He is too eager to please
> . . . Franklin D. Roosevelt is no crusader. He is no enemy of en-
> trenched privilege. He is a pleasant man who, without any important
> qualifications for the office, would very much like to be President.[1]

Following World War I a wave of isolationist sentiment permeated both
national parties, and in 1932 many Americans remained convinced that

arms and munitions makers were responsible for a foreign war which we had no business getting into in the first place.

In an announcement aimed toward dampening this powerful isolationist sentiment, Roosevelt declared that he no longer favored American entry into the League of Nations. His statement helped convince doubters that down deep he was not a "Wilson internationalist," and party regulars began rallying around him.

John Nance Garner of Texas, his chief rival for the nomination, did not want the vice-presidency but was a loyal Democrat who chose not to risk party divisions that might result in President Herbert Hoover's return for another four years. When Garner was persuaded to accept second place on the ticket, the way was cleared to nominate Roosevelt.

Every move in Roosevelt's campaign that fall was designed to show him as a man of action. He and his family had remained in Albany listening to radio and telephone reports from the convention, but he already had planned a dramatic gesture—an airplane was gassed and waiting to carry him, his wife, and others of his staff to Chicago, where he intended to deliver his acceptance speech. Not only was the flight itself compelling news, but the very idea of a nominee appearing in person was a defiant break with tradition. Until that time the custom was for candidates to stay home until officially "notified" of their nomination. Then they would deliver an "acceptance" speech from their front porch, the town square, or some other appropriate rostrum.

Buffeted by strong head winds, Roosevelt's flimsy trimotor plane was three hours late in reaching its destination. By that time, convention attendees had grown tired of speeches and had turned to bandleaders and songsters in attempts to bolster flagging spirits.

Frequent radio reports had kept delegates and the public informed of the plane's westward progress, and when at last it landed, a huge crowd was waiting at the airport. A triumphant motorcade snaked its way to the convention hall, where after an enthusiastic introduction, Roosevelt delivered one of the most highly acclaimed speeches of his long career.

He began with an ad-libbed apology, saying that he had no control over "the winds of heaven," but the rest of his address had been carefully scripted in close collaboration with Louis Howe and Sam Rosenman. The peroration caught on immediately and became the trademark of Roosevelt's subsequent administrations:

Never before in modern history have the essential differences between the two major parties stood out in such striking contrast as they do today. . . . I pledge you, I pledge myself, to a *NEW DEAL* [italics supplied] for the American people. . . . This is more than a political campaign; it is a call to arms. Give me your help, not to win votes alone, but to win in this crusade to restore America to its own people.[2]

Throughout the campaign, FDR found it easier to assail the policies of President Hoover than to spell out his own. In point of fact, in 1932, Roosevelt's opinions did not seem very different from Hoover's. At the time, FDR believed in keeping expenditures within income, so he repeatedly denounced President Hoover for failing to balance the federal budget.

Every important speech given by FDR that fall dealt with a major topic. In Topeka, it was the farm problem: he promised to reorganize the Department of Agriculture, reduce taxes for farmers, offer federal help in refinancing mortgages, and lower tariffs, and he hinted about a government allotment plan to handle farm surpluses. In Salt Lake City he suggested an idea for revitalizing the railroad industry. In Seattle he attacked high tariffs, and in Portland he demanded disclosure of the financial dealings of public utilities. In Detroit, without giving details as to how it might be done, he called for removing the causes of poverty.

The 1932 campaign was confusing but boisterous and invigorating. November produced the first of FDR's enormous victories. He and his running mate, Garner, won 22,815,539 votes to Hoover's 15,759,930, while capturing 472 electoral votes in carrying forty-two of the forty-eight states.

FDR loved giving speeches, and many of his best ones were delivered during campaign stints. He had become an orator of rank soon after being elected governor of New York. That campaign had given him practical lessons in public speaking. In those early speeches he kept trying to make his messages warm, intimate, and aimed at specific individuals in his audience, believing that if he could rivet their attention others would pay close heed. Hence he tried to gauge the impact of his speeches by observing reactions of persons he deliberately watched during the time he was talking. Once after speaking to several thousand people in Philadelphia, as he was leaving in his automobile, he turned to his son Franklin, Jr., and asked, "Did you see that funny hat the woman in fourteenth row was wearing?"[3]

Shackled by heavy steel braces on both legs after the disastrous polio attack in 1921, FDR sometimes tried to be jocular about his condition and might interject such remarks as "Really, it's as funny as a crutch" or "Sorry, but I have to run now."

He usually used one arm to rest on the lectern, steadying himself as he spoke, and the other hand then was free to turn the pages of his manuscript.

In his day there were no such contrivances as teleprompters, so he spoke either extemporaneously or from a manuscript. He preferred the latter for several reasons, one of which was the confidence that came from his superb ability to read with feeling. Whatever he lacked in bodily gestures while speaking he made up for with his resonant voice and expressive vocal features.[4]

Frequently in campaigning, FDR popularized such striking phrases as "the do-nothing-or-wait-and-see policy," "the well-upholstered, hindsight critic," and "an every-man-for-himself kind of society." He felt no embarrassment at using words such as "shenanigans," "botch," "jazz," and "chisel," which many persons at the time considered slang. Vernacular was well understood by his diverse listeners and reinforced his image as a man in close touch with them.

On the hustings, where image-provoking language not only is permissible but expected, FDR displayed talents for analogy, hyperbole, oversimplification, or sarcasm whenever the occasion demanded. Phrases and slogans were not the only elements making up his eloquence, of course, and no matter how carefully appeals were selected and refined by aides, the words did not become speeches until uttered by Roosevelt himself.

In addition to language, he had other undeniable assets for communication. Among them was good judgment in knowing when and where to make his speeches. He also had a flair for the dramatic. Beyond these two natural gifts was his exceptional ability to read aloud. His mobile face could reflect a wide variety of reactions and seemed to lead the changes in his vocal stress and intonations. Through his voice he could portray amusement, solemnity, empathy, ridicule, or exasperation, and he was never dull. He considered the rostrum his stage and once said to Orson Welles, "You know, Orson, you and I are the two best actors in America."

Roosevelt's tenor voice was widely praised even by those Midwestern critics who sometimes mocked his Eastern pronunciations. One distinguished speech teacher and poet, Lew Sarett, observed:

> The President spoke over the air for a few minutes, and millions of Americans had a new light in their eyes, new confidence in their hearts . . . if Herbert Hoover had spoken the same words into the microphone . . . the stock market would have fallen another notch and public confidence with it. The cues in Franklin D. Roosevelt's voice—the voice alone—inspired confidence.[5]

Few public persons have demonstrated greater respect for the power of the spoken word or worked harder to use it effectively than did Franklin

Roosevelt. The emergence of radio as a widespread means of communication had much to do with his success. His conversational speaking style, distinct pronunciation, mellifluous voice, and ability to read with feeling were excellently adapted to the new medium.

Beyond whatever immediate audience he might be addressing, millions of listeners sat by their radios and got the impression FDR was talking directly to them. The speaking style and related techniques which won him the White House in 1932 would be used again throughout his campaigns in 1936, 1940, and to a somewhat lesser degree in 1944 when fatal illness was sapping his once limitless energies.*

HARRY TRUMAN

In contrast with Roosevelt, who entered active politics at the age of twenty-eight, Harry Truman was thirty-eight before he made his first bid for public office. And even then it was for an office that would have warranted only a microscopic dot on a map of national politics.

Just as a wartime friendship had been the impetus for starting his clothing business, Truman's unique ties with Battery D of World War I helped launch his first campaign. This opening shot must have resembled a veterans' reunion almost as much as a political rally, for through a fortuitous combination of politics and the military, Jim Pendergast, son of Mike and nephew of Big Tom, had been a second lieutenant in Truman's army battalion. The fact that Truman was picked by the Pendergasts is attested by several sources, but the versions differ somewhat.[6]

Democrats in Jackson County then were divided into two main factions: the "Goats" and the "Rabbits." The "Goats," led by the Pendergasts, included a large Irish population, many of whom had served in Truman's regiment. Years later HST gave his version of why he decided to run:

> Mr. Wm. Southern, editor and publisher of the INDEPENDENCE EXAMINER, the most widely read paper in Jackson County outside of Kansas City, suggested to some of the Eastern Jackson County politicians, that if they wanted a candidate for Eastern Judge who could win they should take an ex-soldier of the late war. He suggested Harry Truman.

---

*It is not the purpose of this book to dwell at length on particular speeches delivered by Franklin Roosevelt or to describe in detail each of his four campaigns for the presidency. Readers who want to pursue such topics are encouraged to consult the book's bibliography.

I knew nothing of this until a delegation of men from the County came into my store on 12th Street and asked me to run. My father having been road overseer, and both of us having always been interested in politics to some extent, I knew all the men in the delegation personally. They told me about Mr. Southern's suggestion to the "Goat" faction of the Democrats and urged me to go.

They told me that the Eastern Jackson County "Goat" faction would back me tooth and nail, and that if I won the nomination the "Rabbits" had agreed to support me.[7]

Winning a Democratic nomination in Jackson County, Missouri, in 1922 was tantamount to winning the office, and by running an aggressive race in a hotly contested primary, Truman beat out four other candidates. His advertisements stressed that he was a native son, a veteran, a farmer, and a businessman.

Far from being as glib and polished as FDR on the platform, it would never be said that Truman's oratory by itself won him many votes. His presentations, although factual, were not particularly impressive, and his very first one bordered on disaster.

The day on which Truman made his first political speech was also the day on which he took his first airplane ride. He had initiated a promotion stunt by getting Eddie McKim, a military buddy, to swing a deal with a former army pilot to fly over the crowd and drop circulars. The pilot and Truman went up in an old jenny plane "held together with baling wire" and dropped the leaflets somewhat as planned.

McKim later described the event:

Well, we got them started off and got the leaflets loaded in; they took off from the pasture, and circled around this picnic in Oak Grove. They came down all right, but Clarence [the pilot] had a little trouble stopping the plane, and it ended up about three feet from a barbed wire fence. Our candidate got out and gave forth with a lot of things I know he didn't eat! He was as green as grass. I think it was his first flight, but he mounted the rostrum and made a speech.[8]

Even the most ardent Republicans around Kansas City at the time conceded that the forthcoming election would show a Democratic sweep, particularly in county offices. Their predictions proved accurate, for when the votes began coming in, it was apparent that the Democrats would garner a huge victory. Truman won handily over his Republican opponent. Thus in November 1922, when FDR was crippled by polio and reentering the practice of law, Harry Truman, a man who eight months earlier had been forced to close his failing business, became the county judge for the Eastern District of Jackson County.

Two years later, Truman ran for reelection, but there were national circumstances beyond his control. It was a presidential election year, and prosperity was in the saddle. Business was booming, prices were high, and new technologies captured the public's attention. The Democratic party of Woodrow Wilson was in shambles, while national support for Calvin Coolidge, who declared "the business of America is business," rose quickly and swept him into office.

The Republican wave reached into Jackson County, where voting was exceedingly heavy. Almost as soon as the first returns began coming in, the trend was obvious. Republicans would capture the county just as Democrats had done two years earlier.

Factors other than the national mood contributed to Truman's losing his seat. The former alliance of "Goats" and "Rabbits" within the Democrats broke down, and accompanying fissures made a victory for their party most unlikely. Moreover, Truman's public statements criticizing the Ku Klux Klan probably cost him at the time more votes than they won. The loss taught him a lot about campaigning. Without realizing it, he had practiced even then certain aggressive tactics which he would strengthen and use in future contests.

Startled by their earlier losses, in 1926 Jackson County Democrats drew the party together in order to back a winning candidate. With a united party behind him and with good marks for his previous two-year term, Harry Truman was easily elected presiding judge of the Jackson County Court— a position he held for the next eight years.

The political talks Truman gave during the time he was a county judge were largely ones of explanation, description, or defense of the court's record. Just as the condition of county roads had been a frequent theme during his campaigns, the subject also served as the main topic in many subsequent speeches.

It was his practice during this period to write his speeches in longhand before they were delivered. The drafts of these talks indicate that he wrote them in a manner similar to the way in which he spoke—rapidly, and often unmindful of nuances and wording. The sentences were short and choppy, with scant attention paid to the niceties of conjunctives or transitions. There is little evidence that he ever gave the speeches much polish or editing, for seldom are his first words or phrases changed. The result was a pattern of speaking that was terse, dry, and lacking in much intellectual stimulation.

Truman's persuasive strength sprang not from eloquence but from his exemplification of the ordinary person. He was the citizen who dared to reach a little farther than the persons around him. Moreover, he had shown himself and others that he could win at the polls. The resultant public image was a persuasive plus that would follow him throughout his political career.

The off-year election of 1934 produced great congressional gains for the Roosevelt administration. Among the freshmen senators was Harry S. Truman of Missouri. Because he was a gregarious politician with an excellent record, again with strong backing from the Pendergasts, Truman had won the Democratic nomination over two other strong contenders. As a result of his primary victory, he was in an advantageous position, for President Roosevelt and the Democrats were at the height of popularity. Truman unequivocally endorsed Roosevelt's leadership and praised all the national relief programs. So solid was his backing of Roosevelt's programs, it was said that he approved in advance all that the administration thereafter would do.[9]

To voters in Missouri the choice in 1934 seemed clear, and they went the same way as did voters in Pennsylvania, Indiana, and other states where established conservatives met and were defeated by comparative unknowns who unequivocally lauded FDR and the New Deal.

During his first term, Senator Truman focused most of his attention on matters of transportation, interstate finance, and regulation of corporate practices. By the spring of 1940 there was no doubt he would run for reelection, and at a carefully selected spot in central Missouri (Sedalia), he formally announced his candidacy. Again, he appealed to groups that had backed him earlier: "I have been faithful to my promises of 1934 to veterans, to labor, to the farmers, to the Administration. I have supported the leadership of the Democratic Party in the Senate and have upheld the President in all matters of National Policy."[10]

Truman felt that he deserved Roosevelt's backing because of his faithful New Deal voting record. Furthermore, he had praised FDR on many occasions and had been particularly laudatory at the Missouri Democratic Convention in 1936 where he characterized the president as the "Bonhomie Roosevelt."

The popular Roosevelt wore long coattails in 1940, and most Democrats grabbed eagerly at them. In one speech, Truman remarked rather breezily: "Just the other day I spent a very pleasant hour with the President at the White House, discussing various bills pending in Congress, and he expressed the hope that I would come back to the Senate next year."[11]

Truman was unsuccessful, however, in getting a public endorsement from the politically astute Roosevelt, who refused to be led into an open avowal of any of the contenders among Missouri Democrats.

The president's failure to back him publicly in the Missouri primary struck at Truman's confidence, and he admitted that "it looked very dark for the junior senator from Missouri." On the night of the primary he went to bed believing he had lost the race. However, when the smoke cleared and results were announced, a jubilant HST discovered he had won the nomination with a plurality of nearly 8,000 votes.

In the general election he was opposed by Manvel Davis, a Kansas City Republican, who made the grave mistake of running as much against FDR as he did against Senator Truman. Truman gained reelection by a vote of 930,775 to Davis' 886,376. The margin was closer than Democrats in Missouri had experienced for many years, but Truman had kept his Senate seat.

Four years later, when Truman became the vice-presidential nominee, FDR encouraged him to do "some campaigning," saying, "I don't feel like going everywhere," and in fact, FDR that year campaigned only in New York, Chicago, Boston, and Philadelphia.

Dramatic events occurring throughout the world in the fall of 1944 made it difficult for either major political party to arouse public interest over domestic policies, and it was no great surprise when Roosevelt won another electoral landslide.

FDR seems never to have discussed anything important with his third vice president and apparently did not look upon Truman as a deputy head of government any more than he had regarded Truman's two predecessors, John Nance Garner and Henry Agard Wallace, as vital members of the New Deal administration. In his mind all three were merely vice presidents, likely to sink into obscurity along with the others who had occupied that office. Nor was there much evidence that Truman overestimated his new role; he knew American history too well to do that. "I'll bet you can't name the names of half a dozen vice presidents," he told his sister.

The story of how Truman became president of the United States has been told many times, and yet it keeps its fascination, for it is a story of both inevitability and surprise. In that spring of 1945 it was evident to many Americans that the once robust health of Franklin Roosevelt had weakened. His eloquent, moving radio voice had lost its vigor; the famous smile and friendly warmth were displayed infrequently. With his energy gone but optimistic as always, in April he went to Warm Springs, Georgia, to recuperate. About 1:15 in the afternoon of April 12, the impending disaster struck. Only a few hours later a stunned world heard the first network radio newsman stumble slightly over the pronunciation of *cerebral* but announce, "President Roosevelt has died of a *cerebral* hemorrhage!"[12] It was the end of an epoch.

Truman trailed none of his predecessor's clouds of glory. Early in his administration he was fond of saying that he had been elected on the Roosevelt platform and that he meant to continue those programs. It was typical Truman—frank, simple, and honest.

Truman lacked Roosevelt's style, his prestige, and his informal, patrician grandeur. Yet the Missourian had talents of his own that soon began to surface. As a result of his grounding in American history, Truman understood the role of the presidency.

There is no hard evidence that he needed encouragement to run for a full term of his own, but an initial show of support came from a small unofficial group that began meeting early in 1947. The so-called liberal wing of advisers formed the group's nucleus, and it included Oscar Ewing, Charles S. Murphy, Matt Connelly, Leon Keyserling, and Robert Hannegan, who then was chairman of the Democratic National Committee and had helped engineer Truman's selection as FDR's vice president. Clark Clifford, who had started as Truman's speech writer but who by then was one of his closest and most trusted advisers, frequently joined the informal gatherings.

James Rowe, an early administrative assistant to FDR, later an employee of the Justice Department, and by 1947 in private practice with Tommy "the Cork" Corcoran, summarized the views of Ewing, Murphy, Keyserling, and certain other Truman advisers at the time. Rowe's lengthy thirty-three-page single-spaced summary entitled "The Politics of 1948" was funneled through Clifford, who changed very little except to add a section on civil rights.

This Rowe-Clifford memorandum—which was sent to President Truman almost a full year before the 1948 election took place—set forth seven major assumptions:

1. Governor Thomas Dewey of New York would be the nominee of the Republican party.

2. President Truman would be elected if the administration would concentrate on the Democratic alliance between the South and West.

3. Henry Wallace would become the candidate of a third party.

4. The independent voter in 1948 would hold the balance of power and would not actively support President Truman unless a great effort were made.

5. The foreign policy issues of the campaign would center on relations with the Soviet Union and the administration's handling of foreign reconstruction and relief.

6. The domestic issues of the campaign would be high prices and housing.

7. Tensions and conflict between the president and the legislative branch of the government would increase during the Congressional sessions of 1948.

Even more important than the Rowe-Clifford memo was the drum-beat emanating from the liberal Ewing group. Although not openly identified in the manner of FDR's "brain trust," these close advisers were the ones who pressed their conclusions upon a receptive HST. In essence, the battle for Truman's mind was won by this wing of advisers over conservative opposition from Cabinet members such as Treasury Secretary John Synder and Agriculture Secretary Clinton Anderson.

President Truman not only had the Republicans to contend with in 1948; the two extreme wings of the Democratic party fielded candidates as well. Dixiecrats representing a conservative bloc in the South bolted and nominated Governor Strom Thurmond of South Carolina. At the other end of the spectrum, liberals formed the Progressive party and chose Henry Wallace as their standard bearer. HST, though, refused to quit. At the age of sixty-four, a mere two years younger than his fallen predecessor, he threw his full energies into the fight and simply outhustled all opponents.

He also polished his earthy, combative speaking style, which audiences loved. His sixteen-car train, dubbed the *Truman Special* with its Pullman sleeping car in the rear called the *Ferdinand Magellan*, traveled 31,700 miles in thirty-five days that fall, and by Truman's count he made 356 speeches. His fiery rhetoric scorched the "do-nothing Congress" and the Republican party while enthusiastic listeners shouted the familiar, "Give 'em hell, Harry!"

On most days there would be one or two outdoor rallies or even a major speech off the train. Then there would be a rush back to the railroad station to keep the campaign on its tight schedule. Truman had used an extemporaneous delivery during a warm-up trip in June when he went to California to give the commencement address at the University of California, and it was this seemingly off-the-cuff presentation that he used throughout his fall campaign.

Senator Robert Taft, leader of the opposition Republicans in that body, helped bring a new term into popular usage—a term that worked greatly to Truman's advantage. The Ohio senator criticized the president for "blackguarding Congress at every whistle station [sic] in the West." This reference gave the doughty Truman an opportunity too good to pass up. He and his staff immediately seized upon the Ohioan's blundering language. In telegrams to thirty-five mayors of towns where Truman spoke, civic leaders were asked if they agreed with Taft's description of their town as a whistle station. The bulk of the answers made Taft look ridiculous; typical responses include the following:

(From Seattle) Seattle is not a whistle stop, but everyone who sees her stops and whistles, including Presidents and Senators.

(From Grand Island, Nebraska) Grand Island was never a whistle stop. Third largest city in Nebraska with 25,000 of the finest people in the midwest.

(From Gary, Indiana) Senator Taft in very poor taste to refer to Gary as quote whistle stop unquote. 135,000 citizens of America's greatest steel city resent this slur.

(From Los Angeles) The term hardly applies to the Los Angeles metropolitan area in which presently live one-thirty-fifth of all the people in the United States, considerably more than half of the population of Ohio.

(From Crestline, Ohio) Senator Taft's description of our town as a whistle stop is rather misleading in view of the fact that Crestline, Ohio, a town of 5,000 population, is served by two of the world's greatest transportation systems, Pennsylvania Railroad Company and the New York Central ... suggest Senator Taft consult time tables of the above referred to transportation systems for a proper classification, proper description of a "whistle stop."[13]

The strategy planned and adopted by Truman a year in advance proved eminently productive, and the election results of 1948 are well-known history. To the utter dismay of pundits and pollsters, Truman pulled off a stunning upset, capturing 24,105,000 popular votes and 303 electoral ones while Dewey collected 21,969,000 popular votes and 189 electoral ones.

Throughout the campaign, it seemed the platitudes of Dewey could not stand against the commonsense utterances of Truman. In the last analysis, the slim margin of victory might have been provided by the personalities of the two men. Truman seemed more warm and human than did the detached and lofty Dewey. No one could gainsay the adroitly planned campaign conducted by the president and his aides, but the bottom line of the final report showed that Truman did just what he had done in nine earlier political races—talk oftener, talk plainer, and work harder than the person running against him.[14]

Chapter 7

FDR: Economics

The year of 1932 was one of the gloomiest in America's history, and when Franklin Roosevelt was inaugurated as the nation's thirty-first president in March 1933, his most critical crisis by far was an internal one—a depression so deep there were alarming signs of revolt.

Unruly demonstrations by idled workers had broken out in Seattle, Los Angeles, and Chicago, and bread lines in the Bowery of lower Manhattan were drawing two thousand hungry people daily. Milwaukee, Denver, Detroit, Philadelphia, and Kansas City, along with countless other cities, opened municipal soup kitchens; formerly employed men were selling apples on street corners; dispossessed families shivered in makeshift hovels in the dead of winter; and itinerants bivouacked around wood fires at the railroad tracks.

Smaller industrial towns also suffered. In Muncie, Indiana—the Middletown of sociological America—every third factory worker had lost his job. Unskilled workers were first to feel the shocks from the nation's plummeting economy. Makers of ready-to-wear clothing, bakery and confectionery helpers, field hands, cannery employees, and other seasonal workers were callously exploited.

Those lucky enough to have a job—any kind of job—were forced to take pay cuts of monstrous proportions. Department store clerks were paid as little as five or ten dollars weekly, and an investigation of a group of working girls in Chicago revealed that the great majority of them were working for less than twenty-five cents an hour, a fourth of them for less than ten cents. Stenographers' and secretaries' salaries fell from thirty-five and forty-five dollars a week to sixteen dollars a week.

Professional classes likewise found their incomes drastically reduced as fees became increasingly hard to collect. Physicians' incomes were a third of what they had been prior to 1929, and the income of lawyers showed a similar drop.

In the heartlands, where farmers had outlasted eight years of high industrial prices and depressed agricultural markets even before the advent of the Great Depression, the picture was even grimmer. Tumbling farm prices touched off waves of mortgage foreclosures that cost thousands of farmers their homes. There seemed to be never-ending problems of supply and demand, middlemen's costs and profits, tariffs, farm abandonments, and creeping urbanization with its accompanying complexities.

Across the country, a so-called Farm Holiday, loosely organized for the purpose of bolstering farm prices, spread rapidly. Unfortunately, the movement soon spawned incidents of violence.

In Iowa—a state boasting more than one-quarter of all the grade A agricultural land in America—the danger to established government was clearly evident. At Le Mars, a town in the northwestern part of that Hawkeye State, an angry gang of normally law-abiding citizens broke into foreclosure hearings in the courtroom of District Judge C. C. Bradley and dragged him out into the countryside where, with encouragement from onlookers, the crowd's leaders placed a noose around his neck, smeared grease in his hair, and threatened him with other indignities.

In scattered parts of the state, railroad bridges were burned, and special deputies had numerous clashes with roadside pickets gathered to stop farmers daring enough to try to get their products to markets. As larger crowds rallied, the violence increased. A milk hauler from South Dakota was shot and killed when he attempted to bring a truckload of milk into nearby Sioux City.[1]

The worsening economy was also choking the life out of the nation's financial and free enterprise system. More than eighty-five thousand business failures had been recorded along with the suspension of five thousand banks. Wage losses were upward of $26 billion, and savings accounts representing the toil and sweat of more than 9 million workers had been wiped out.

Like a physician confronted by a patient with multiple diseases, the new president was hard pressed to know which symptoms of the nation's economic illness ought to be treated first. Fever over the banking system seemed the most dangerous.

A few hours before Roosevelt's inauguration, every bank in America had closed its doors, and no one could be sure if and when they might reopen.

Inauguration Day, Saturday, March 4, 1933, set off a whirlwind of activity among incoming administrators. Late in the afternoon, after Washington streets had cleared of celebrants, FDR brought together members of his new cabinet and had them sworn in en masse—a dramatic procedure never done before.

The next afternoon, he convened them in the Oval Room of the White House and disclosed two proclamations he had prepared: one calling Congress into a special session, and the other declaring a bank holiday and controlling the export of gold.

To a depressed citizenry the news that a cabinet meeting was being held on a Sunday afternoon seemed a sign of the new administration's vigorous intentions, and that belief was heightened on Monday when FDR's two proclamations were duly issued.

The Banking Bill, the first of multitudinous ones FDR would sign in the next thirteen years, owed its legitimacy to an obscure item in the Trading with the Enemy Act dating back to 1917. FDR's proposal called for giving the president authority to control transactions in foreign exchange as well as the right to take possession of all gold in the country and to keep a bank closed for any period he directed.

A special session of Congress convened four days later on Thursday, March 9, and received Roosevelt's urgent plea to take "immediate action" to halt the run on banks and the hoarding of gold. Accordingly, amid an atmosphere of hysteria and with less than eight hours of debate, both Houses of Congress passed the Emergency Banking Act. The bill was not referred to a standing committee; there was no minority caucus or strategy session. Banking was so technical that even most of those who voted for it did not understand it.

On Sunday, March 12, President Roosevelt in another dramatic move took to the microphone and held his first "fireside chat" with the American people. In it he analyzed the banking crisis and forecast other steps that lay ahead, and he assured the American people that their savings in closed banks were secure. "Let us unite in banishing fear," the president declared, "it is your problem no less than it is mine. Together we cannot fail."

On this precedent-setting occasion, he discussed legislation for the control of federal reserve banks and announced that he had ordered a bank holiday to stop the run on banks. His talk on the complicated subject of banking was worded so simply that it led America's celebrated humorist

Will Rogers to observe, "He made everybody understand it, even the bankers!"

President Hoover once had proposed a similar banking moratorium, but his term carried connotations of deaths and crematoriums. At any rate, Hoover's suggestion had gone unheeded until Roosevelt phrased the same idea in plainer language and treated it merely as a bank holiday.

In the momentous three months following his inauguration—a period historians came to term the Hundred Days—FDR sent fifteen messages to Congress, guided fifteen major laws into action, delivered ten speeches, held press conferences and cabinet meetings twice a week, and made major decisions affecting economic and domestic policies.

He had come into office during a time of domestic peril, and he channeled his dynamic energy toward those concerns. By the time the 73rd Congress, goaded by the president, adjourned on June 15, 1933, it had passed the following measures:

1. Emergency Banking Act
2. Economy Act
3. Establishment of the Civilian Conservation Corps
4. Abandonment of the Gold Standard
5. Federal Emergency Relief Act (creating a national relief system)
6. Agricultural Adjustment Act
7. Emergency Farm Mortgage Act (providing for refinancing of farm mortgages)
8. Tennessee Valley Authority Act
9. Truth-in-Securities Act (requiring disclosure in the issuance of new securities)
10. Abrogation of the gold clause in public and private contracts
11. Home Owners' Loan Act (providing for refinancing of home mortgages)
12. National Industrial Recovery Act (NRA—providing for industrial self-government under federal supervision and for a $3.3 billion public works program)
13. Glass-Stegall Banking Act (divorcing commercial and investment banking and guaranteeing bank deposits)
14. Farm Credit Act (providing for the reorganization of agricultural credit agencies)

15. Railroad Coordination Act (creating a federal coordinator of transportation).

The Democratic Convention in the fall of 1932 had called for the repeal of the Eighteenth Amendment to the Constitution, the amendment that banned the manufacture and sale of alcohol. No matter how well-intentioned, Prohibition's Volstead Act failed to reduce the country's consumption of alcoholic beverages; in fact, the actual consumption had increased. Moreover, the amendment had proved to be impossible to enforce and had led to unforeseen corruption and violence.

Prohibition had hardly been enacted before a new occupation, bootlegging, had sprung up to quench the public thirst. The federal government in ten years made over half a million arrests for violating Prohibition laws, but the number of infractions kept growing. Smuggling increased along Canadian and Mexican borders; mountain moonshiners multiplied; and obliging vineyards in California and New York provided unlimited grape juice which, with a little time, yeast, and minimal knowledge, one could quickly sell as a top-grade product. Every city became studded with speakeasies, and those who chose not to patronize such places made their own bathtub gin or got along with home-brewed beer and cider.

Roosevelt's decisive victory made it almost certain that he would attempt to end the Prohibition Era, and he did so by urging Congress to pass a law legalizing the sale of light wines and beer. Congress readily obliged—in the House without even a roll call—and also recommended the Twenty-First Amendment to the U.S. Constitution. The amendment, repealing federal Prohibition, was prepared and promptly ratified the following December.

The most ambitious of President Roosevelt's early proposals was the National Industrial Recovery Act which Congress passed in June 1933. Known as the NRA, this cornucopia of New Deal programs was aimed at mollifying both industrial leaders and labor factions. To industry, it promised government enforcement of price and production agreements, and to labor it established wages-and-hours regulations along with other concessions. Proponents argued that the act would stabilize production and cause prices and wages to go up. The New Dealers drafting the bill added another fillip, namely, a large-scale public-works spending program.

With the act's passage, President Roosevelt called upon the citizenry to accept a blanket code, providing minimum wages of thirty cents or forty cents per hour, maximum working hours of thirty-five or forty per week, and the abolition of child labor. Employers who agreed with the code displayed the NRA blue-eagle symbol, and all consumers who cooperated were to sign pledges that they would buy only from blue-eagle establishments.

The NRA not only established minimum wages and maximum hours for workers; even more important, it affirmed organized labor's right to bargain collectively and led to the passage of the even stronger Wagner Act (1935), providing effective government protection for unions.

The NRA represented the heart and soul of President Roosevelt's early New Deal; however, at the time he and Congress were moving to the left, the Supreme Court was heading to the right. A test case involving the NRA code and collective-bargaining systems finally reached the Supreme Court in 1935, and to Roosevelt's great chagrin the court in a unanimous decision ruled that the NRA was an unconstitutional delegation of legislative power and an unwarranted effort to control interstate commerce.

FDR's anger simmered for four days and then boiled over. He held a press conference and castigated the Court, declaring that its ruling meant that the country had been "relegated to the horse-and-buggy definition of interstate commerce." He intended to carry the fight further but would have to wait until a more propitious time.

Notwithstanding the court's invalidation of the NRA, most of FDR's vigorous reform programs, including the monumental Social Security Act, had been enacted by the time his first term ended. Of all New Deal measures, the Social Security Act of 1935 was the most fundamental. Even before the Great Depression struck, the United States lagged behind the industrial nations of Europe in offering protection against unemployment or in making provisions for old age.

Sentiment for such legislation had been voiced occasionally in Congress even before President Roosevelt took office, but no pertinent legislation had been developed. FDR was generally sympathetic to the idea of more protection for the unemployed and the aged, but he moved cautiously. It was not until January 1935 that he recommended the relevant legislation.

Congress debated his proposal for six months before both Houses overwhelmingly passed it in August. A jubilant FDR proclaimed Social Security "the supreme achievement of the New Deal," and he may have been right, for the act immediately won praise and universal acceptance. Moreover, there were political gains inasmuch as the Social Security Act dampened the clamor from Townsendites advocating federal grants to all persons over the age of sixty and at the same time burst the "share-the-wealth" bubble of flamboyant Senator Huey Long of Louisiana.

The 1936 election represented the zenith of the New Deal; in Roosevelt's following administrations, there would be no such spate of legislation, particularly in economic fields.

Until FDR's second term, few Americans had heard of John Maynard Keynes, a British economist who advocated large-scale economic planning by governments instead of the traditional concept of laissez-faire capitalism. Democratic governments, it was argued, should be less concerned over balanced budgets; the solution to periodic depressions lay in deficit spending. The best way to get prices up was to stimulate national purchasing power, not the other way around. The surest way to promote employment, according to Keynes and his followers, was to institute a program of government spending on public works, for such spending would increase national purchasing power as well as expand employment in private industry.

For governments struggling to climb out of the worldwide depression, Keynesian arguments for a planned economy were very appealing, nowhere more than in the United States. During Franklin Roosevelt's first year in office, Felix Frankfurter, one of his advisers then at Oxford, had several talks with Keynes. In December, Frankfurter forwarded to Roosevelt an open letter from Keynes. The letter was scheduled to appear in the *New York Times* and contained the rationale for deficit spending. A few months later, when Keynes came to the United States to receive an honorary degree from Columbia, he visited the White House to have tea and chat with FDR.

Most of Roosevelt's early advisers on economics were dyed-in-the-wool Keynesians, several of whom were professors at Columbia University—men such as Raymond Moley; Rexford Guy Tugwell, an expert on agriculture; and Adolph A. Berle, Jr., from the law school. FDR termed them his "brain trust." Such advisers encouraged him to turn abstract economic theories into political actions. The resultant actions became known as "pump-priming," and were built on the conviction that to relieve unemployment it was essential to use government funds to subsidize private enterprise even when the practice demanded deficit financing.

Pump-priming and alphabetical agencies cost money, however, and the primary source of revenue was taxation. Increasing the government's income, therefore, had to be a continuing priority for President Roosevelt. During his terms, federal tax revenues showed a massive increase from $1.9 billion in 1933 (about 3 percent of the gross national product) to $44.1 billion in 1945 (about 21 percent of the gross national product).[2]

FDR valued taxes more for their ability to fund new programs than for their capacity to redistribute income and wealth. He had campaigned first on a balanced budget, and during the New Deal years he sought to achieve that goal by stepping up levels of taxation. From 1933 through 1938 he made determined, though largely unsuccessful, efforts to shift the tax burden to the wealthiest individuals and corporations. Then with the coming of World War II, he endeavored to hold down inflation by ever-rising tax rates.

Barely two months into his first administration, FDR brought Harry Hopkins into his administration, and it was Hopkins who became FDR's chief apostle of the New Deal and the most cordially hated by its enemies. Hopkins was an administrator rather than a planner; his forte was getting things done quickly.

Three weeks after he entered government service, Hopkins went to Detroit where he spoke out in favor of relief as a duty the federal government owed its citizens. Benevolent private agencies might be useful, but the major responsibility for meeting the needs of the unemployed rested on the shoulders of elected officials. Without realizing it, Hopkins voiced what became the Roosevelt doctrine, namely, that federal relief was a sacred trust, an obligation rather than mere charitable alleviation of suffering.

Hopkins inherited scattered previous government relief organizations headed by dedicated social workers like himself. Then in the fall of 1933, during a lunch with the president, he proposed a gigantic program that would entail creating 4 million new jobs. FDR said that number of jobs would cost somewhere around $400 million, and he thought that amount might be provided from the Public Works fund under the guardianship of Harold Ickes.

This initial transfer, which required delicate maneuvering and explanation by FDR because it encroached on directions he previously had given to Ickes, his secretary of the interior, became the genesis of the Works Progress Administration (WPA).

Ickes directed the Public Works Administration (PWA) and was a meticulous administrator concerned about returns of investments made with taxpayers' dollars. By contrast, Hopkins "did not give a damn about the return; his approach was that of a social worker who was interested only in getting relief to the miserable and getting it there quickly."[3]

During the years from 1933 to 1938, Hopkins administered the Federal Emergency Relief Administration, the Civil Works Administration, the Federal Surplus Relief Administration, and the gigantic Works Progress

Administration. These were controversial agencies; as a result, he became a favorite target for New Deal critics.

The WPA established in 1935 epitomized the New Deal and became the largest work-relief program in the history of the country. Led by the resourceful Hopkins, this agency alone employed more than 2 million people a month. Under its aegis were built thousands of schools, libraries, parks, sidewalks, and hospitals. It put hundreds of poverty-stricken writers, musicians, and artists to work, and also provided hot lunches for children of the poor.

Contemptuous of bureaucratic procedures, Hopkins proved to Roosevelt that he was "utterly trustworthy." Often regarded as a sinister figure, a backstairs intriguer, an Iowan combination of Machiavelli, Svengali, and Rasputin, Hopkins won FDR's confidence so entirely that for many years he lived at the White House. Although administering programs that took billions of dollars from the federal treasury, Hopkins asked and received almost nothing for himself. One cartoonist portrayed his record by showing a door outside an office prominently marked WPA. A printed notice on the wall read: "To the everlasting honor of HARRY L. HOPKINS—an American boy from Iowa who spent 9 billions of his country's money and not a dollar stuck to his fingers!"[4]

By 1938, the middle of FDR's second term, virtually all the alphabetical agencies that made up the New Deal's approach to economic problems had been enacted: Works Progress Administration (WPA), Civilian Conservation Corps (CCC), Public Works Administration (PWA), Agricultural Adjustment Act (AAA), Home Owners' Loan Act (HOLA), Tennessee Valley Authority (TVA), and the ill-fated National Recovery Act (NRA).

By 1939 and with the coming of war prosperity the Great Depression had run its course; relief and recovery problems disappeared as spirits for reform ebbed. New Deal Congresses, under continual pressure from the man in the White House, had enacted an unprecedented series of laws—laws which among other actions regulated the securities market, established a minimum wage, guaranteed labor's right to collective bargaining, set up controls over the nation's money supply, and originated a long-range system of social security. William Leuchtenberg, historian of the New Deal, later evaluated the era: "It is hard to think of another period in the whole history of the republic that was so fruitful or of a crisis that was met with such imagination."[5]

By the middle of FDR's second administration, America's economic problems had lessened only to be replaced by events occurring in Europe and Asia. Even by 1939 no one could be sure where such happenings might lead, but the outlook was ominous. Few persons at the time understood the peril better than President Roosevelt, and thereafter his attention along with that of the public would turn increasingly toward foreign affairs.

Chapter 8

HST: Economics

In contrast to the Great Depression that confronted Franklin Roosevelt in 1932, when Harry Truman came into the presidency war's prosperity had swept over the country. Truman entered office with an outlook shaped by his Middlewestern background. His forte was practical politics. In most economic matters his orientation was more akin to that of the small businessman than to that of the Eastern New Dealers who dominated FDR's brain trust. Truman felt most at home with those who shared his pragmatic middle-of-the-road philosophies, but he was quite comfortable with conservatives who championed the role of business in American society.

Well aware that he had been chosen largely because of his excellent reputation in the Senate where he consistently had supported legislation proposed by the liberal wing of the Democratic party, Truman insisted that he meant to follow Roosevelt's general course.

Almost immediately upon his elevation to the Oval Office, however, Truman gave out conflicting signals. True enough a few liberal advisers, such as David Lilienthal, Henry Morgenthau, Jr., Chester Bowles, Leon Henderson, William O. Douglas, and other doctrinaire New Dealers were still around, but Truman also chose some predominantly conservative administrators and cabinet members, including John Snyder and Clinton Anderson.

An incident that revealed Truman's determination to be his own man despite his admiration for Roosevelt's accomplishments happened during his second day as president. Truman was in his office with one of his oldest and closest friends, John W. Snyder of Saint Louis, with whom he had much in common. They were about the same age; they were both from Missouri; each had been a captain in the field artillery during World War I and had kept active in the Missouri National Guard ever since; both were enthusiastic members of various veterans' organizations; and they both enjoyed playing poker, which they called their study in probabilities.

Truman told Snyder he was going to appoint him federal loan administrator, a high-ranking post within the Reconstruction Finance Corporation (RFC). The chief of the RFC at the time was Jesse Jones, a hard, cautious banker from Houston, Texas.

The RFC, although established by Herbert Hoover in January 1932, had become a main pivot of the New Deal in that it worked to restore the shattered banking system, made loans to over 7,000 banks, lent money to millions of farmers, raised the prices of commodities, and saved several railroads as well as many insurance companies.

With Snyder sitting before him, Truman telephoned Jones to tell him the "president" had appointed Snyder as federal loan administrator. "Oh," asked Jones, "did he make that appointment before he died?" "No," was President Truman's grim reply. "He made it just now."[1]

Truman gave staunch conservative Snyder the only important post immediately vacant, but three months later Snyder's job was changed when he became director of the Office of War Mobilization and Reconversion. Then in June 1946 Truman appointed him secretary of the treasury. This old friend's role during the first Truman administration was more important than his titles suggest, for as a close confidant John Snyder was in on nearly all of President Truman's early strategies and decisions.

Truman picked another conservative Democrat, Clinton Anderson, a congressman from New Mexico who had served well on the House Agriculture Committee, as his secretary of agriculture. In no way a vociferous liberal, Anderson was relied upon by Truman for advice in matters far beyond agriculture. For instance, in the fall of 1945, Patrick J. Hurley, President Roosevelt's personal representative and then ambassador to China, infuriated Truman by publicly charging that "a considerable section of our State Department is endeavoring to support Communism generally as well as specifically in China." It was Secretary of Agriculture Anderson who suggested that Truman take the play away from Hurley by immediately naming the highly esteemed General George Marshall as the flamboyant ambassador's successor.[2]

In April, when Truman came into the presidency, there were no unemployment lines, no closed banks, no stagnant businesses, nor low public morale—problems that had challenged Roosevelt a dozen years earlier.

In that spring of 1945 the outcome of the war was far from certain, however, so Truman's overriding objective was to end it quickly and with as little cost in lives as possible. During the morning of his first day in office, Truman was told by his chiefs of staff that fighting in Europe could go on for another six months; war in the Pacific might last for another year and a half.

Even while facing decisions about ending the war, Truman did not forget the hard times that followed in the wake of World War I. Memory of his subsequent failed business venture in Kansas City as well as the specter of unemployment during the Great Depression haunted him.

He had promised to carry on with Roosevelt's policies, and to fulfill that pledge he quickly endorsed the Bretton Woods monetary program, which had created the International Monetary Fund and the World Bank. He also wanted passage of more reciprocal trade agreements, then pending in the Senate.

In another move, President Truman made it clear that he intended to continue Roosevelt's aims for public power. When David Lilienthal's term as head of the Tennessee Valley Authority was about to expire, the untried president was under great pressure from conservative Democrats to dump him. Instead, Truman called the idealistic, avowedly liberal Lilienthal to the White House to tell him he was doing a first rate job.

Truman endorsed the idea behind full employment and unequivocally backed efforts to expand the Social Security Act of 1935. He asked Congress to extend price controls and related economic measures, including a proposal to establish unemployment benefits of twenty-five dollars a week for twenty-six weeks for persons without work. The measures were ones initiated under the Roosevelt administrations.

Whereas Roosevelt's economic programs had been piecemeal, Truman chose to send Congress a comprehensive message setting forth his own philosophies and long-range goals. The message was drafted and edited numerous times by Samuel Irving Rosenman, a former judge and President Roosevelt's veteran speech writer.

Rosenman was known as an aide who "could peg a grammatical solecism or a dubious bit of political policy as unerringly as he could pick a flaw in a law brief." He had served Roosevelt for almost two decades and was thoroughly familiar with the history and facts of the New Deal.

During his first four months, President Truman's attention had centered on foreign affairs; it was the area in which he had the most to learn, and there had been one crisis after another. Then came July and his meeting at Potsdam with Stalin and Churchill (replaced by Clement Attlee while the conference was still in session). Sam Rosenman was among the select few President Truman asked to accompany him on the trip to Germany, and aboard the *Augusta* enroute home the two of them had their first chance for an extended talk about domestic affairs. That shipboard discussion was the genesis of what became known as Truman's "Fair Deal."

Aware that men who did not believe in the New Deal were swarming around the new president, Rosenman had reason to expect that Truman would be more conservative than his predecessor. Fred Vinson, who later became chief justice, Matt Connelly, Jake Vardaman, and other presidential intimates at the time were among those who were only lukewarm toward most of FDR's reform programs. John Snyder, Truman's closest confidant during the first months, was convinced that continuation of Roosevelt's domestic programs would be a disaster for the president as well as for the country.

Aboard the *Augusta*, when President Truman sketched his personal views of social and economic problems facing the nation, Rosenman was agreeably surprised to learn that far from moving in the direction of "normalcy," Truman wanted a liberal program in internal affairs.

Truman asked Rosenman to begin preparing a sort of state of the union message on domestic matters, and in so doing Rosenman consulted with a great many government officials, seeking memoranda summarizing the main problems as they saw them from their respective viewpoints. Then he melded the memoranda into twenty-one related points and set to work drafting the message.

When Rosenman's first draft was submitted to President Truman, he said he would like to circulate it among people with whom he worked. Subsequently, there were several meetings in which various points of the draft were discussed. John Snyder, Fred Vinson, Matt Connelly, and Jake Vardaman, as well as the president and Rosenman, were usually present.

In his *Memoirs*, President Truman wrote that most of his aides agreed with tenets in the proposed document. Rosenman's recall was different, for he insisted:

> "Most of my [Truman's] advisers agreed with the message" is not accurate. I think that the majority disagreed. The statement is accurate when he says that one of those who advised him against it was John Snyder. In fact, that is quite an understatement by the President. Snyder was not only opposed to it, but he became quite emotional about it. I'm sure that at the time the President put an end to the discussion and signed the instrument, John Snyder had tears in his eyes.[3]

The message that resulted from numerous discussions and revisions was sent to Congress on September 6, 1945. The president chose to send the document in its written form rather than present it as a public address. When he failed to appear in person, some of his former colleagues were miffed enough to recall that Thomas Jefferson, too, had felt that as president he ought not go in person to the Congress. One congressman quoted Jefferson and referred to Truman's message as "the speech from the throne." Such criticism was unjustified because the biggest single reason Truman chose not to put the message in speech form was its length. It contained more than 21,000 words, and even at Truman's rapid speaking rate would have required more than two hours to deliver.

The message is the best expression of Truman's economic philosophy. Its first substantive points concerned dislocations in the national economy caused by the swift end of the war. Cutbacks in war orders already had occurred, and most workers had returned to normal workweeks with resultant reductions in pay. Also, many workers were between jobs as industries moved from a military footing toward peacetime production. These dislocations demanded unemployment compensation, increase in the minimum wage, and extension of selected wartime controls in order to protect against inflation.

Truman identified his goal of full employment with that of Roosevelt and quoted the former president's "Bill of Economic Rights," which called, among other things, for the right to a remunerative job, a decent home, a good education, and adequate medical care. Truman urged Congress to enact legislation that would provide for full employment necessary if these rights were to be secured for all citizens. He called for a Fair Employment Practices Committee to remove more of the injustices based on race, religion, or color. He challenged Congress to set up new and more effective agencies to deal with labor disputes and to find jobs for veterans. He endorsed the continuation of the selective service and announced that he was preparing plans for a comprehensive, long-range, military training program, and for the unification of the armed services.

Near the end of this foretelling message, the president stressed the need to continue shipments abroad in some revised form of the former lend-lease arrangement and in an expansion of the nation's merchant marine.

The scope of the message was so broad it was hard to grasp immediately. When it did begin to sink in, observers recognized it as more than an outline for postwar conversions; it was a comprehensive statement of the Fair Deal.

One scholar of the period saw the document as heralding Truman's new independence:

Beyond this, the new President had a very personal stake in his September message: reaffirmation of his own philosophy, his own commitments, his own social outlook; denial of the complacent understandings, the comfortable assertions that now with "That Man" gone, the White House would be "reasonable," "sound" and "safe." Harry Truman wanted, as he used to say, to separate the "men" from the "boys" among his summertime supporters.[4]

In the preceding April, Truman had become president by chance, but this September message announced that he was going to be an aggressive leader by choice. The event marked the end of the honeymoon he had enjoyed with a sympathetic Congress since his inauguration. In the months ahead he bombarded Congress with special messages, usually detailing the general program he had sketched in September. There was no order or particular timing; proposals came swiftly in scattershot fashion and eventually covered the boundaries of social welfare and economic development marked out earlier. As a practical politician, he knew he was asking for more than he could hope to get, but he stubbornly insisted that under his administration the nation was not going to return to "normalcy."

Truman was acutely aware of FDR's success in shepherding labor groups into the Democratic fold. Nevertheless, in 1945, Truman saw labor factions threatening chances for smooth reconversion to a peacetime economy. Labor's pent-up grievances were being released and his administration was being criticized for lack of supporting action. Unions seethed over the fact that a wartime freeze on wages had not affected executive compensations, which in many cases had soared during the war. Now strident labor voices were demanding at least a 30 percent increase for their workers.

Truman lacked Roosevelt's willingness to bypass party beliefs in order to achieve an immediate goal. For instance, in the summer of 1940, when many of the country's largest corporations refused to sign defense contracts until they got pro-business tax legislation, President Roosevelt had urged Congress to pass laws permitting large corporations to build new plants and acquire new equipment while amortizing such capital expenses over a period of five years or less.

Liberals, including Eleanor Roosevelt, Treasury Secretary Henry Morgenthau, Jr., and Secretary of Interior Harold Ickes, who had unreservedly praised FDR's acceptance speech four years earlier when he had excoriated "economic royalists" and those "privileged princes of . . . new economic dynasties thirsting for power," were driven into deep dismay by what they considered their leader's capitulation to big business. Morgenthau complained bitterly that the law would award the largest corporations a near monopoly in their industries, and that the amortization scheme made government responsible for building and equipping new plants while permitting corporations to make huge profits at virtually no risks.

Roosevelt had turned back their protests with a demanding: "I want a tax bill; I want one damned quick; I don't care what is in it; I don't want to know. . . . The contracts are being held up, and I want a tax bill."[5]

In retrospect, FDR undoubtedly was right, for when the revenue bill finally passed that fall the rapid write-off of expenses induced businesses to expand quickly, and war contracts were accepted with amazing speed. Without such expansion, production of planes, tanks, ships, guns, ordnance, and all the supplies for modern war would have fallen even farther behind.

However, it was not in Harry Truman's nature to make such compromises. His stalwart veto of the Taft-Hartley Act in 1947 as well as his earlier actions during threats of strikes in the coal and railroad industries—normally bastions of power for his Democratic party—stand in sharp contrast to Roosevelt's expediencies.

In May 1946 Truman's administration was plagued by threatened strikes from both railroad workers and coal miners. When two major railroad unions rejected President Truman's demands that they call off their intended strike, he signed an executive order for the government to take over the roads.

Angered by the union leaders' refusal to accept the government's directive, Truman decided to go to Congress in person the next day and ask for the stiffest laws in history. The heart of his message, which he first scribbled out on tablet paper, was a request for authority to draft strikers into the armed services without respect to age or dependency if the strike was judged to be a national emergency.

The original draft that Truman penned is a rare and remarkable document, for it reveals his basic attitudes and naked passions unadorned by restraints from family or advisers. His intended talk praised citizens and soldiers for winning "the greatest war in history," claimed that labor strikes were "worse than bullets in the back of our soldiers," condemned strikers "and their demigog [sic] leaders," and closed with a rabid appeal:

Let's give the country back to the people. Let's put transportation and production back to work, hang a few traitors and make our own country safe for democracy, tell Russia where to get off and make the United Nations work. Come on boys, let's do the job.[6]

It's difficult to imagine what might have occurred had the president of the United States actually given this rabble-rousing speech over national radio. Fortunately for the welfare of the country and for the good of his presidency, Truman's outburst was cooled by a few hours of more careful consideration.

Clark Clifford, Truman's closest adviser at the time, and others persuaded the feisty president to accept a rewritten draft, which they got to him about an hour before he was scheduled to go on the air. Although still one of the most emphatic indictments ever uttered by a president, this final version was nowhere near the savage attack he had penned earlier.

The two speeches President Truman gave on the railroad strike in 1946—one over the radio and one to Congress—were successful by nearly every measure. While Truman was in the middle of his address to Congress, Clifford received a telephone call telling him that the strike was over. He hastily scribbled a note on a scrap of paper, "Mr. President, Agreement signed, strike over." The secretary of the Senate carried the note to Truman at the lectern, who interrupted his address long enough to declare, "Gentlemen, the strike has been settled!" There was a thunderous ovation from the packed chamber, and the remainder of his speech was anticlimactic.

President Truman encountered another confrontation with organized labor in November 1946, when the United Mine Workers went out on strike. In the preceding May, he had signed an executive order seizing the coal mines in order to end a forty-five-day work stoppage in the bituminous industry.

The head of the United Mine Workers was the formidable John L. Lewis, son of a miner and a former miner himself. Lewis had led his union so successfully for thirty years that he had become its undisputed chief. As the date of the threatened coal strike approached, some of Truman's advisers warned him not to risk a showdown with this powerful figure.

Late in October, Lewis demanded that contract talks be reopened or else his miners would consider all contracts void—no contract, no work. His ultimatum was a bold stroke because in effect it challenged the authority of the federal government.

The first step in President Truman's defense strategy was to have the courts issue an injunction restraining the miners' chief from breaking his union's contract with the government. The injunction affected more than 400 thousand United Mine Workers.

The use of injunction, which unions regarded as the most hated maneuver in the antilabor arsenal, so angered the miners that virtually every soft coal mine in the country was immediately shut down.

Then President Truman instructed the Department of Justice to press contempt charges against Lewis for defiance of the antistrike injunction. The contempt action was successfully carried through the U.S. District Court of the District of Columbia, Justice Alan T. Goldsborough presiding, and culminated in a judgment fining the mine workers' boss $10,000 and his union a whopping $3,500,000.

The little man from Missouri, whom most people expected to be a caretaker president, had won another major showdown. He had challenged and triumphed over two of America's strongest unions. Moreover, as shown in the election two years later, Truman had suffered little loss in his standing with rank-and-file members.

In 1947 another huge crisis involving organized labor confronted him, and this time HST was on the side of labor, leading assaults upon the Taft-Hartley Act.

The final Taft-Hartley Act, although modifying even harsher restrictions in an original bill, was passed by both Houses of Congress and was sent to Truman for signature on June 9, 1947. Among the bill's provisions was a ban against the closed shop—a shop in which membership in a particular union was a prerequisite for being hired. Labor regarded this as the most odious section of the bill because it also permitted states to pass their own "right-to-work" laws—laws which, if enacted by state legislatures, could forbid even the requirements that workers in a given industry must belong to a union. Other restrictions included one that, in the event of a national emergency, the president, through his attorney general, could seek a court injunction to prevent strikes or lockouts.

While the Taft-Hartley bill was first being debated in Congress, Truman remained out of the public controversy, but as the legislation gained steam a mass of lobbyists and pressure communications descended upon him. The overwhelming portion of these efforts urged a veto. The bill carried heavy political baggage when it finally reached his desk. If he signed it after his stand against railroad strikers a year and a half earlier, traditional labor support for his party was sure to evaporate; on the other hand, if he vetoed it, his standing with organized labor would improve. Everything in the bill was against his basic nature; it represented an attempt to take away labor's gains; it favored employers while penalizing workers; furthermore, he and his Democratic party's tenets were being challenged by a Republican majority in Congress—a majority eager to make political capital of the bill in future elections.

Since Truman owed many of his political triumphs to labor anyway, it was no great strain for him to decide on a veto. When the sealed envelope containing his decision was opened and read by the clerk in the House of

Representatives that body voted immediately (331 to 83) to override the veto. Action in the Senate took slightly longer because of filibusters by the bill's opponents, but two days later that body, too, voted (68 to 25) to override the president's decision.

Before the Senate's vote on the issue, Truman delivered a national radio speech explaining his action. Among other contentions, he declared,

> I vetoed this bill because I am convinced it is a bad bill. It is bad for labor, bad for management, and bad for the country . . . a shocking piece of legislation . . . unfair to working people . . . deliberately designed to weaken labor unions.[7]

HST's efforts to kill the Taft-Hartley bill proved futile, but his unequivocal criticisms of it won great support from labor unions and individual workers. More than political expediency, his forthright arguments against the act grew from his basic economic beliefs and were thoroughly consistent with the bluntness in his nature.

Chapter 9

FDR: Politician

Twenty-three hundred years have passed since Aristotle, sage of Athens, declared, "Man is by nature a political animal." Since Aristotle's time, countless others have commented on politics. Views range from Finley Peter Dunne's fictional Mr. Dooley's charge that "Politics is still th' same ol' spoort iv highway robb'ry" to Sidney Hillman's credo: "Politics is the science of how who gets what and why."

Hillman's definition is more pertinent because he was a contemporary of Franklin Roosevelt and a strong backer of most New Deal measures. Moreover, few persons would be so brash as to deny that FDR was a political animal who succeeded in getting things done.

Although rich, well born, and inbred, FDR was never without ambition; nor was he idle. During his childhood, Sara's rigorous schedule ensured against that, and at Groton the inexorable routine of chapel, classes, sports, study hall, and evening readings kept the pupils busy from early morning until bedtime.

The transition from Groton to Harvard University had been easy for him. At Harvard such extracurricular activities as the glee club, rowing team, cheer leading, and especially the student newspaper captured his interest more than any intellectual stimulation from books or classes. There also were plenty of opportunities for golf, tennis, travel, and other pastimes.

The Boston-Cambridge area featured a very attractive social circuit, and seldom a week went by when the handsome young man with the distinguished name was not handing his card to a butler who would duly announce his presence to one of the Brahmin families. Some of these acquaintances later sneered that Roosevelt had become a "traitor to his class," but for FDR the early contacts proved to be a laboratory in which he honed his skills of dealing with people.

By 1910, when he ran for the New York Senate, he was poised, confident, and articulate in almost every situation. His upright posture, handsome head—hair parted in the middle—deep-set eyes, long, lean nose and chin, sensitive lips, and ready smile presented an impressive appearance on the platform.

There is an apocryphal story about FDR's debut as a member of the New York Assembly. In early January 1911, a Tammany boss named Big Tim Sullivan sat talking with a cohort in the lobby of an Albany hotel when the newly elected Roosevelt walked across the room. The tall FDR with his strong face, gold bowed spectacles, and frock coat looked more like a student of divinity than a budding politician. Tammany regulars took note of his well-modeled features, lithe figure, and slightly curling hair; one reporter gushed that Roosevelt's appearance was enough "to set the matinee girl's heart throbbing with subtle and happy emotion."

Big Tim was not equally impressed; instead, he saw a cocky, arrogant, "college kid," still wet behind the ears. "You know these Roosevelts," he growled to his partner. "This fellow is still young. Wouldn't it be safer to drown him before he grows up?"[1]

Louis McHenry Howe and others looked at young Roosevelt differently. Howe had latched onto Roosevelt in 1912 when the latter was in the middle of his campaign for reelection to the state senate. FDR, stricken by typhoid and out of action, lay in bed while the astute Howe ran his campaign. Howe sent thousands of "personal" letters from the candidate to voters throughout the district, published huge advertisements in newspapers, played up specific measures that Roosevelt had endorsed, and dealt with complaints about FDR's handling of patronage during his first two years in the legislature. The strategy worked, for Roosevelt won the race and Howe had carved an important niche for himself in FDR's plans.

The assistance this shrewd and tireless aide gave Franklin Roosevelt is impossible to exaggerate. Louis Howe had started his newspaper career with the *Saratoga Sun*, later moving to Albany where he became a stringer for the *New York Herald*. When Roosevelt arrived in 1910 to begin his term in the state assembly, Howe was a capital fixture, known for searching out facts behind the political stories he filed. He also had won a reputation for assessing public moods and for predicting political races.

After fastening his star to Roosevelt in those early Albany days, Howe went with him to Washington during the time FDR was assistant secretary of the navy. Howe tutored him throughout the vice-presidential run in 1920, helped him rebuild the shattered Democratic party following the disastrous 1920 election, was Roosevelt's chief mentor during his governorship of New York, and guided him through political maelstroms encountered on his course to the White House.

In February 1925, following his highly successful nominating speech for Al Smith the previous year, Roosevelt went to Florida and boarded his yacht, *The Larooco*, for an extended vacation. Howe remained in New York scanning newspapers and collecting political reports to send the chief. They had vowed to rebuild the Democratic party from its nadir of 1920.

Under Howe's goading, FDR kept urging party leaders to hold conferences that would serve to bring warring factions together. He also pushed for the establishment of a full-time national office which, he argued, would bring financial contributions from the largest possible number of ordinary citizens and not just a handful of rich supporters. The goal, he said, was to make Democrats clearly the party "of progressive and liberal thought."

Efforts to rebuild the party doubled in 1924 when, under FDR's approval, Howe sent letters to every delegate who attended the New York convention, asking each for suggestions as to how the Democratic party could be better managed. Massive responses indicated how deep were the rifts; Southerners believed Northerners ignored their concerns; Westerners charged there was a coalition between North and South; and earlier failures were blamed on such Democrats as Bryan, Smith, and McAdoo or upon groups like the Socialists, Wets, Drys, immigrants, or farmers.

For a half dozen years, FDR's pleas for party unity seemed to fall upon deaf ears. Divisions were too deep, and besides, he was suspected as being a stalking horse for Al Smith. Some of FDR's arguments persisted, however, and slowly began to win converts. His election as New York's governor gave him a more solid base from which to operate.

His next goal—and a very big one at that—was to win the presidential nomination in 1932. The climax came that June when the convention met in Chicago. Nine candidates vied for the nomination and helped make it one of the most exciting fights in the history of American politics.

Al Smith, the leading candidate when the convention opened, arrived in Chicago confident that he could stop FDR because Roosevelt at the time was hated by several other contenders who were willing to yield their own chances just to keep him from getting the nod.

Roosevelt remained in Albany but by telephone directed every move made by aides in Chicago, talking for hours on end with Howe, Farley, Edward J. Flynn, and other sachems at the convention site.

On the first ballot, Roosevelt was 104 votes short of the necessary 770. In retrospect, it seems incredible that Huey Long of Louisiana, Burton Wheeler of Montana, and newspaper mogul William Randolph Hearst—men who would later become FDR's bitter critics—threw their support to him at the 1932 convention; yet they did.

Also, Jim Farley masterminded a finesse by which he persuaded McAdoo of California and Garner of Texas that neither could win; each would gain more by backing FDR. McAdoo finally was persuaded and gave California to Roosevelt on the fourth ballot. Garner agreed to accept the vice-presidential slot and release his Texas delegation. Careful maneuvering and more than a dozen years of political fence building had paid off; Roosevelt was nominated and broke all precedents by flying to Chicago to accept the endorsement in person.

After the 1932 election, Louis Howe was deemed so valuable that he was given a bedroom on the second floor of the White House just 200 feet from the president's own. Howe's small room, originally designed as a dressing room for the larger Lincoln bedroom adjoining it, meant that he was accessible for the president twenty-four hours a day, which suited both just fine.

One of Roosevelt's first tasks as president was to select his cabinet, and before making the appointments he solicited advice from numerous sources. No one was more influential or more persistent than Howe, who pushed his personal recommendations and was not shy about stating his objections to others.

With the country mired in its worst financial crisis, the secretary of the treasury was Roosevelt's most critical appointment. He needed a person already known to the public, a person with experience in money matters and likely to bring respect for whatever financial programs the administration enacted.

No one seemed to fit the bill better than the white-maned Senator Carter Glass of Virginia. Glass had been one of the architects of the Federal Reserve System and throughout his several terms in the Senate had been an outspoken advocate of financial conservatism.

Over the objections of Howe, Roosevelt offered the position to Glass but made the tender on his own terms, carefully avoiding any definite assurances that the new administration's approaches to the nation's economic plight would be built upon conservative financial principles. Glass was wary and asked for more time to consider the offer.

Meanwhile, Howe, joined by Raymond Moley, by this time the acknowledged head of several idea men advising the new president, strongly recommended William Woodin, a man experienced in big business dealings and past president of the American Car and Foundry Company. Two weeks before inauguration FDR agreed with Howe to dump Glass. However, in attempts to avoid outright alienation from the powerful Virginia senator, Roosevelt, aboard his yacht in the Potomac, carried on a charade of negotiations. Howe sent his chief a radiogram purportedly referring to a new White House installation: "Prefer a wooden roof to a glass roof over swimming pool." Roosevelt puzzled over the cryptic message before roaring with delight.[2]

Although having decided against Glass, FDR had to wait until Glass gave an answer of some sort. When Glass finally told Moley he did not want to accept the appointment, Roosevelt offered the position to Woodin that very evening.

Long before FDR reached the White House he had come to depend upon Howe's judgments about public relations—judgments that sometimes merged with personal goals and family relations. For example, in 1918, when Eleanor discovered the incriminating love letters from Lucy Mercer, Howe sided with Sara, Franklin's mother, who was aghast over the impact a divorce would have on the family name. Howe put the matter in a different focus, warning FDR that a divorce would bring his promising political career to an abrupt end.

By 1935 Louis Howe was lying in the White House critically ill but continuing to be as involved as possible in FDR's political affairs. Howe had survived a close brush with death in the spring of that year but rallied enough that by summer he could talk strategy for the forthcoming campaign. In August, however, his condition was so extreme that he had to be moved out of the White House to the nearby Naval Hospital where he could be given more constant care.

Throughout the fall of 1935 Howe put up a pretense that he intended to go to New York City the next year for the Democratic National Convention and once again direct his champion's campaign. President Roosevelt and Eleanor encouraged such talk although both realized that Howe's physical condition would never permit such an endeavor.

On the afternoon of April 18, 1936, Roosevelt visited Howe in his hospital room and talked with his faithful adviser for the last time; later that same day Louis Howe passed away silently in his sleep. Following a state funeral in the East Room of the White House, President Roosevelt and his wife went to a cemetery at Fall River, Massachusetts, where with bowed heads they stood among others watching the coffin being lowered into the gravesite.

Eleanor had lost a friend and Franklin his longtime aide. Eleanor had come to appreciate Howe's unflinching loyalty to her husband, and by the time Howe moved into the White House she regarded him as someone in whom she could confide even though she recognized his yen to play the role of kingmaker. She once wrote to her friend Lorena Hickok that "he [Howe] was interested in his power to create personages more than in a person. . . . Sheer need on his part I imagine!"[3]

Harold Ickes, secretary of the interior, believed that Howe was an unusually keen judge of men and political trends. The acknowledged curmudgeon of the New Deal paid further tribute to FDR's political tutor by writing:

> It was loudly proclaimed that Louie Howe had supplied most of the political strategy that resulted in the nomination and election of President Roosevelt. . . . I do know that Howe was the only one who dared to talk to him frankly and fearlessly. He not only could tell him what he believed to be the truth, but he could hang on like a pup to a root until he got results. He could reach him not only directly but through Mrs. Roosevelt. Jim Farley tries to please the President. He will state a point of view and if the President takes issue with him, Jim will drop the subject.[4]

Howe, by no means, was FDR's only political guide. Sam Rosenman, a former state legislator who once had served on the New York Assembly's bill drafting commission, joined Roosevelt's team when he began his governorship of the Empire State. FDR asked Rosenman to start assembling a group of first-class men from every field pertinent to the campaign—men who would dig out material for speeches, submit ideas, and otherwise give succor and advice.

Thus by 1932 FDR already had the nucleus of a team of excellent advisers. James A. Farley, a contractor and state boxing commissioner as well as secretary of the state Democratic committee, was put in charge of Roosevelt's headquarters in New York City. In New York also was Edward J. Flynn, boss of the turbulent party faction in the Bronx. Others included five Columbia University professors: Raymond Moley, Rexford Guy Tugwell, Adolf A. Berle, Jr., Joseph McGoldrick, and Lindsay Rogers.

Roosevelt's advisers tended to fall in one of two camps: idea men from the universities or "pros" like Farley, Flynn, and Howe from the school of practical politics. Moley acted as head of the university team and tried to bring the factions together, not always with success. The term "brain trust" originally had come from Howe in a moment of ridicule for the professors, but reporters liked it and gave the term wide circulation. FDR's preference—in the early days at least—was "Privy Council."

It was not in FDR's nature to pay elaborate tribute to aides, but there was an exception the night of his first election as president. Appearing at a triumphant celebration in the grand ballroom of the Baltimore Hotel in New York City, the exuberant president-elect declared, "There are two people in the United States more than anybody else who are responsible for this great victory. One is my old friend and associate, Colonel Louis McHenry Howe, and the other is that splendid American, Jim Farley."[5]

Roosevelt's coattails were especially long in that election of 1932, for along with the capture of the White House came gigantic gains in the Congress. Not since the beginning of President Wilson's second term (1917) had Democrats controlled both houses of Congress. The new Senate was composed of 59 Democrats and 36 Republicans, while in the House the Democrats held a majority of 313 Democrats to the Republicans' 117.

An occasional Republican voice complained about White House pressures and the ramrodding of New Deal measures through the Congress, but those few voices were drowned out by the chorus insisting on reforms and actions. Throughout the New Deal years nearly everyone with political aspirations, including three presidents-to-be (a Missouri county judge named Harry Truman, a young congressional aide from Texas named Lyndon Johnson, and a beginning radio announcer named Ronald Reagan) strove to identify themselves with FDR.

Roosevelt's sweeping victory in 1932 marked a complete restructuring of his party. Democrats no longer were dependent upon the Solid South and three or four pivotal states. And geography was not the only aspect of the new unified party; each New Deal measure seemed to shepherd another flock of voters into the party's fold.

The Emergency Banking Relief Act, affecting all national banks and the Federal Reserve, pleased financiers because it succeeded in checking the money panic. The Beer-Wine Revenue Act, passed in March 1932, which legalized sale of some alcoholic beverages, delighted the Wets, and even Drys were somewhat mollified knowing the act would secure additional revenue.

Most farmers believed their incomes would be helped by the Triple A (Agricultural Adjustment Act). The Triple A was designed to eliminate surplus crops by curtailing production and by establishing parity prices. A parity price was based on the purchasing power of the farmers' dollars at the level of 100 cents during a base period of 1909–1914 for corn, cotton, wheat, rice, hogs, and dairy products; for tobacco a base period of 1919–1929 was used.

FDR was slower to act on the labor front because he failed at first to recognize the political strength that lay in the expanding labor movement. When he finally threw his weight behind the Wagner bill, a bill strongly endorsed by labor unions, the Democratic party's broad base was complete.

Roosevelt initially put his faith in Section 7a of the NRA program, which provided that "employees shall have the right to organize and bargain collectively through representatives of their own choosing, and shall be free from interference, restraint or coercion of employers of labor, or their agents."

When business improved somewhat in 1933, labor leaders expanded Section 7a by telling their organizers "to hell with the legal talk; unionism was good Americanism!" Posters by the thousands proclaimed, "President Roosevelt Wants You to Join the Union."

Along with increased union membership came more intransigence as strikes broke out in scattered industries. Within the mediation machinery set up by the NRA was a feeble National Labor Board, but this board soon drew fire from employers and the press. The president vacillated while labor crises continued to build.

Other pluses, though, drew additional enthusiasm for the Democratic party. The National Youth Administration (NYA), with its work-relief and employment programs for persons between the ages of sixteen and twenty-five, was established during June of Roosevelt's first year. The forward-looking endeavor enabled thousands of needy secondary, college, and graduate students to continue their education.

The Tennessee Valley Authority (TVA), created in May 1933, proved to be an even bigger success. During World War I the government had built a large hydroelectric power plant and two munitions plants at Muscle Shoals on the Tennessee River in Alabama. In the late 1920s and again in 1931 legislators led by Senator George Norris of Nebraska introduced bills that would place the power resources of the Tennessee River at the service of the watershed inhabitants and would convert the munitions plants to manufacturing fertilizer. Presidents Coolidge and Hoover successively had vetoed the measures on grounds that government operation would constitute competition with private enterprise.

President Roosevelt with Norris's invaluable guidance prepared an ambitious plan that went beyond merely supplying power. The program included measures for flood control, land reclamation, the prevention of soil erosion, afforestation, elimination of marginal lands from cultivation, distribution of diversified industries, and generally aimed at advancing the social and economic welfare of the region. The independent corporation established by the TVA was authorized to produce, distribute, and sell electric power and nitrogen fertilizer to people of the region as well as explosives to the government. The TVA soon showed itself to be the boon its sponsors had promised.

Work-relief measures also drew people toward the Democrats. A new federal program for constructing bridges, dams, buildings, and roads came out in 1933. This program, labeled the Public Works Administration (PWA), was conceived as part of the NRA, but FDR was not inclined to give so much responsibility to the NRA director, the flamboyant Hugh Johnson. Instead, he placed the PWA under the supervision of the secretary of the interior.

Although not aimed directly at easing unemployment, the PWA as a "pump-priming" measure did create additional jobs and increase business activity. Public works of every description (lighthouse beacons, municipal sewage systems, hospitals, dams, battleships, and bridges) were undertaken all across the country. From July 1933 to March 1939, the PWA financed construction of more than 34,000 public projects at a cost of over $6 billion.

Primary and more direct work-relief measures came under the Works Project Administration (WPA). In the late summer of 1933, it became apparent that unemployment was not decreasing as quickly as NRA proponents had hoped; in fact, the number of people on relief actually seemed to be rising. Harry Hopkins, who had been in charge of New York State's Temporary Emergency Relief Administration, along with several of his associates, was instrumental in laying plans for a huge federal jobs program that would shift millions of people from relief rolls onto payrolls. President Roosevelt and Hopkins were opposed to the dole, or direct handouts to men and women able and willing to work.

In late October, Hopkins lunched with the president and described a plan for putting people to work and at the same time injecting a great quantity of purchasing power into the economy. FDR wanted to know how many federal jobs would be needed. About 4 million came Hopkins' reply. "Let's see," FDR mused. "Four million people—that means roughly four hundred million dollars."[6]

Apparently he was thinking of a sixty-day emergency period and that the $400 million would be in addition to direct relief money already provided by the Federal Emergency Relief Administration (FERA). Where was the extra money to come from? He thought the most obvious place was the PWA under Secretary Ickes which so far had not spent much of its allotment.

The new agency, named the Civil Works Administration (CWA), was intended only as a short-term emergency project. In March 1934, the CWA was terminated, but the program continued under the previously established FERA (May 1933). Then in 1935, as the federal government withdrew from the arena of direct relief, the same moneys were provided to states and local communities to continue the large-scale national program for jobless employables. The continuation first became the Works Progress Administration and was modified slightly in 1939 to be the Works Projects Administration.

Before it officially ended in June 1943, the WPA had employed more than 8,500,000 different persons on 1,410,000 individual projects and had spent about $11 billion. Although its fundamental purpose was work relief, by providing jobs to millions of unemployed men and women, FDR won votes from the bulk of them and their extended families. It was further demonstration of his remarkable success in widening the base of his Democratic party.

One of the biggest challenges facing any president is his relationship with Congress. The relationship also is one in which he can win or lose status. Few presidents have understood that relationship better than Franklin Roosevelt or have used it as effectively. During his stint as a navy bureaucrat, FDR had witnessed firsthand President Wilson's troubles with an angry Congress; in 1933, as the nation's thirty-first president, Roosevelt realized how much he would have to depend upon congressional leaders for enactment of his programs.

He capitalized on the huge Democratic majority in Congress, knowing that those members were under great pressure from voters back home. Most legislators were demanding action of some sort; the government had been passive too long.

FDR entered the White House with no overall plan except determination to meet each problem as it came up. His method was to draft measures in the executive branch and then apply constant pressure, including patronage and face-to-face persuasiveness, on members of Congress for quick enactment.

There were still a few conservatives in Congress who opposed almost any reform measure, but Roosevelt had some very astute and powerful allies. In the Senate there were men like the majority leader, Joe Robinson of Arkansas, Robert Wagner (New York), Key Pittman (Nevada), and on some measures even Republicans like George Norris (Nebraska) and Hiram Johnson (California). Of the 435 members in the House of Representatives, 150 were impressionable freshmen congressmen, washed in on the tide.

The House membership with its more than two to one Democratic majority quickly elected a notable Roosevelt supporter, Henry T. Rainey of Illinois, as speaker, the first northern Democrat so chosen in over half a century. Rainey lost no time in identifying the majority party's goals with those of the administration, and from his lofty position promised, "We will put over Mr. Roosevelt's program."

No matter how shrewdly conceived were the programs coming from the chief executive nor how unified the Congress, the New Deal could not have succeeded if its leader had not won overwhelming support from the citizenry. To win such support, Franklin took cues from his colorful cousin, Theodore. Both viewed the presidency as preeminently a place for dominant leadership. "I want to be a *preaching* president," FDR once said, "like my cousin." And preach he did—preachments that attempted to lay a moral basis for proposals from his administration.

"Power," wrote Karl Marx over a hundred years ago, "is control over the means of production." From a different viewpoint, Franklin Roosevelt saw effective communication as the primary avenue leading to power in democratic government.

No previous American president placed so much faith and importance in the spoken word as he did. Whenever a new issue or event took place, FDR talked to the people. One of America's most quotable historians, Charles A. Beard, attached great significance to Roosevelt's oral communications, praising him for speaking "with courage and great appeal."[7]

It would serve no purpose to argue that a particular address delivered by Franklin Roosevelt during his twelve years in office was his "greatest" one. He gave thousands of public talks, and among them were many that must be judged truly eloquent. His inaugural address on March 4, 1933, is worthy of note, however, because if for no other reason it contained all the elements of the New Deal. In this talk he acknowledged the need for bold action, demonstrated his understanding of the nation's ills, and sought broad acceptance of remedial measures.

The address attempted to boost national morale, was in the spirit of a crusade, and nearly every statement was meant to compare a vigorous new Democratic administration with Republican inaction. Rarely if ever has a single speech foreshadowed the use of such broad executive power. The one thought that remained uppermost in the minds of most Americans after they had sifted through the address was the arresting assertion: "The only thing we have to fear is fear itself."

Like most eloquence, particularly that coming from presidents who have a battery of aides to help refine wording, this expression was no spur-of-the-moment statement. Other speakers and writers had embodied the idea in similar vocabulary. There was Saint Theresa of Avila (circa 1575): "Whenever conscience commands any thing, there is only one thing to fear, and that is fear." The French essayist Montaigne (1580) echoed: "That of which I stand most in fear is fear." Francis Bacon (1625) wrote, "Nothing is so terrible except fear itself." And in our American record stands Thoreau's version: "Nothing is so much to be feared as fear."

During Roosevelt's first term, when he was solidifying his position as party leader, most of his rhetoric understandably dealt with the country's economic condition. In the first Hundred Days he delivered ten major public addresses, sent to Congress fifteen important messages, persuaded legislators to enact many new laws, talked to the press twice a week, conferred personally or by phone with foreign statesmen, and made decisions that were to have profound consequences.

A week into his presidency, he gave his initial fireside chat. The adaptation to radio listeners that had begun to show up in all of his talks was clearly evident in this first fireside address. He believed that the attention of radio listeners seated comfortably at home could not be held for any long period of time. Consequently, the fireside chats were short; none lasted more than thirty minutes.

Sunday evenings at 10:00 P.M. Eastern Standard Time was the preferred schedule because the president and confidants believed the radio audience then was relaxed and at its peak. The term "fireside chat" was given impetus by Harry Butcher, manager of CBS, who began using it to refer to FDR's style as well as to specific occasions. Butcher lifted the phrase from a description Press Secretary Stephen Early had given him to the effect that the "President likes to think of his audience as being a few people around his fireside." The phrase became common and helped advance the image of a popular, friendly person talking intimately from the White House.

Early was adept in helping build audiences for these fireside chats. Every hour or so on the day preceding a scheduled fireside, he would release to the press a new statement about the forthcoming talk. His releases built public interest to a climax so that across the land that night millions of listeners were sitting before their receiving sets waiting for their president to talk to them.

The fireside chats were not addressed toward any special interest group; instead, FDR used the occasions to reach across class and regional lines, to make people identify with larger aims, and to give them a sense of the nation. He thought of the talks as direct communication with the American people, and judging by mail responses, so did they.

The volume of mail Roosevelt received during his first term was nearly four times as large as all the mail received by presidents William Howard Taft through Herbert Hoover. Much of FDR's mail came in on ruled paper of the type used by schoolchildren or found in homes where writing was not a regular practice. Immediately after his first fireside talk, he received approximately eight thousand letters and telegrams, nearly every one of which expressed approval.[8]

Roosevelt's masterful communications before assemblages, as well as his intimate messages over the microphone to millions of radio listeners, buttressed his relations with Congress. Brilliant communication was the asset that enabled him to weld within the Democratic party such diverse groups as labor and agriculture, North and South, East and West, loyal Democrats and dispirited Republicans, financiers and ordinary citizens. Through his persuasions was built a coalition so powerful and effective that it stayed in power for the next twenty years.

Labor's vote was vital to Roosevelt's twelve-year tenure, and throughout it he carefully wooed labor's most powerful leaders—John L. Lewis, William Green, and Sidney Hillman. Hillman, president of the Amalgamated Clothing Workers, played a role in the 1944 political campaign because of a private remark FDR made regarding the selection of a vice-presidential candidate.

At the time the Democrats were in Chicago and gearing up for their convention, President Roosevelt was enroute by train to San Diego, where a cruiser was waiting to take him to Hawaii to meet with General Douglas MacArthur and Admiral Chester Nimitz. The two commanders in the Pacific theater differed over military strategy, and FDR wanted to hear their views in a face-to-face situation. The train stopped in Chicago where FDR held a quick tête-à-tête aboard with close lieutenants working the convention, among them Robert Hannegan, National Chairman of the Democratic Party.

The main purpose of the tête-à-tête was to secure FDR's approval of a running mate, and he agreed that Harry Truman of Missouri was one of two acceptable candidates. (The other was William O. Douglas.) Much that was said between Roosevelt and Hannegan during this half-hour meeting remained secret although it was disclosed that the president instructed subordinates to "clear everything with Sidney."

Sidney Hillman was head of the CIO's well-heeled political action committee (PAC), and when Republicans learned of Roosevelt's demand, "Clear everything with Sidney" became their battle cry throughout the subsequent campaign.

FDR's political mastery relied upon good timing, compromise, manipulation, and dashes of deviousness. Although there were many instances of deviousness, few were more revealing or typical than one reported by Henry Morgenthau, Jr., whom FDR in 1934 chose as secretary of the treasury to replace the desperately ill William Woodin.

In May of the next year, Roosevelt was under pressure to sign a veterans' bonus bill. Morgenthau, the voice of Roosevelt's conservative conscience in most matters, urged him to veto it and then fight vigorously against a congressional override which was certain to follow. FDR delayed but asked Morgenthau to build a "bonfire of support" for the veto message when it came. Soon thereafter Senator Wright Patman (Texas) and twenty of his colleagues came to see Roosevelt hoping to win approval for the bonus. FDR hinted there might be a compromise.

Morgenthau, privileged to lunch often alone with the president, was thunderstruck when he met with FDR shortly after the congressional delegation left. When FDR mentioned "compromise," Morgenthau asked if in the light of that he should continue building the "bonfire" as originally instructed.

"Of course," insisted Roosevelt, but without mentioning "bonfire" to him again. He promised in return not to use the word "compromise." Then with his mischievous grin, FDR added, "In other words, never let your left hand know what your right hand is doing."

The normally humorless Morgenthau, trying to match the president's levity, asked, "And which hand am I, Mr. President?"

"My right hand," FDR promptly replied. "But I keep my left hand under the table."[9]

When the election year of 1936 rolled around, the economic surge that Roosevelt had led was unmistakable. Unemployment had dropped by about 4 million; payrolls in manufacturing industries had doubled; stock prices had done even better than that; total cash income of farmers had risen by $3 billion; commercial and industrial failures were only one-third of what they had been four years earlier; industrial production had doubled. By almost any test or measurement, Roosevelt's New Deal was doing what he had promised.

Despite the *Literary Digest*'s widely publicized poll predicting a Democratic defeat—a poll flawed by an egregious sampling error—the election results were a landslide. President Roosevelt carried every state but Maine and Vermont, swamping his Republican challenger, Alf M. Landon, by 523 to 8 electoral votes, the biggest margin since 1820.

Buoyed by victory but still smarting from the rebuff of the Supreme Court in striking down the NRA, Roosevelt made his biggest political blunder—a blunder that he might not have made or at least plunged into so recklessly if his mentor Louis Howe had still been around.

The scheme was launched in February 1935, when without advance notice Roosevelt sent Congress an astonishing proposal for a drastic overhaul of the judicial system. The ages of several leading justices exacerbated the ensuing dispute. The last-ditch "horse and buggy" obstructionists on the Court were Willis Van Devanter, James McReynolds, George Sutherland, and Pierce Butler; FDR was determined to get rid of them somehow.

Roosevelt argued that the Court was composed entirely of "nine old men," whom he tried to picture as outdated and overworked.[10]

His stratagem had four prongs. The first was that if a judge of any federal court who had been on the bench more than ten years failed to resign six months following his seventieth birthday, the president could appoint a sort of coadjudicator for him in the same court. Second, the proposal authorized appointment of additional judges, but the number of the Supreme Court could not be increased by more than six. (In effect, the Supreme Court might be as large as fifteen; hence, the label "court-packing.") Third, the Chief Justice could assign extra circuit judges to any circuit court of appeals that was behind in its work. Fourth, FDR proposed that the Supreme Court appoint a proctor to watch over litigation and investigate the need for assigning additional judges.

In the Supreme Court episode, FDR's touted political sixth sense seems to have deserted him, for his message set off a groundswell of criticism that crossed all geographic borders and party lines.

The manner in which he presented the ideas revealed his worst traits: deviousness and manipulativeness. Roosevelt and Attorney General Homer Cummings had drafted the plan in utter secrecy; nobody in Congress was informed until almost the last moment. On the morning of February 5, FDR assembled his cabinet and a few chosen congressional leaders where, to their astonishment, he read the message that would be delivered to both houses of Congress two hours later. The message already had been mimeographed and released to the press, so there was no chance for discussion.

Roosevelt's attempted retaliation immediately sowed dissension among his party's strongest supporters; the coalition so carefully built began coming apart. Public opinion was expressed emphatically against him, and with brilliant rebuttals Chief Justice Charles Evans Hughes exposed the shallowness of the president's arguments.

Democrats, enjoying their huge congressional majority, nevertheless resented the cavalier way FDR had thrown the plan at them. Heated exchanges over the court-packing scheme went on in Congress for 168 days, but eventually, despite tremendous pressure from the president, the Judiciary Committee of the Senate rejected the bill by a vote of ten to eight, and it had to be dropped.

The Supreme Court plan was the biggest mistake in FDR's peacetime presidency, and the resulting imbroglio signaled the end of the period when New Deal legislation was rubber-stamped with little or no debate. FDR himself had put the indelible blemish on his otherwise brilliant record as a masterful politician. Henceforth, motives and underlying philosophies would be questioned more closely.

Chapter 10

HST: Politician

At the time Franklin Roosevelt took his initial plunge into politics he had to convince Democratic party leaders that he merited their support. By contrast, when Harry Truman first entered the lists it was because party leaders urged him to do so.

Indisputably, when Truman first ran for the U.S. Senate he was a "machine" candidate pushed by the powerful confederation that controlled western Missouri; however, the Pendergast connection that helped send him to Washington was a liability Truman had to live with for nearly half his tenure in Congress.

Truman's mettle was tested during the middle of his first year in the Senate when the Public Utility Holding Company Act came up for debate. The act was intended to curb such abuses as excessive management and control by holding companies, to reduce their exorbitant fees, and to nullify the practice of using the mammoth corporations in order to bypass the regulatory power of states. Truman favored the bill despite enormous pressures put on him by its opponents in his home state.

The *Kansas City Journal Post*, a newspaper very friendly to Pendergast, strongly opposed the bill and in this instance was joined by the influential *Kansas City Star*. When Truman voted for regulation, the wrath of the Kansas City press descended upon him. Charges bloomed that he was nothing but a stooge of the Roosevelt administration. Four months earlier, the *Journal Post* had praised him and his colleague Bennett Clark as the "two best senators from Missouri in a generation."

After Truman's vote on the Holding Company Act, this same newspaper began its denunciatory editorial by saying: "Harry S. Truman . . . became United States Senator from Missouri by default, so to speak, getting the Democratic nomination in 1934 because there were no other takers."[1]

Actually, Truman was caught in a bind. In this case, when he favored the act he was labeled an "unthinking tool of the administration." If he disagreed with the administration, he was accused of being unfaithful to campaign promises and not a man of his word.

In France, Captain Truman had been ready to drink cognac, vin rouge, or vin blanc with any or all of his friends, and he could match the profanity of any of them. Nevertheless, he had not hesitated to use the guardhouse when one of them got out of line. In the military Truman had made decisions irrespective of friendships; he had every intention of doing the same in his political jobs.

The Pendergast connection popped up to give him another headache during the Milligan entanglement. After 1934, efforts to uncover crime and bossism in Kansas City intensified, and two years later a federal judge empaneled a grand jury to investigate vote frauds there. Maurice Milligan, an ambitious district attorney, handled the prosecution as well as directed the government's case against Boss Tom Pendergast for income tax evasion.

Although the tax case dragged on for nearly three years, Milligan's efforts were so successful that Pendergast pleaded guilty in 1939 and was sentenced to prison.

When Milligan's term as district attorney ended, Senator Truman opposed his reappointment, insisting that Milligan was neither professionally nor morally qualified for the job, that the newspapers had created a hero out of him, and that government prosecutors had intimidated defense attorneys and jurors chosen from nonresidents of Jackson County.

Growing ever more intemperate, Truman charged, "I say to the Senate, Mr. President, that a Jackson County, Mo., Democrat has as much chance of a fair trial in the Federal District Court of Western Missouri as a Jew would have in a Hitler court or a Trotsky follower before Stalin."[2]

The Senate, unswayed by such hyperbole, approved Milligan's confirmation, and Truman's speech proved to be a setback in his attempts to get rid of his Pendergast linkage. Edgar Bergen, a radio entertainer and ventriloquist very popular at the time, put on a skit for the Advertising Club in Saint Louis. In the skit, Bergen's wooden dummy, Charlie McCarthy, was asked, "What is Senator Truman's relationship to Tom Pendergast?" Charlie replied mischievously, "I'll give you the real low-down if it kills me. You know my relationship to Edgar Bergen. Wellllll—."

A cartoon, with the caption, "Charlie McTruman does his stuff," showed a McCarthy-type dummy on a knee saying, ""Milligan and those Judges are railroading the Democrats."[3]

Even newspapers normally friendly to Truman conceded that his violent attack on Milligan had peeled off the Pendergast scab again and "had done his [Truman's] cause no particular good."

Truman's performance in the imbroglio caused him further embarrassment when it was learned that he had come home to Kansas City to confer with Pendergast. When their conference ended, the wily Boss Pendergast told reporters, "I have nothing to say. Whatever is said will be said by Senator Truman on the floor of the Senate."[4]

Truman outlasted the Pendergast stigma, but if it had not been for later accomplishments his first term in Congress would have to be judged undistinguished. During those six years, however, he made some very important contacts. His easy-going, gregarious nature got him into the poker-playing, cloakroom-chatting coterie that dominated the Senate. Known as a hard worker ready to go down the line for Roosevelt's programs, Truman chose friends from both parties, among them Vice President Cactus Jack Garner, Carl Hayden of Arizona, Burton K. Wheeler of Montana, Arthur Vandenberg of Michigan, Charles McNary of Oregon, and William Borah of Idaho.

In 1940 Senator Truman ran spirited campaigns for reelection, both in the primary and in the general election which followed. The primary race was the deciding one because he faced two strong Democratic contenders: Maurice Milligan, who was at a peak in his crime-busting success, and Governor Lloyd Stark, a name well known because of Stark apples, who tried to portray himself as President Roosevelt's choice.

As it turned out, having Milligan and Stark as challengers was probably pure luck because the two of them in effect split the anti-Pendergast vote thus enabling Truman to win the nomination.

In the general election Truman, ever conscientious about his duties in the Senate, spent much of the campaign in Washington where because of the international crisis Congress was unwilling to adjourn.

His opponent Manvel Davis and fellow Republicans were unsuccessful in their campaign against Roosevelt and Truman. Having kept his Senate seat, Truman prepared to return to that body for another six years.

He also enjoyed a sip from a brand of glee he would savor again eight years later for, on the night of the Missouri primary in 1940, both the *St. Louis Post Dispatch* and the *Kansas City Star* put out extras announcing that Senator Truman had been defeated.

Years afterward HST penned his version of that primary win:

I was nominated by a plurality of 8400 votes [the actual plurality was 7976] in the August primary, after the most bitter mud slinging campaign in Missouri's history of dirty campaigns. At eleven o'clock on the night of the primary vote I went to bed eleven thousand votes behind and supposedly defeated. The KANSAS CITY STAR and the ST. LOUIS POST DISPATCH had extras out telling how happy they were and safe Missouri was from my slimy person as Senator. A lying press cannot fool the people. I came back to the Senate and the doublecrossing ingrate of a Governor was sent back to the nursery.[5]

It was largely Truman's zeal that created the Senate Special Committee to Investigate the National Defense Program, and there is no doubt that the work of this committee served to propel him into the vice presidency. One careful student of the Truman Committee summarized: "In a very real sense he [Senator Truman] was the Committee; he was responsible for its creation, for its organization, its accomplishments and its influence."[6]

Nearly all accounts describe Truman as coming into the presidency entirely surprised and unsuspecting. Admittedly, he had no way of knowing he would be called upon less than four months after assuming the vice presidency, yet no normal man, and certainly not a seasoned politician with twenty-three years of practical experience, is immune from the human urge for higher office. For every vice president, the White House is a magnet, to which that urge, no matter how small or unrestrained, must be drawn.

After being selected as FDR's running mate, Truman, on August 18, 1944, met with Roosevelt for lunch on the South Lawn of the White House. The contrast in the appearance of the two men was striking. FDR although only two years older than HST was a sickly, haggard old man with deep circles under his eyes, sagging shoulders, and purple spots dotting his face. Truman, dapper and robust, looked younger than his age.

According to Margaret Truman, her father did not divulge the whole truth to reporters waiting for him outside the White House when the luncheon ended. "He's still the leader he's always been, and don't let anybody kid you about it. He's keen as briar," HST told them.[7]

In private, however, HST shared a different impression, telling close friends that throughout the luncheon the president talked with difficulty and his hands shook so badly he could not get the cream from the pitcher into his coffee, spilling most of it into the saucer. "It doesn't seem to be any mental lapse of any kind, but physically he's just going to pieces. I'm very much concerned about him," HST confided.[8]

Truman's perception of FDR's health during this time can be inferred further from entries in his *Memoirs* and from remarks made to close friends. Among the latter was Eddie McKim who in September accompanied HST to a White House reception. McKim had been shocked by Roosevelt's physical appearance, and as the two old friends were walking out the gate, McKim told Truman to look back because that's where he would be living before long. "I'm afraid you're right, Eddie," Truman replied, "and it scares the hell out of me."[9]

Unknown to the public at the time, Roosevelt was under the constant supervision of a cardiologist, Dr. Howard Bruenn, who advised that given proper care FDR might live for a year.[10]

Among the leaders conferring almost daily with Roosevelt were General George Marshall, Harry Hopkins, Jimmy Byrnes, Speaker Sam Rayburn, House Majority Leader John McCormack, and speech writer Sam Rosenman. These and a few others had to be aware of Roosevelt's rapidly declining health, but otherwise his arteriosclerosis and its seriousness was a carefully guarded secret.

Except for the lunch on August 18, there was little or no communication between Roosevelt and Truman throughout the 1944 campaign. If Truman felt slighted by such indignity, he never let it show publicly. His first official speech of the campaign was delivered in front of the old red-brick courthouse in Lamar, Missouri, just a stone's throw from where he had been born.

He was not an exciting speaker, but whenever he spoke that fall he hammered on the theme that Roosevelt should be reelected in order to win the war and establish the peace. Because of FDR's popularity, Republicans tried to make Truman an issue, and it was the old Pendergast linkage on which he was most vulnerable.

The *Chicago Tribune* led the attack by declaring:

If they confess that there is the slightest chance that Mr. Roosevelt may die or become incapacitated in the next four years, they [Democrats] are faced with the grinning skeleton of Truman the bankrupt, Truman the pliant tool of Boss Pendergast in looting Kansas City's county government, Truman the yes-man and apologist in the Senate for political gangsters.[11]

After his inauguration on January 20, 1945, Truman did exactly what FDR expected of his vice presidents—preside over the Senate, attend parties and receptions, shake hands, and mingle with politicians from both sides of the aisle in Congress.

Often it seemed that Harry Truman could turn a liability into a political plus. An example of that knack occurred late in January 1945, when Tom

Pendergast, broke after being released from prison and deserted by friends and nearly all of his own family, died in Kansas City. Truman decided to attend the funeral, where he was photographed talking with other mourners or paying his respects to the family. The stories and photographs triggered another barrage from people who deemed it unforgivable for a vice president to honor the memory of a convicted criminal. Others, however, awarded Truman good marks for the spunk he showed in refusing to turn his back on an old friend.

Vice President Truman was not included among the hundred or more Americans who accompanied Roosevelt to the Yalta Conference in late January 1945. Nor did he ever receive a special account from FDR about this historic meeting. However, a short time after Roosevelt's return to Washington, the two of them met briefly, and again the president's physical condition did not go unnoticed by his vice president, who recalled, "I met with the President a week later and was shocked by his appearance. His eyes were sunken. His magnificent smile was missing from his careworn face. He seemed a spent man. I had a hollow feeling within me, for I saw that the journey to Yalta must have been a terrible ordeal."[12]

When the first waves of dismay over Roosevelt's death began to settle, the prevalent feeling in America was one of uncertainty about the man who followed him. As a result of his grounding in American history, Truman understood the role of the presidency. He was better read, particularly in history and biography, than FDR.

Truman went to the Constitution often in order to make certain he was right in interpreting his presidential responsibilities. He understood there was only one president in the White House, and this understanding gave him opportunity to draw upon his natural preference for fast and decisive action.

He brought with him into office definite ideas about presidential leadership in the American system of government. He respected the presidency, almost seemed in awe of it, but he was seldom timid about using it. The famous sign on his desk—The Buck Stops Here—provided the best summary of the way his White House staff operated. That sign was more than a simple slogan; it was the unforgettable dictum of his administration.

It is a mistake to think that Truman came into the presidency inept and ill-prepared. True, he had not been privy to Roosevelt's ideas and methods, and if that lockout had not occurred, he would have been more schooled in such matters as the Teheran agreements, the overall relations with Russia, and particularly the Yalta Conference.

In a technical sense, no one can prepare for the presidency in the way a dentist or a lawyer can be said to be trained by several years of experience to extract a tooth or build a legal case. Truman lacked a college degree but certainly could not be considered uneducated. Not a man of brilliant intellectual gifts, he nevertheless was smart and had spent his life in serious reading and studying. Insights gained from his self-imposed discipline coupled with a background in practical politics formed the bedrock for his values and judgments.

Truman came into the Oval Office as a seasoned politician with twenty-three years of practical experience behind him and a better acquaintanceship with the workings of government than Lincoln, Hoover, Eisenhower, Carter, and many other presidents. He had served in the U.S. Senate, where his dedication and leadership had given him a better grasp of domestic problems connected with the war than nearly any other public official.

A president is by virtue of office the country's number one politician, and that role calls for the establishment of strong defenses on three interrelated fronts: Congress, the press, and the public.

TRUMAN AND CONGRESS

President Truman's overall relations with Congress would have to be considered at best a mixed bag.

When he took office in April 1945, most observers anticipated a period of congressional-executive harmony. He had been a well-liked and respected two-term senator. Moreover, Democrats were in the majority and would likely protect one of their own who was expected to serve as a caretaker through 1948 anyway.

Within six months, however, President Truman ran into fierce congressional opposition made up of a coalition of Republicans and Southern Democrats. The flash point came with the presentation of his Fair Deal. This ambitious twenty-one-point program created an impasse that would last throughout his presidency.

Fortunately, Truman could count on a loyal and able congressional leadership team—veteran Sam Rayburn in the House and Alben Barkley in the Senate. It was Truman's good luck, too, that except for two powerful individuals in the Senate—Robert Taft and Arthur Vandenberg—Republican leadership was lackluster.

In the important area of foreign policy, Truman's relations with Congress were different and more productive. First, across the country there was fervent determination to back the new president in order to end the war as quickly as possible. Second, the onset of the Cold War gave him greater latitude for actions which won strong support from the most influential leaders in the Congress.

The only Republican-controlled Congress that Truman had to deal with during his nearly eight years in office was the Eightieth (1947–1949). The GOP appeal throughout the 1946 campaign had been the simple slogan, "Had Enough?" Several factors had contributed to Republican congressional gains. First, there had been a growing feeling among both Republicans and Democrats that during the Depression and World War II, the executive branch of government had usurped some of the responsibilities of Congress. Second, it was clear to all that Harry Truman believed in a strong executive and intended no retrenchment in that office. Third, President Truman's proposals relating to Social Security, national health insurance, aid to education, regional power development, full employment, and civil rights raised the hackles of conservative forces.

HST's main clashes with Congress were over domestic policies, most notably the Taft-Hartley Act. The philosophy behind this act, which was passed over his veto, was that the federal government during the Depression and World War II had favored labor unions with the result that their leaders had amassed uncontrollable powers. The act outlawed the closed shop and permitted a union shop only through petition and election. Another section allowed states to enact right-to-work laws which banned compulsory union membership. Unions could not refuse to bargain collectively, use secondary boycotts, engage in jurisdictional strikes, or curtail an employer's right to free speech. National government employees were forbidden to strike, and union officials had to sign a non-Communist affidavit.

There is considerable evidence that President Truman agreed with many aspects of the Taft-Hartley Act, but when union officials denounced it as a "slave labor law," he took up the cry, realizing full well that Democrats needed labor's support at the polls. He was certain that Congress would pass the act over his veto anyway, and that is precisely what happened. He vetoed the measure, and Congress promptly overrode his decision by four-to-one majorities.

Never hesitant about voicing displeasure over legislative action or inaction, President Truman in 1948 made the Republican-controlled "Awful, Do-Nothing Eightieth Congress" and the Taft-Hartley Act favorite targets in his successful "Give 'Em Hell" presidential campaign.

As the first president to face the problems of governing a superpower in a global age, Truman welded a bulwark of bipartisanship and gained approval for numerous innovative and far-reaching programs—programs such as Greek-Turkish Aid, the European Recovery Program, the Atlantic Treaty Organization, the Berlin Airlift, and Point Four calling for aid and technical assistance to underdeveloped countries. Even for the "police action" in Korea, he won grudging votes from a sizable bloc of reluctant Republicans in both Senate and House. Thus the pattern he set for executive-legislative action, notwithstanding party loyalties, enabled subsequent presidents to meet later challenges that developed in the course of the Cold War.

TRUMAN AND THE PRESS

The second front Truman faced as the nation's number one politician was his relations with the press—a term generally used at the time he was in office to refer to both print and radio; "media" as a popular term arose later. Television then was in its infancy although when Truman gave his Navy Day Speech on October 27, 1945, he became the first American president to speak over the rapidly expanding electronic wizardry, thus ushering in a new era of reporting public affairs. Through an experimental hookup, viewers in New York, Philadelphia, and Schenectady were able to see and hear their nation's chief executive at the very time he was speaking.[13]

HST was keenly aware that even as president his speeches and remarks would have only minimal significance until they were converted into newspaper paragraphs and radio reports. His relationship with the working press had been extremely good during his years in the Senate, and in the Oval Office he moved quickly to maintain those healthy contacts. Newsman James E. Pollard quoted *Editor & Publisher* as stating that Truman began his presidency "with a larger acquaintance among newspaper men than Hoover or Coolidge ever enjoyed or than Roosevelt had in 1933."[14]

There were differences between Presidents Truman and Roosevelt in their attitudes toward the press. When FDR criticized the press he included everyone connected with it. In contrast, while Truman might flay publishers and columnists, he usually held to his belief that the reporters covering his speeches and conferences were fair.

President Truman's relations with the press revolved around three basic factors: respect for the office he held, the persuasiveness of facts, and his predilection for efficient administration.

HST held his first press conference five days after taking office; he held his last one as president just five days before leaving the White House in

January 1953. In the intervening period, he met reporters in a total of 324 press conferences at fairly regular intervals.

Usually his manner in conducting the conferences was relaxed but confident and authoritative. Douglass Cater, who was Washington bureau chief for the *Reporter* magazine during the Truman years, once characterized him at press conferences as "the backwoods Baptist laying down a personal testament of God and Mammon to the congregated reporters."[15]

Most of the time, HST was patient with journalists, although he could be sharp if he thought they were trying to pressure him or if he felt they were attempting to take control of the meeting. He brought to the press conferences a bluntness bred in the army and nurtured in the rough and tumble of politics. His comments and conduct put reporters at ease but also demanded respect. He demanded that respect not so much for himself as for the office he held, and he was quick to defend himself if he felt presidential authority was being questioned.

The second factor that marked Truman's relations with the press was his reliance upon facts. His belief in the persuasiveness of specific data has become almost legendary. Aides were expected to provide him with information he needed in contacts with Congress and the press. He was sure he could sustain his views only when he had enough facts on his side.

George Elsey, one of President Truman's most stalwart White House aides, said that he and other assistants were not policy makers but seekers of information:

Truman had an appetite for facts, plain and unvarnished, and lots of them. He studied documents late at night and early in the morning, and it was a rare day when White House staff members failed to start the morning with a note or two from "the Boss" asking for more information on matters he had been poring over since the official close of business the evening before.[16]

The third characteristic which helped HST win respect from the working press was his penchant for efficient administration. This insistence meant that in those rare instances when he could not answer a question properly himself, he knew exactly who in his administration could. Reporters appreciated such straight talk from the nation's highest official—again, a decided contrast to FDR's lack of straightforwardness.

HST understood that efficient administration meant choosing capable and loyal subordinates; his success would not have been possible had he chosen otherwise. Moreover, in relations with the press he relied heavily upon men such as his first press secretary, Charles G. Ross, and later his special counsel, Clark Clifford—both of whom had grown wise in public relations and often cautioned restraint in presidential utterances.

Most of HST's press conferences were conducted around his desk in the Oval Office, where the atmosphere was intimate and frequently preceded by relaxed banter. The reading public might occasionally be misled into believing such conferences were spontaneous and ill-considered, but in truth they were neither. Truman liked to hold a briefing session with key staff members about one week prior to a scheduled press conference. At these meetings Clifford, Ross, and in later years Press Secretaries Joseph Short, Roger Tubby, or Irving Perlmeter would submit notes of points or questions likely to be raised. Aides would be collecting information to give the president on these matters, and then Truman would hold a second briefing session, usually on the day of the scheduled press conference. The two sessions enabled him to respond succinctly to most questions, and while it was impossible to anticipate every question, aides who participated felt there was great merit in the practice and that their batting average was quite high.

Like other presidents before him, HST smarted under newspaper or radio criticisms, but he seldom went for the jugular in his tiffs with the press. The exceptions occurred when a member of his family was criticized publicly; then he became truly angry. A case in point was his furious reaction to the *Washington Post* music critic's unfavorable review of his daughter's singing.

Despite his occasional battles with the press, most reporters gave Truman very high marks for his honesty with them. In the judgment of most of them, even to those who disagreed with his policies, he came across as a knowledgeable, competent leader who knew the facts before making his decisions.

TRUMAN AND THE PUBLIC

Harry Truman in public was very much like Harry Truman in private. Capable of stubborn enmity or unflinching loyalty, he was a man whose emotions often surfaced. To political foes he was a tough opponent who asked no quarter, and associates knew him to be like Marc Antony, "a plain blunt man that love my friend."[17]

The Republican sweep of Congress in 1946 gave most political observers reason to think that Truman would be soundly defeated when he ran for election two years later, but the stubborn fighter from Missouri refused to admit defeat. His "Give 'em Hell" tactics carried him through one of the most vigorous campaigns in history.

Nearly every student of the presidency regards HST's upset of the pollsters in 1948 as one of the most remarkable episodes in the record of American politics. No other president, even Franklin Roosevelt with his unprecedented four victories, ever won over such seemingly insurmountable odds.

Contrary to popular explanations, HST's win was not just another example of his "luck"; nor did it happen because Thomas Dewey was a weak opponent. Such explanations are misleading in their simplicity, and they ignore the shrewd analyses and meticulous staff work that lay behind Truman's masterful campaign.

The lengthy Rowe-Clifford memorandum of 1947 was a coldly pragmatic document that exemplified beliefs of advisers and confidants within the Ewing group. These beliefs helped devise a pattern of tactics that closely fitted HST's personality and charted a course the 1948 campaign followed.

There was a strong demagogic flavor in advising that the Taft-Hartley Act ought to be played up as a "slave-labor act" even though President Truman himself had benefited from its provisions several times earlier. There was further demagoguery in trying to garner all the victories in foreign affairs—victories which had come about through congressional bipartisanship—and then implying that such cooperation would vanish if Republicans were elected. Perhaps the most Machiavellian aspects of the strategy lay in proposing that President Truman submit legislative programs to Congress even when he knew they would be defeated.

The real heat of the campaign came from the civil rights issue. In December 1946, Truman issued an executive order creating the Committee on Civil Rights, and this group had prepared a lengthy, widely publicized report—To Secure These Rights—which among other things called on the federal government to take the initiative in trying to end discriminatory employment practices, in protecting the right to vote by establishing an anti-poll tax law, in seeking enactment of anti-lynching laws, and in setting up a permanent commission on civil rights.

Judged by today's standards, HST's call for action on civil rights in 1948 seems rather innocuous, but it was an audacious document at the time he issued it. Southern conservatives announced they would boycott any ticket with Truman on it, and many did just that. When, in July 1948, Democrats held their convention in Philadelphia, Strom Thurmond of South Carolina, followed by a phalanx of delegates from the deepest parts of Dixie, walked out of the convention hall and away from the Democratic party.

By the time Truman had received the nomination and had galvanized an otherwise apathetic crowd in convention hall with his bold call for a special session of Congress, his Republican opponent, Governor Thomas E. Dewey of New York, already had determined the broad outlines of the battle he meant to wage. He intended to run a "dignified" campaign and remain aloof from specific controversies.

Truman's campaign train consisted of sixteen cars, including a Pullman that had been especially adapted for FDR during the war. This car with its armor plating and bulletproof glass carried HST and his family. The train left Washington on Sunday, September 5, and it wasn't long before the journey began following a definite pattern. Stopovers were usually ten minutes long, and HST's appearance took up about half that time. His extempore remarks always began with references to local scenery, industry, agriculture, or history, and his detailed knowledge of small towns and regions seldom failed to surprise and delight listeners.

After concluding his four-to-five minute talk, HST would ask the crowd: "How would you like to meet my family?" Then he'd say something like, "First, Mizz Truman." Right on cue, Mrs. Truman would come through the door and stand on the right side of her husband. A moment or two later, the proud father would announce, "And now I'd like to have you meet my daughter, Margaret." Some observers noticed that when he was in border or Southern states, the president referred to his daughter as "Miss Margaret."

President Truman gave twenty-six major addresses that fall, and with the exception of ones in Detroit, Dexter (Iowa), Denver, Oklahoma City, Miami, and Raleigh, all were delivered at night in order to take advantage of extensive radio coverage. The train trip was what would go down in history, however, for thousands of American voters would always remember the image of a smiling, waving President Truman standing alone beneath a striped canopy on the rear platform as his train pulled slowly away and faded from sight.[18]

As the campaign intensified, it became clear that Truman was aiming his appeals at four distinct groups: farmers, laboring men and women, blacks, and consumers. Sometimes the groups would overlap, but usually in the large cities he could be counted upon to put heaviest stress on labor themes. The more HST poured it on about Taft-Hartley the more organized labor responded. Opponent Dewey lamented, "I wondered whether I was running against labor or the Democratic Party."

The results are well-known history. To the astonishment and chagrin of pundits and pollsters, HST won despite the loss of four of the largest industrial states: New York, Pennsylvania, Michigan, and New Jersey.

For years to come, analysts would attempt to explain his surprising victory. Fundamental to all explanations lay the political strategy adopted a year earlier, but more important than all strategies was the public persona of vigor and forthright honesty on the part of the man from Missouri.

Chapter 11

FDR: Foreign Policies
(1933–1936)

On March 4, 1933, the day Franklin Roosevelt took his first oath of office, Germany, 5,000 miles away in Western Europe, was awash in political upheaval. The country had held five national elections the preceding year, and finally in a desperate, reluctant move President Hindenburg on January 30, 1933, consented to accept Adolph Hitler as the new chancellor.

Hitler moved rapidly, ordering an immediate roundup of private weapons; all meetings or demonstrations against the government were forbidden, and exultant columns of the National Socialist Party staged nightly homages to their party and Fuehrer.

The climax came on the evening of February 27 when the Reichstag building burst into flames. Hitler and his henchmen blamed the Communists, and in retaliation four thousand arrests were made within the next twenty-four hours. With removal of the most formidable opposition to the new regime, Adolph Hitler's power base was unchallenged.

The sudden turn in German politics occasioned no great stir in the American press; certainly seizure of power by the Nazis aroused little sense of foreboding with respect to the future. Americans were less interested in what was happening in other parts of the world than in what Franklin Roosevelt's promised New Deal was going to bring.

Nor was FDR under any illusion as to what must come first. Foreign relations paled when compared with America's hunger, unemployment, and financial crisis. He stated as much in his Inaugural Address:

Our international trade relations are in point of time and necessity secondary to the establishment of a sound national economy. I favor as a practical policy putting of first things first. I shall spare no effort to restore world trade by international economic readjustment, but the emergency at home cannot wait on that accomplishment.[1]

FDR dealt with each domestic crisis as it arose, and foreign policies during his first four years were developed in similar fashion, improvised from one situation to another in the absence of any overall plan. The result was an administration that veered back and forth between isolationism and internationalism.

Throughout his presidencies, FDR made maximum use of his powers as chief of state, supremely confident that he could solve every international problem if only he could meet his adversaries face to face across a conference table. He greatly enjoyed conferring with potentates from abroad and went into such meetings assuming that he could deal with foreign adversaries as he did with political rivals at home, charming them into friendship and vague agreements which subordinates could later translate into binding language. Nowhere can his attitude be better illustrated than in his relations with the Soviet Union, beginning with diplomatic recognition of that government in 1933 and ending with the Yalta meeting of 1945.

Official recognition of the Soviet Union had been withheld since the Bolshevik revolution of November 1917, but by 1933 many Americans were convinced that Russia was headed the same way the French Revolution had gone 150 years earlier. FDR and several New Deal advisers believed, too, that improvement in world commerce called for normal relations with the Soviet government.

Accordingly, in November 1933, official recognition of Soviet Russia was given largely in the hope of improving trade but also because there was little to be gained by refusing to accept the fact of complete control by the Communist regime there.

Constitutionally, the president has exclusive power to grant or withhold recognition of foreign governments, but in this case Roosevelt's use of the power did not go without protests, including the disapproval of his mother and friends. Father Edmund Walsh, rector of Georgetown University and a friendly adviser to FDR at the time, revealed that President Roosevelt had invited him to the White House where he disclosed his intention to recognize the Soviet government.

"Mr. President, don't do it," the Catholic father remonstrated. "It will be the biggest mistake you could make."

"Don't worry, Father," Roosevelt smiled his reply. "I'm a good horse trader."[2]

America's domestic economy was intimately linked with imports and exports, so although during the Hundred Days while FDR was aiming his main volleys at internal economic problems, he was forced to act on foreign trade. Secretary of State Cordell Hull persistently pleaded for lower tariffs, but his efforts were rebuffed not only by powerful Republicans but also by Democrats who felt that New Deal programs like the Triple A and the NRA would be in jeopardy if foreign imports were allowed to flow easily into American markets.

Cordell Hull, born in a log cabin in backwoods Tennessee, had been elected to Congress in 1907, and as FDR's secretary of state twenty-six years later he was one of the earliest to warn of the dangers of the rapidly developing breakdown of international law. Hull's rigid, somewhat doctrinaire approach called for reaffirming traditional standards of justice, peaceful conferences to settle international disputes, and acceptance of liberal trade agreements as the best method for easing world tensions.

Hull finally won Roosevelt's agreement that domestic recovery would not be possible without restoring America's badly shrunken world commerce, and in March 1934, FDR sent Congress a reciprocal trade proposal.

Hull and most Congressional Democrats argued that the bill was a necessary step toward international tariff reductions and expansion of world trade. Opponents saw it differently; only five Republicans voted for the bill, with most of the others denouncing it as "Fascist," "palpably unconstitutional," or as "economic dictatorship come to America."

To the press and public FDR seemed ambivalent, simultaneously encouraging both international and nationalist interpretations of the trade bill's benefits, but when it became law on June 12, it represented the earliest achievement of his administration's foreign policies.

Passage of the Reciprocal Trade Agreements encouraged Roosevelt after months of preoccupation with internal matters to give more attention to foreign relations. Uppermost was the problem of international arms traffic.

In 1933 if there was any consensus in America regarding foreign relations it was disillusionment with European politics. America had rejected both the peace treaty and the League of Nations and, in 1928, had given overwhelming support to the Kellogg-Briand Pact, which supposedly outlawed aggressive war.

The cult of neutrality swelled to unrealistic proportions; Wilsonian dreams had evaporated and been replaced by a hope to trade with all nations but to avoid alliances with any of them; pundits in press and rostrums kept reminding everyone of President George Washington's dictum: "The great rule of conduct for us in regard to foreign nations is, in extending our commercial relations, to have with them as little political connection as possible."[3] Individual citizens and organized groups warned government officials to be on guard against the slick Europeans who had misled the country once before and would try to do so again.

Never immune to the public mood, Franklin Roosevelt began working toward arms control and antiwar covenants. From his bully pulpit, he tried to assert a strong moral position in favor of substantial disarmament, but the new Reich under Adolph Hitler was bent on rearming, and in October 1933 when Germany withdrew from both the Geneva Peace Conference and the League of Nations, the arms race got under way.

If worsening world commerce contributed to the collapse of disarmament plans, President Roosevelt's waffling came in for a share of the blame. His predecessor, Herbert Hoover, had initiated plans for a World Economic Conference to meet in June 1933, and Roosevelt's early endorsement of this meeting kindled hopes that it would light the way toward better economic relations among the major nations.

On several occasions, FDR stated that currency stabilization was essential to "establish order in place of the present chaos," and when representatives of eleven countries visited him in advance of the London conference, he gave each of them vague assurances that he would work toward that goal.

This was the policy that Secretary of State Hull, who led the American delegation to London, believed was his mandate. By mid-May, however, FDR was giving currency stabilization a reassessment. The dollar had slid downward along with a simultaneous rise in stock, bond, and commodity prices. These factors helped him change his mind and decide that currency stabilization would be unwise until the dollar had fallen to a more competitive position on the world market. Roosevelt told Brain Truster Raymond Moley that he was in no hurry to stabilize until he was sure he was going to get the best bargain there was to be got. New purchasing power was being created in this country and "this stimulating movement must not be stopped."[4]

Shortly thereafter, the president sent Moley to join the Hull delegation in London—a delegation churning with confusion and conflicting signals. On July 3, FDR sent a blunt message to Hull and his contingent in effect criticizing the conference for attempting to create artificial currency stability "on the part of a few large countries only."

Roosevelt's sudden switch dealt a death blow to the World Economic Conference. In the words of one of his most respected biographers, "It [the Conference] went on twitching for a few days . . . before it rolled over and died, amid savage recriminations and general hopelessness."[5]

When it came to dealing with the expanding international arms traffic, Roosevelt's approaches throughout most of his first administration were tied to his foreign policies in trade matters and reflected the isolationist mood prevailing in the country.

In October 1935, Benito Mussolini sent his troops into Ethiopia in a vainglorious attempt to restore Italy to a more dominant world position. Pictures of Il Duce resplendent in uniform and arrogance while speaking from a balcony in the piazza or goose-stepping in parades through the streets of Rome suggested a buffoon more than a threat to the world, and at a cabinet meeting on August 27, FDR joked that in Ethiopia, "the Italian army of occupation places most of its orders for supplies in the British colony of Kenya and that recently the first item on a large order that went to the suppliers in Kenya was for five hundred women of easy virtue."[6]

The road to Addis Ababa was neither long nor difficult for the Italians though. Ethiopia's pitiful army had no chance against Italy's mechanized forces, and the world soon learned of massacres taking place in the African nation. Emperor Haile Selassie's mobilization order was enough to win his case in the court of world opinion:

When this order is received all men and boys able to carry a spear will go to Addis Ababa. Every married man will bring his wife to cook and wash for him. Every unmarried man will bring any unmarried woman he can find to cook and wash for him. Women with babies, the blind, and those too aged or infirm to carry a spear are excused. Anyone found at home after receiving this order will be hanged.[7]

The numerous reports of sadistic dive-bombing raids upon the hapless Ethiopians left Americans shocked and outraged. Nor did it help the Italian image when Count Ciano, Mussolini's son-in-law and one of the pilots, called such sorties "magnificent sport" and offered journalists his heartless version: "one group of horsemen gave me the impression of a budding rose unfolding as the bomb fell in their midst and blew them up."

The next year, 1936, brought a clear violation in Europe of the Versailles Treaty when Hitler moved German troops into the Rhineland. When that thrust went unchallenged, he and his Italian counterpart threw their support to the forces of Francisco Franco, who was waging a rebellion against the liberal democratic government of Spain—a war that culminated in Franco's Fascist victory in 1939.

These violations of the peace structure seemed only to reinforce the determination of most Americans to stay out of foreign wars no matter what the cost or cause. The attitude was buttressed by uncritical acceptance of reports from Senate investigators under the aggressive leadership of Senator Gerald P. Nye of North Dakota. Nye and fellow committee members disclosed that dealers in arms and munitions throughout World War I had amassed exorbitant profits and by seamy tactics had avoided paying taxes. The revelations led the bulk of the public to believe that entrance into World War I had been a mistake and the only way to avoid its repetition was to legislate the pitfalls out of existence.

Opposition to Woodrow Wilson's internationalism enveloped the nation and became a powerful factor in American political life. Money, it was argued, not noble purpose had led to involvement in the Great War. The influential Kansas editorialist William Allen White summed up feelings of the era: "The boys who died just went and died. And for what?"[8]

In retrospect, there can be little question that Franklin Roosevelt's daring leadership in his first administration saved the country from economic chaos. Those were isolationist years though, and FDR in the main flowed with the public tide. He and the citizenry were preoccupied with internal problems anyway, and foreign affairs seemed of secondary importance. One exception came in the form of what the administration labeled America's "Good Neighbor" policy.

Again Cordell Hull took the lead in promoting the doctrine, but this time he had FDR's full backing. Latin America, torn by strife but ever resentful of intrusions by its Big Brother to the north, was skeptical of promises not to meddle in its internal affairs. Cuba, long a ward of the United States, was the administration's first test.

In 1933 rioting and revolt by the Cuban army threatened America's commercial stakes in that island country. The ambassador there, Sumner Welles, hurriedly proposed "limited intervention," but FDR and Secretary Hull refused and ordered the ambassador to undertake peaceful negotiations without the customary use of U.S. Marines. The next year, when a more conservative government came to power in Cuba, FDR announced that the United States was giving up its right of intervention under the earlier Platt Amendment, which had restricted Cuba's sovereignty. That same year the last Marines were withdrawn from Haiti, and in 1936 a treaty was negotiated relaxing the restrictions upon Panama.

Along with nonintervention promises of the Good Neighbor policy toward Latin America came emphasis upon cooperation toward mutually beneficial trade policies. Then as threats of war in Europe increased, the policy began emphasizing mutual defense, and this aspect eventually became paramount.

By the summer of 1936, when his campaign for reelection was under way, FDR had settled into a routine which remained the pattern throughout his presidential years. He ate breakfast in bed at 8:30 while skimming newspapers from New York, Washington, Baltimore, and Chicago. Immediately afterward, he usually conferred with aides about the day's schedule.

Examination of FDR's daily calendar as well as memoirs from his closest advisers during his first term reveal the dominance of domestic concerns if compared with foreign affairs. But while President Roosevelt was concentrating on domestic programs, leaders in other lands were bent on expansion.

In October 1935, when the attack upon Ethiopia was launched, the League of Nations branded Italy an aggressor and voted sanctions which proved toothless. England and France refused to impose an oil embargo against Italy for fear of antagonizing Hitler, who was consolidating his control and enlarging the Third Reich with every passing month. Also, sanctions against Italy risked alienating Russia, which supplied oil for Mussolini's army and dive bombers. Secretary of State Hull's "moral embargo" became an empty gesture, and the outcome was that the Italian dictator easily conquered Ethiopia and boasted of a Second Roman Empire.

The fatuous policies of England and France during the period, however, cannot be judged too harshly and must be placed alongside American inaction. A few voices cried that the emerging Berlin-Rome axis was threatening world peace, but those voices were drowned by an overwhelming chorus to stay out of war. Polls indicated top-heavy opinion against any kind of involvement. Most surveys showed that the American people wanted a larger army and navy; however, they were thinking not of foreign involvement but in terms of defending American shorelines. For example, a September 1936 poll reported that 71 percent favored a national referendum on any question of declaring war. In March 1936 no less than 82 percent of the respondents wanted to prohibit the manufacture and sale of arms and munitions. In November of that year, 95 percent thought that the United States should not take part in another conflict like World War I, and in April 1937 it was the belief of 70 percent of those responding that the nation had made a mistake in entering the war in 1917.[9]

Throughout the 1936 presidential campaign and his second term, Franklin Roosevelt was in the prime of his life and administration. Whether dictating little notes to friends and subordinates, splashing for an hour in the White House pool, showing visitors the gewgaws that littered his desk, chiding reporters at press conferences, bantering with congressional leaders, party sachems, and foreign emissaries, or sharing anecdotes about his ancestors—whatever the daily tasks called for—FDR did it with exuberance. He loved being president.

He was not unaware of the clamor against him—much of which was intensely personal. Businessmen angry over NRA codes or bankers irked about SEC regulations claimed "that man" in the White House was dictating their lives. It was understandable, therefore, that the campaign of 1936 would become extremely heated, yet certain facts in the nation's economy were inescapable.

Unemployment had dropped from 12 to 4 million; the stock market was up; payrolls had doubled; cash income of farmers had done the same; Social Security, financed through payroll taxes, was operating and winning approval.

It was odd because the more the economy improved, the more vicious became the attacks upon Roosevelt and the New Deal. Roosevelt supporters explained the phenomenon as being like a drunk picked up from the gutter who later turned resentful because he had been found in a degrading position.

The Republicans nominated Governor Alfred M. Landon of Kansas as their candidate, and Democrats in a jubilant mood at their convention renominated Roosevelt by acclamation. Many polls, including a particularly egregious sampling by the *Literary Digest*, predicted a Republican victory, but in one of the greatest landslides in history, FDR received 60.7 percent of the popular vote and 523 electoral ones out of 531. His opponent carried only two states: Maine and Vermont.

While Roosevelt was concentrating on the domestic economy and reelection, events were moving rapidly toward a European war. Although American feelings had been riled by the Italian-Ethiopian fiasco, those feelings were submerged in passionate and widespread anti-involvement sentiment. Roosevelt made an oblique attack upon this majority attitude when in August 1936, a month after the Spanish civil war broke out, he spoke at Chautauqua, New York. "We are not isolationists," he asserted, "except to isolate ourselves completely from war. Yet we must remember that so long as war exists on earth there will be some danger that even the nation which most ardently desires peace may be drawn into war."[10]

In an emotional passage that exaggerated his actual record during World War I, he declared, "I have seen war. I have seen war on land and sea. I have seen blood running from the wounded. I have seen men coughing out their gassed lungs. I have seen the dead in the mud. . . . I have seen children starving. I have seen the agony of mothers and wives. I hate war."[11]

President Roosevelt thought this speech at Chautauqua, New York, was one of his most important, and the following Christmas he sent several friends a specially printed and inscribed copy of it. Although in retrospect the address can be viewed as a forerunner of later positions, his words on this occasion were too indirect to be of great significance.

Embroiled as he was in fierce controversy over the Supreme Court issue, FDR did not speak out strongly against Hitler's and Mussolini's marches of conquest until more than a year later.

Europe was not the only place darkened by clouds of war. In July 1937, an incident at the Marco Polo bridge, ten miles west of Peking, led to Japanese occupation of the entire Peking area. This occupation turned out to be a prelude to the swift Japanese thrust into five northern provinces of China. At first, FDR and the State Department tried to pursue a middle-of-the road policy, favoring neither Japan nor China, and because Japan studiously avoided declaring its invasion a "war," Roosevelt did not invoke the Neutrality Act then in place. As a result, American ships continued to carry arms and munitions to both nations.

The consensus among the president's advisers was that Japan was a mediocre military power, so it was not until October that FDR spoke out more forcibly. Heading east from a speaking tour in the Western United States, he stopped in Chicago to give a dedicatory speech upon the occasion of opening a PWA bridge on the lakeshore drive.

Hundreds of thousands lined his route to the bridge where he told the crowd that the increasing hostilities in Spain and China threatened the very foundations of civilization. America was not immune, and if conditions got worse the whole Western Hemisphere would be endangered. "No nation," he declared, "could isolate itself from international anarchy." Then came his stirring climax:

When an epidemic of physical disease starts to spread, the community approves and joins in a quarantine of the patients in order to protect the health of the community against the disease.[12]

The "quarantine" expression, which was headlined throughout the world, had been suggested to Roosevelt by Secretary of the Interior Harold Ickes:

I [Harold Ickes] remarked [October 3, 1937] that the international situation was just like a case of contagious disease in a community.

... I suggested that householders in a neighborhood had a right to quarantine themselves against a threatened infection. The President interrupted, "That's a good word; I will write it down and some day I will use it." Drawing one of his little scratch pads to him, he did write it down.[13]

When Roosevelt used the "quarantine" analogy in this landmark speech, he also insisted that he would do everything practicable to avoid involvement in war, thus ending the address on a mixed note. His warning of danger was clear enough, but what did his administration intend to do? Was he repudiating neutrality and aligning America with one group of belligerents? The immediate crowd had shouted its approval, but within hours opposition erupted.

Back in Washington, Secretary of State Hull remained quiet, shocked by the president's strong words. Reactions from others were widespread, vehement, and nearly uniform in calling Roosevelt's idea war mongering or saber rattling. Opinion polls showed a heavy majority against common action with the League of Nations regarding the crisis in the Far East, and FDR's staunchest allies in Congress kept out of the fray. Pacifists charged he was leading the country down the path to war, and isolationists cried for his impeachment.

Surprised at the intensity of criticism and disappointed that party leaders would not share his alarm, FDR decided he had made a mistake in attempting to lead the country too quickly; the public simply was not ready for such arguments. "It's a terrible thing," he said to speech writer Rosenman, "to look over your shoulder when you are trying to lead—and to find no one there."[14]

Adverse public reactions convinced Roosevelt that gradualism would win more converts than forceful flourishes, and thereafter he was very careful not to recommend any drastic action without first tilling the soil on which his seeds of persuasion were to be sown. Despite the clamor it produced, FDR's "quarantine of aggressor nations" speech was his first direct public appeal in behalf of collective security, and it marked an end to the tepid foreign policies followed throughout his first presidential term.

Chapter 12

FDR: Foreign Policies (1937–1945)

The court-packing controversy soured relations between President Roosevelt and many of his key supporters in Congress, and as a result of this embitterment legislative matters during the early months of 1937 were brought to a virtual standstill. The only accomplishment of note was the enactment of two revised neutrality laws: (1) emergency legislation to embargo shipment of arms to both sides in Spain's civil war and (2) the Neutrality Act of 1937.

The Spanish civil war—a squall line forerunning the storm of World War II—was in its second year. Soon after this war began, a so-called Non-Intervention Committee led by Britain and France had been organized. Representatives from Germany and Italy signed the Committee's declaration promising absolute neutrality toward the Spanish conflict, but such pledges proved hollow. Both dictators flagrantly violated the pact and supplied not only arms and war matériel to the Spanish Fascists but sent them units of the air forces and infantry from Italy and the Reich as well.

As an outgrowth of widespread isolationist sentiment in America, Congress in 1935 and 1936 had passed a series of neutrality laws—in actuality a scissors-and-paste combination of legislative resolutions—which among other provisions mandated an arms embargo requiring the president, whenever he found a state of war existing anywhere, to prohibit the sale of arms and munitions to belligerents of either side.

These temporary laws failed to quell arguments or to satisfy critics who wanted assurances that policy makers would not be "suckered again" into a European war. Some groups advocated mandatory laws that would leave the president no discretion in case of the outbreak of hostilities; others wanted more flexible rules which would permit him to handle each case as it arose.

A compromise came in the form of the War Policy Act of May 1, 1937, which granted the president the all-important power of deciding when war actually existed and whether the law was to be put into effect. Prior to 1937 Franklin Roosevelt's public references to foreign problems had been few and comparatively mild, but as war clouds thickened, his speeches and the foreign policies they enunciated changed dramatically. The evolution of this turnabout is thoroughly compatible with the boldness he displayed in domestic matters as well as with his willingness to be inconsistent when necessary in order to attain ultimate goals.

In 1937, isolationists had momentum on their side, and after fierce debate in both House and Senate, Congress passed a "permanent" Neutrality Act, which the president signed into law on May 1. This act retained many provisions of earlier laws—a mandatory arms embargo, a ban on loans and credits to belligerents, continuation of the National Munitions Control Board, a ban on travel by Americans on belligerent ships, and prohibition from arming American ships trading with belligerents as well as the use of American ships for transporting munitions to belligerents. The biggest change brought about by the act was the authority given the president to put the sale of nonembargoed goods to belligerents on a cash-and-carry basis—that is, title to the goods had to be transferred to non-American hands, and the goods had to be carried to the belligerent in non-American ships. The new law also gave Roosevelt discretionary authority to prohibit use of American ports by armed belligerent ships.

The next January FDR proposed that a conference of leading powers meet in Washington to discuss the growing threats to peace in Europe, but the British government thought little of the idea; Prime Minister Chamberlain feared antagonizing Hitler and felt that Japan's doings in China did not concern his country.

Meanwhile, Adolph Hitler had rebuilt his armies and air forces so rapidly that he was ready to embark upon a course of conquest. In February, he forced collapse of the Austrian government under Kurt von Schuschnigg, and a month later German soldiers made their triumphant entry into Vienna.

German control of Austria put Czechoslovakia in the jaws of a Nazi vise. The Czechs were ready to resist, but Western nations, appalled at the threat of another world conflict, demurred and pushed for settlement on almost any terms.

Roosevelt unsuccessfully appealed for continued international negotiations regarding the Czechoslovakian Sudetenland dispute, also reminding signatory European nations that under the Kellogg-Briand Pact war had been "outlawed."

British Prime Minister Neville Chamberlain and French Premier Edouard Daladier met with Hitler and Mussolini in Munich on September 29. No invitation was extended to Russia nor were any Czechs permitted to attend this meeting where the so-called Big Four determined their country's fate. The Munich agreement allowed Germany to set new frontiers for Czechoslovakia and to conduct a plebisicite for a new government. Essentially the "agreement" was nothing more than acceptance of an ultimatum der Fuehrer had laid down earlier.

"This is the last territorial claim I have to make in Europe," Hitler declared. Prime Minister Chamberlain returned to cheering crowds in London and announced, "This is the second time there has come back from Germany peace with honour. I believe it is peace in our time."

But it was not to be. Within weeks, the once strong Czechoslovakia was whittled down to impotence, and in March 1939, Hitler, demonstrating the folly of the previous Munich agreement, took over all the country.

"The bloodless solution of the Czech conflict in the autumn of 1938 and spring of 1939 and the annexation of Slovakia," declared German General von Jodl in a postwar lecture, "rounded off the territory of Greater Germany in such a way that it now became possible to consider the Polish problem on the basis of more or less favourable strategic premises."[1]

A few members of the German General Staff opposed Hitler's aggrandizements, but his judgment that the West would do nothing to halt bold actions had been vindicated in both Austria and Czechoslovakia. Following the latter coup, German military chiefs, longing to see the Fatherland regain its position in the world, smothered their personal dislike for der Fuehrer and decided to cast their lots with him and his henchmen. Thus did Adolph Hitler become undisputed master of the Third Reich and establish a path for his grandiose designs.

In April 1939, after the German Protectorate of Czechoslovakia was completed, FDR sent Hitler and Mussolini an extraordinary public letter which was broadcast to all parts of the world. Recounting the loss of independence by three nations in Europe, one in Africa, and the occupation of a large part of China by Japan, FDR cited reports of plans for further aggressions and then urged the two dictators to pledge themselves to peace.

"Are you willing," asked the American president, "to give assurance that your armed forces will not attack or invade the territory or possessions" of thirty-one specific nations for "ten or even twenty-five years, if we are to look that far ahead?"

FDR knew that his appeal would arouse great popular enthusiasm in America and much of Europe, so his message was aimed more at rallying Western resolve than at obtaining cooperation from either Germany or Italy. He told confidants that it was a way of putting both dictators on the spot.

Reacting to Roosevelt's ploy, Mussolini in Rome declared his indifference to "press campaigns . . . or Messiah-like messages" and at first even refused to read the document. To German Air Marshall Hermann Goering, who was meeting with him at the time, he sneered that the request was the "result of infantile paralysis!"[2]

In Berlin, Hitler's reaction was even more insulting. Though claiming to be reluctant to respond to a "communication from so contemptible a creature as the present President of the United States," Hitler convened the Reichstag and treated them to a sarcastic harangue that drew roars of malicious laughter.[3]

"If all problems could be solved around a conference table as Roosevelt believed, why," der Fuehrer shouted, "had the United States rejected the League of Nations? If Germans had asked about American intentions in Latin America they most certainly would have been told to mind their own business." Furthermore, Hitler maintained that each of the thirty-one states mentioned in FDR's message had been asked if it felt threatened by Germany, and all replies had been negative. To the delight of the wildly applauding members of the Reichstag, Hitler ranted further, eliciting more ridicule with each thrust.

The German dictator denied that he wanted to start a war, explained his actions as simply the righting of past wrongs, and insisted that Germany's moves were indistinguishable from past self-interested deeds of America, Britain, and France.

The Nazi leader's rebuttal appealed to American isolationists, who refused to believe that a European conflict was in the offing. President Roosevelt, they insisted, was trying to deflect problems at home by meddling abroad.

Senator Hiram Johnson of California wrote to his son, "Hitler had all the better of the argument. . . . Roosevelt put his chin out and got a resounding whack. I have reached the conclusion that there will be no war."[4]

As Hitler moved toward further expansions in the spring and summer of 1939, Roosevelt stepped up his arguments that the arms embargo actually encouraged Germany and that it was in America's best interests to send arms to Britain and France. As was his practice, he preferred a backstairs approach, meeting often with party stalwarts and wavering senators and representatives.

A great believer in opinion polls, FDR sensed that public sentiment was turning in his favor, and as war became increasingly likely he increased efforts to get the embargo repealed.

British and French governments at the time had recovered from earlier delusions about Nazi intentions and had signed pacts with Poland and Romania guaranteeing them against aggression. The Soviet Union was willing to join as an additional signatory to the pacts but again was ignored by the two Western governments.[5]

Romania was included in the treaty because of extensive oil fields at Ploesti. Ploesti's refineries produced one-third of Adolph Hitler's high-octane aviation gasoline, panzer fuel, benzine, and lubricants. From there would come more than half the oil that later kept Rommel's armor running on the sand plains of Mediterranean Africa.

Realizing Ploesti's importance to Hitler's Wehrmacht, Britain and France paid a staggering sum into Romania's King Carol's privy purse, and the resultant pact guaranteed military aid for his country in case of attack. The treaty also contained a secret proviso that if Hitler tried to seize the refineries, Allied technicians might destroy them.

Hitler, his appetite whetted by Austria and Czechoslovakia, turned hungry eyes toward Poland. From Paris, American Ambassador William Bullitt reported that the Polish government viewed the chances of war by no later than mid-August as eighty out of a hundred. Unknown then to Bullitt and the Poles, Hitler on April 1 had given orders to his generals setting September 1 as the invasion date.

On July 18, FDR arranged a private arm-twisting session in the White House. Senate Majority Leader Alben Barkley rounded up five influential colleagues to meet with the president and Secretary of State Hull. After drinks had been mixed and served, Roosevelt turned serious, sharing his alarm about the likelihood of war and describing the consequences of a possible British-French defeat. Hull gave salty concurrence by saying that the legislators were making the mistake of their lives if they thought the European crisis was "another goddamned piddling dispute over a boundary line."[6]

Roosevelt, knowing how pitifully short of men and matériel the Western Allies were, presented his case as best he could: the only way to avert war was to repeal the Neutrality Act so that Britain and France could get needed equipment.

A majority of the legislative leaders in attendance, however, were unconvinced, and Vice President John Nance Garner ended the meeting by turning to the president and saying, "Well, Captain, we may as well face the facts. You haven't got the votes, and that's all there is to it."[7]

William E. Borah of Idaho, one of the senators present, insisted that he had private sources of information. He assured the group and later offered such assurance to the entire country that there would be no war. Meanwhile, France equivocated, Chamberlain's government in Britain fiddled, and Poland quibbled.

Then, on August 24, 1939, the standoff took a sudden turn for the worse when Soviet Premier Joseph Stalin did an about-face and signed a peace treaty with Hitler. The diplomatic world was stunned, for the two dictators had been violently abusing each other for the past five years. Their pact promised each other nonaggression and included secret clauses for the partition of Poland. The way now was clear for another German conquest.

At dawn on September 1, 1939, Nazi armed forces crossed the border to attack Poland, thereby setting off the debacle that would take the lives of more than 14 million men and women under arms as well as countless civilians killed either by deliberate intent or as innocent victims of modern weapons.

At 2:50 A.M. on September 2, the American ambassador in Warsaw, Anthony J. Drexel Biddle, managed to telephone Ambassador Bullitt in Paris who immediately called Roosevelt to report that Germany had invaded Poland. At the presidential press conference held later that day, most discussion understandably was about the ominous happening. The overriding question was "Can we stay out?" In answer, FDR kept repeating, "I believe so . . . every effort will be made by this Administration to do so."

Despite the seriousness of the situation, he was not above taking a shot at Senator Borah, one of his isolationist adversaries. A reporter said that the senator was very sick and had gone to Poland Springs, Maine, for treatment. "Oh," jibed Roosevelt, "I thought you said Poland. That would have been news!"[8]

Two days later FDR gave a fireside chat to the American people. His words were carefully crafted in order to win more public support and at the same time not rile unduly the isolationist faction.

> This nation will remain a neutral nation, but I cannot ask that every
> American remain neutral in thought as well. Even a neutral has a right

to take account of facts. Even a neutral cannot be asked to close his mind or his conscience. . . .

I hope the United States will keep out of this war. I believe it will. And I give you assurance and reassurance that every effort of your Government will be directed toward that end.[9]

Roosevelt must have felt compelled to make such dissembling if not actually misleading remarks in order to bolster support for repeal of the embargo. Two weeks later he called Congress into a special session. It became a month-long fight; congressmen were flooded with letters and telegrams against repeal, many of them echoing lines from a popular radio priest, Father Coughlin of Detroit, and the hero of the 1920s, Charles A. Lindbergh, both of whom strongly opposed aiding the Western allies.

Isolationists insisted that FDR was planning "to send the boys of American mothers to fight on the battlefields of Europe," but the president met daily with individual senators and used all his matchless personal persuasions to bring them around to his side. After a month of behind-the-scenes meetings in the White House, the Senate went along and repealed the arms embargo by a vote of sixty-three to thirty. The House followed suit a few days later. President Roosevelt had won another tremendous debate.

Almost as soon as German armies blitzed into Poland, FDR ordered a huge war map mounted on an office wall so that he would be given an up-to-the-hour view of military actions. The Poles though brave and determined were no match for the Nazi blitzkrieg. Stukas, screaming as they dived to drop bombs that spread flame and terror, and divisions of machine-gun spouting tanks quickly overpowered the horse-drawn artillery and World War I rifles of the hapless Poles.

After the initial onslaught against Poland, the major belligerents—Germany, Britain, and France—allowed the war to settle into a stalemate. Though Soviets were crushing their way into Finland, the rest of Europe bogged down in what American journalists called "the Phony War."

In England, Winston Churchill was returned to being First Lord of the Admiralty. Shortly thereafter, FDR wrote a letter to him, which began a relationship that would grow ever stronger throughout the war.

September 11, 1939

My dear Churchill:

It is because you and I occupied similar positions in the World War that I want you to know how glad I am that you are back again in the

Admiralty. Your problems are, I realize, complicated by new factors, but the essential is not very different. What I want you to know is that I shall at all times welcome it if you will keep in touch with me personally with anything you want me to know about. You can always send sealed letters through your pouch or my pouch.

I am glad you did the Marlboro [*sic*] volumes before this thing started—and I much enjoyed reading them.

Franklin D. Roosevelt[10]

The sincerity as well as the purpose of this missive from FDR are questionable, for in private he expressed quite a different opinion.

Joseph P. Kennedy at that time was the American ambassador to the Court of Saint James, having been appointed two years earlier in repayment for political support he had given FDR in 1932 and 1936. The appointment had not been granted without misgivings, however, for Roosevelt distrusted Kennedy personally and resented demands the rich, influential, and crusty Irishman consistently made. According to Morgenthau, FDR deemed Kennedy "a very dangerous man—too dangerous to have around here" (i.e., in Washington).[11]

In January 1940, when Ambassador Kennedy returned from London, he brought along a personal message from Churchill expressing British intention to disrupt German ore shipments by mining Norwegian waters. Kennedy, aware of the growing linkage between the president and Churchill, asked about Churchill's role.

"I have always disliked him since the time I went to England in 1918," Roosevelt declared. "He acted like a stinker at a dinner I attended, lording it all over us. . . . I've given him attention now because there is a strong possibility that he will become the prime minister and I want to get my hand in now."[12]

Europe in 1940 was not the only continent darkened by war. In the Far East, Japanese conquests that had begun with the rape of Nanking in 1937 were continuing almost unimpeded. With the forces of Britain and France desperately needed at home, the Empire of the Rising Sun saw an opportunity to achieve its goal of making all of Southeast Asia a part of the Empire's autonomy.

It cannot be said that Japanese purposes were entirely unsuspected by the Roosevelt administration, for from listening posts scattered around the Pacific the U.S. Navy was eavesdropping on messages out of Tokyo. Furthermore, since 1935, cryptographers in Washington were on the trail of breaking secret codes Japan was using for military and diplomatic messages.

In the fall of 1940, Joseph C. Grew, America's ambassador to Japan, returned to meet with President Roosevelt and express alarm over Japanese moves. FDR in response spoke confidently of intercepting the Japanese fleet if it moved southward, of reinforcing U.S. troops stationed in Manila and Pearl Harbor, and of impressive naval maneuvers soon to be displayed in the Pacific. It would be U.S. policy to avoid confronting the Japanese while setting in place machinery to assist the British in Europe.

Grew went back to Tokyo where he gave a carefully planned address to the American-Japan Society—a prestigious group that included American businessmen and their wives, along with Japanese from the highest financial, diplomatic, and court circles.

With the president's prior approval, Grew told his listeners that American opinion resented Japanese aggression in China and that his government favored economic retaliation against further violations of American rights or international law.

Back in America, the ambassador's remarks received enthusiastic editorial endorsements, but in fact there was no retaliation. Oil, gasoline, and finished steel continued to be sent to Japan. The Japanese, who depended on imports for 90 percent of their gasoline, were known to be stockpiling petroleum products, but throughout 1940 and the first half of 1941, when their intentions became more evident, American oil continued to be sold to them. Thus the arsenal of democracy was also the service station for fascism.

From his post in Tokyo, Ambassador Grew repeatedly warned that Japan was continuing its depredations and was preparing to move southward, that the Japanese army was capable of surprise actions, and that Japanese leaders were trumpeting that a showdown with the United States was unavoidable.

At the opening of 1941 (January 17), Grew sent Roosevelt an ominous report he had obtained from the Peruvian minister in Tokyo: "There is a lot of talk around town to the effect that the Japanese, in case of a break with the United States, are planning to go all out in a surprise mass attack on Pearl Harbor. I rather guess that the boys in Hawaii are not precisely asleep."[13]

The State Department took no more notice of this warning that it did other similar warnings.

April 1940 marked the end of the Phony War, for in that month the Germans launched invasions of Norway and Denmark. A month later, Wehrmacht tanks rumbled into the Low Countries: Holland, Belgium, and Luxembourg. France was scheduled to be the next victim.

Dunkirk, a French industrial town on the North Sea coast, was the last remaining port of evacuation for British troops trapped by the German encirclement. Through Herculean efforts and sheer courage, in late May over 335,585 men were rescued from the entrapment and returned to England to fight again.

Italy's dictator Benito Mussolini, watching the Nazi blitzkrieg, knew he could not delay much longer if he hoped to share in the spoils, so on June 10 he strutted onto his balcony in Rome's Piazza Venezia to announce that he, too, was sending troops into France.

Roosevelt received news of this announcement just an hour before he left Washington for a speech at the University of Virginia in Charlottesville. There speaking in his habitual slow rate for emphasis and in a voice heavy with contempt, he declared, "On this tenth day of June 1940, the hand that held the dagger has struck it into the back of its neighbor."

Wirephotos four days later showed Germans entering Paris and victorious Nazi troops parading in the Place de la Concorde; Le Havre was gone, so was Verdun, and Hitler's legions were about to capture the vaunted Maginot Line from the rear.

Americans watched these momentous happenings with a growing sense of foreboding. Public opinion, strongly shaped by FDR's rhetoric and that of interventionist committees, began shifting away from the isolationists.

The public was unaware that behind the scenes Roosevelt was seeking ways to circumvent legal stumbling blocks that might keep him from aiding beleaguered Britain. One of the first priorities was to shore up Britain's naval strength.

Five days after Churchill became prime minister he had sent FDR a desperate request for fifty or sixty destroyers. Private negotiations on this matter continued until September 5, 1 940, when the agreement to transfer fifty "overaged" destroyers was completed, and Churchill could disingenuously tell the House of Commons that "by the long arm of coincidence" the destroyers already were in ports where they could be turned over to British crews.

In that summer and fall, while Roosevelt was doing all he could to help countries being overrun by the Nazis, he also had to campaign for reelection. In deciding to run for a third term, he had broken tradition and faced a formidable Republican opponent in Wendell Wilkie. Despite his own earlier stances against Hitler and his statements that fascism was a menace to democracy everywhere, Wilkie made a flat prediction that electing Roosevelt to a third term would surely mean dictatorship, war, and the sending of "American boys into foreign wars."

Wilkie's candidacy raised GOP hopes everywhere, and indeed he garnered more popular votes that November than any Republican in history, but he was up against Franklin Roosevelt—the most masterful politician the country had ever known and an incumbent president at the height of his power and prestige. The popular vote was relatively close, but the electoral vote was more decisive: 449 to 82.

Almost as soon as results were in, FDR put aside remarks his opponent had made during the campaign and, largely because of Wilkie's internationalist outlook, brought him into the administration's fold. Within weeks Wilkie was on his way to England with a letter from Roosevelt to Churchill in his pocket.

By mid-December, the British had nearly exhausted their financial resources. Churchill, acceding to FDR's earlier invitation to correspond often, warned that his country's needs would increase tenfold in the future. While on a cruise following his November victory, FDR pondered Churchill's plea and how the United States could respond.

Toward the end of the cruise, FDR disclosed to Harry Hopkins a new bold, ingenious, and imaginative approach for aid to Britain. As far as can be ascertained, the idea was entirely his—an idea Lord Maynard Keynes characterized as Roosevelt's "brain wave."

FDR introduced the subject at his press conference on December 17 and argued that war materials would be more useful to the defense of the United States "if they were used in Great Britain, than if they were kept in storage here." Then employing his extraordinary talent for homely metaphors, he explained:

> What I am trying to do is to eliminate the dollar sign. Suppose my neighbor's home catches fire, and I have a length of garden hose four or five hundred feet away. If he can take my garden hose and connect it up with his hydrant, I may help him put out his fire. Now what do I do? I don't say to him before that operation, "Neighbor, my garden hose cost me $15; you have to pay me $15 for it." What is the transaction that goes on? I don't want $15—I want my garden hose back after the fire is over.[14]

Roosevelt followed this trial balloon by announcing formation of the Office of Production Management for the purpose of speeding up production of war matériel. Then, on December 29, he delivered one of his most important fireside chats.

In this pivotal talk, FDR began by comparing the world crisis of 1940 to the banking crisis America faced when he came into office. Next he described what would happen if Great Britain were to go down: "the Axis powers will control the continents of Europe, Asia, Africa, Australia, and the high seas. . . . It is no exaggeration to say that all of us, in all the Americas, would be living at the point of a gun—a gun loaded with explosive bullets, economic as well as military."[15]

FDR then gave voice to another of his memorable phrases: "We must be the great *arsenal of democracy*. . . . No dictator, no combination of dictators, will weaken that determination by threats of how they will construe that determination."[16]

The phrase "arsenal of democracy" had been coined by Jean Monnet, a French representative then in Washington. Monnet had used it in conversation with Justice Frankfurter when describing the most effective resistance the United States could provide to European nations struggling against Hitler's tyranny.[17]

On the night FDR gave this talk, the Germans subjected London to one of its heaviest bombings. They and the Japanese, who later adopted similar tactics, used such psychological strategy on frequent occasions when Roosevelt spoke hoping their diversions would blanket the impact of his rhetoric.

The Lend-Lease bill that grew from FDR's "brain wave" was one of the few "irrevocable acts" to which he committed himself prior to the bombing of Pearl Harbor.

FDR's election to an unprecedented third term failed to muffle isolationist voices; there were still influential opponents to be reckoned with. Senator Burton K. Wheeler of Montana, who had just been reelected and was therefore safe from voters for another six years, adopted a slogan asserting that Lend-Lease would mean "ploughing under every fourth American boy." The slogan infuriated FDR, who called it "the most untruthful, the most dastardly, unpatriotic thing that has been said in public in my generation."

Passage of Lend-Lease meant in effect setting up a de facto alliance between the United States and Hitler's foes. From Britain, Churchill weighed in with simple eloquence, "Give us the tools, and we will finish the job."[18]

In America, the Democratic party and the administration, having healed most wounds from the Supreme Court fight, organized a united front, and as a result the Lend-Lease Act (patriotically numbered H.R. 1776) passed Congress in March 1941.

Meanwhile, the Germans were unleashing new offensives. The first week in April they invaded Yugoslavia and killed seventeen thousand civilians in Belgrade during the first twenty-four hours. Eleven days later German armies went on to conquer neighboring Greece and to drive British forces in Libya back to the Egyptian border.

The Allies were being defeated everywhere, and the aid promised by Roosevelt was slow to develop. As more months of 1941 passed, his rhetoric began running ahead of America's war capacity. There were shortages of electric power and war matériel, such as aluminum, vital for airplanes. Industrial production was uneven, and there were threats of a nationwide strike from powerful John L. Lewis, still smarting from his vain efforts to rally United Mine Workers behind Wilkie in order to defeat Roosevelt.

A year earlier FDR dramatically had called for production of fifty thousand planes a year—a staggering number meant to put America ahead of Germany and create an air armada second to none in the world. Although airplane production in 1941 was up more than 20 percent, the big automotive companies were also producing new cars in record numbers and in doing so gobbling up 80 percent of all available rubber, 49 percent of strip steel, 44 percent of sheet metal, and 34 percent of lead.

In August, amidst great secrecy, Roosevelt sailed aboard the U.S.S. *Augusta* to Argentia Harbor off the coast of Newfoundland where the British battleship H.M.S. *Prince of Wales*, still scarred from her encounter with the German *Bismarck*, dropped anchor. British Prime Minister Winston Churchill had come for a top-level tête-à-tête with the American president.

The Atlantic Charter, one of the most compelling statements of the war, grew out of this meeting. The charter's underlying significance lay in strategic decisions and military commitments made there. The British were bent upon bombing, blockading, and wearing down Germany; American military leaders, particularly General George Marshall, contended that it would be necessary for Allied ground forces to invade the Continent and close with the enemy before Germany could be defeated. The American view eventually prevailed.

Churchill pressed for stepped-up American action in the Atlantic and a stronger defense effort in the Pacific. FDR agreed to provide American escorts for all fast convoys between Newfoundland and Iceland. Churchill said Britain planned to occupy the Canary Islands—a move that probably would lead to Spain's counterattack with aid from the Nazis. Later, the British called off the seizure of the Canary Islands, but Roosevelt's willingness to support the Azores shows how far even then he was ready to stretch neutrality interpretations.

Churchill wanted a hard line on Japan, too. He feared Japanese actions could leave Britain standing alone in Southeast Asia. Only the stiffest warning from America, he insisted, would have any deterrent effect on Japanese schemes.

On this subject, Roosevelt demurred, saying he preferred to parley and stall the Japanese, allowing them to save face for at least a while. Instead of agreeing with Churchill's near ultimatum, FDR preferred to inform the Japanese that if they would pull out of Indochina, Washington would be able to settle remaining differences with them. Churchill had little alternative except to go along with this approach, thus leaving the initiative entirely with the American president.

There was ample reason for concern over Japan, for conditions in the Pacific were worsening fast. Admiral Walter Anderson, director of naval intelligence, warned that "Japan will strike soon." Moreover, in May, American experts had decoded a message from Tokyo to Japan's foreign minister in Washington which read, "Should matters [American buildup vis-à-vis Japan] continue unchecked, Japan will be forced to live up to her obligations under the Japan-Germany-Italy Tripartite Pact."[19]

Japanese troops moved into southern Vietnam on July 24, 1941, and President Roosevelt immediately froze Japanese funds in the United States. He also ordered an embargo on shipments of oil to Japan.

Five months later, on December 7, while a navy band on the stern of the U.S.S. *Nevada* was playing "The Star Spangled Banner" for the 8 A.M. flag raising, Japanese bombers roared overhead firing torpedoes at the nearby *Arizona* and other ships at anchor. Pearl Harbor was attacked in a blow that was shattering both physically and psychologically. For years afterward every American alive then would remember what he or she was doing when radio news interrupted that quiet Sunday.

The day after the Japanese struck, round after round of applause greeted President Roosevelt as he slowly made his way to the rostrum of the House of Representatives and delivered his short, emphatic address: "Yesterday, December 7, 1941—a date which will live in infamy—the United States was suddenly and deliberately attacked by the naval and air forces of the Empire of Japan."

More than a declaration of existing war, FDR's message announced onset of a war that would engulf the world and not end until four and a half years later.

In the Atlantic, during the early months of 1942, Nazi submarines attempted to keep American shipping within the Western Hemisphere. The U-boats were so successful in torpedoing American oil tankers silhouetted against the lights of East Coast cities that a critical oil shortage began to be felt throughout the United States.

In May, Soviet Foreign Minister Vyacheslav Molotov arrived in Washington to demand an immediate second front in order to divert at least forty German divisions from the Soviet Union. FDR agreed to do everything possible, including a promise to invade France in 1942, certainly no later than 1943.

When Churchill came to Washington a short time later he strongly urged an invasion of North Africa instead. Accordingly, despite some bungling but gratifyingly few losses, Anglo-American forces landed at Oran and Casablanca in November 1942. As that year drew toward a close, the discouraging months of constant Allied defeats by Axis powers were almost over.

In November, too, FDR proposed to Churchill that the military staffs of the United States, Britain, and the Soviet Union meet in Moscow or Cairo to discuss war strategy. Churchill agreed on a conference but wanted more than just military people. Soviet generals, he said, would simply reiterate demands for a second front and refer every question back to Stalin. Why shouldn't the Big Three leaders meet?

The year of 1943 was one of conferences for Roosevelt. He met with Churchill at Casablanca in January, again at Hyde Park in mid-August, and then at Quebec later that same month. Churchill came to the White House in September. Next was a November meeting of Roosevelt and Churchill in Cairo with Chiang Kai-shek, followed by the Teheran conference where the Big Three—Roosevelt, Churchill, and Stalin—met together for the first time. Finally, in early December, Roosevelt and Churchill again journeyed to Cairo for another of their wartime conferences.

Roosevelt had believed that Stalin would be amenable to meeting with him and Churchill at Casablanca, but he was wrong. The Soviet dictator said he could not leave his country during major military operations, but he wired that he felt confident the promise given by Roosevelt to open a second front in Europe no later than the spring of 1943 would be honored. Thus Stalin laid down the gauntlet for the Casablanca meeting without even attending it.

FDR hoped to keep that conference focused on military issues, but at Casablanca in January 1943 he was entangled with problems of French factionalism. With his usual confidence, he presumed it would be a simple matter to bring together Charles de Gaulle, the touchy leader of the French resistance, and General Henri Giraud, who had been captured by Germans in 1940 and escaped two years later. Roosevelt insisted that de Gaulle come from London to Casablanca; otherwise, important decisions affecting his country would be made without him. De Gaulle came but proved stubborn and bitter; the notion that he was being forced to visit an Anglo-American camp in order to negotiate with another Frenchman deeply offended his Gallic pride.

The most significant public report from the Casablanca meeting came in a press conference held at its conclusion. De Gaulle, Giraud, Churchill, and Roosevelt had posed for pictures, and then the two French generals withdrew, carrying ill-concealed dislike of one another. Churchill and Roosevelt were left, and FDR spoke first, referring to the American Civil War. "Some of you Britishers know the old story—we had a General called U.S. Grant. His name was Ulysses Simpson Grant, but in my and the Prime Minister's early days he was called 'Unconditional Surrender' Grant." FDR went on to say, "The elimination of German, Japanese, and Italian war power means the unconditional surrender of Germany, Italy, and Japan."

Churchill was stunned. He and Roosevelt had discussed unconditional surrender only briefly, and he did not expect the president to refer to it. In explaining his statement later, FDR said that getting de Gaulle and Giraud together had been so difficult it reminded him of Grant and Lee—"and then suddenly the press conference was on, and Winston and I had had no time to prepare for it, and the thought popped into my mind . . . the next thing I knew I had said it."[20]

Throughout 1943 FDR kept trying to arrange a conference that Stalin would attend. Groundwork for such a meeting was laid by Secretary Hull who went to Moscow in October. The result was the Teheran Conference held at the end of November.

The middle of that month found Churchill aboard the H.M.S. *Renown* and Roosevelt aboard the U.S.S. *Iowa* steaming toward Cairo for a preliminary conference before making their way to Teheran for the scheduled summit meeting. In Cairo, FDR and Churchill were joined by Chinese generalissimo Chiang Kai-shek, and the trio drew up plans for the postwar Far East. Japan was to be stripped of her empire in order to restore Manchuria, the Pescadores, and Formosa to China, and a free and independent Korea was to be created.

From Cairo, FDR and Churchill with their respective delegations flew to the historic conference in Iran. In the first session, Soviet dictator Stalin got right to his main point: he wanted the long-promised invasion very soon. The best way to get to the heart of Germany, he insisted, was through northern and southern France, not up the Italian Alps or the "soft underbelly of Europe" proposed by Churchill.

Although Roosevelt presided over the meeting, it was Stalin who forced the important issues. He wanted answers on three questions: (1) the date of OVERLORD (the invasion of Western Europe), (2) landings in southern France, and (3) who would be the commander of OVERLORD. Without a supreme commander, he snapped, "nothing will come of these operations." Stalin's bluntness made it clear he would discuss nothing seriously until he had an Anglo-American commitment for OVERLORD.

After a pause, Churchill replied that at Quebec he and Roosevelt had agreed that the invasion's commander should be American; the Soviet leader would be informed as soon as a final decision was made.

Other specific matters got less attention. Stalin repeatedly sought to couple the treatment of the French nation with that of Poland, thereby inviting the Allies to assume a free hand in France, asserting in turn his own freedom of action in Poland, which was to be liberated by the Red Army.

Stalin reaffirmed his intention to bring the Soviet Union into the Pacific war as soon as hostilities ended in Europe, and in a cordial way the three leaders discussed means of keeping Germany from ever again becoming a menace.

Newspaper and radio reports of the Teheran Conference were glowing enough to raise hopes of war-weary citizens in America, Britain, and the Soviet Union. Shortly after the conference, Stalin wrote to Roosevelt: "Now it is assured that our peoples will act together jointly and in friendship both at the present time and after the end of the war."[21]

On Sunday, January 20, 1945, Roosevelt appeared on the south porch of the White House to take the oath of office for his fourth term. He had won reelection by another smashing victory. America's war on two fronts was winding down; Allied armies were overrunning Germany; Berlin was in ruins from round-the-clock bombing; in the East 180 Soviet divisions were closing in. Tokyo was afire from bombs dropped from gigantic new superforts—the B-29s.

Friends and intimates realized that Roosevelt's health was failing fast; he had lost about twenty pounds, and his body shook as he grasped the rail with his right arm. The new vice president, Harry Truman, standing behind him thought he looked ill and completely worn out.

Notwithstanding Roosevelt's precarious health, there was to be one more Big Three conference. As FDR began his fourth term, he also was making arrangements to go to Yalta, a health resort on the Crimean Peninsula.

Two days after the inauguration Roosevelt left Washington aboard the cruiser *Quincy*. In the Mediterranean he stopped at Malta where Churchill and his entourage were waiting. By this time the American president and the British prime minister were old friends.

From Malta, Roosevelt flew in his presidential plane, *The Sacred Cow*, to an icy runway ninety miles from Yalta. Upon seeing Roosevelt, Charles Wilson, Churchill's doctor, recorded in his dairy:

> To a doctor's eye, the President appears a very sick man. He has all the symptoms of hardening of the arteries of the brain in an advanced stage, so that I give him only a few months to live.[22]

The first session of the Yalta Conference was held on February 4, 1945, and discussion opened with a review of the military situation. The plenary sessions were very tiring for FDR, but he seemed able to regain strength and enjoy the formal dinners, complete with buckets of Caucasian champagne along with thirty or more formal toasts.

Disagreement arose over what role France should play in postwar Europe. On this issue, FDR sided with Churchill instead of Stalin and insisted upon giving France a share in zones of occupation planned for Germany after the war's end.

Roosevelt was flexible in regard to Poland's borders. The Soviet plan essentially called for westward movement of the entire country, thus compensating the Soviet Union at Germany's expense. The critical matter of supervising elections within the borders of redistricted Poland remained unsettled.

Roosevelt next turned the discussion back to his main goal, namely, securing Soviet help in the war against Japan. American military chiefs had warned him repeatedly that the war there would take at least eighteen months after Germany's surrender. Stalin promised to enter the Pacific conflict within two to three months after Germany's defeat, and in return Roosevelt agreed to Russian claims in the Far East.

President Roosevelt's final summit conference became his most controversial one. Harry Hopkins, the president's closest aide at the time, said,

> We really believed in our hearts that this was the dawn of a new day we had all been praying for and talking about for so many years. We were absolutely certain that we had won the first great victory of peace—and by "we" I mean all of us, the whole civilized race.[23]

Others were not so charitable. After public exultation set off by initial reports of the Teheran meeting waned, many of the agreements made at Yalta were harshly criticized. Roosevelt, it was charged, should have insisted upon clear, sharply defined agreements which would have left only one interpretation both in the Soviet Union and in the West. This was especially true of questions of access to Berlin and treatment of Poland. Experience with the Soviets long before Yalta should have pointed out the need for a precise understanding.

It was charged further that FDR had "given away" too much to the Soviets, and because of his overwhelming self-confidence he had been careless in pinning his hopes on a postwar international organization that would preserve peace.

One of FDR's most prominent biographers, James MacGregor Burns, defended his subject's decisions at Yalta and concluded,

His [Roosevelt's] position on Poland resulted not, as many have since charged from naivete, ignorance, illness or perfidy, but from his acceptance of the facts: Russia occupied Poland. Russia distrusted its Western allies. Russia had a million men who could fight Japan. Russia could sabotage the new peace organization. And Russia was absolutely determined about Poland and always had been.[24]

Although the Yalta Conference ended with a signed accord covering Poland, the ink was hardly dry before it became clear that Allied understanding was more apparent than real. None of the signatories interpreted the loosely worded agreement in the same way. Churchill argued for more Western influence; Stalin advocated less. FDR's strategy had been to operate as a mediator between the British and Soviets and to postpone troublesome matters, but death removed him from the inevitable debate over specific decisions.

Chapter 13

HST: Foreign Policies

The death knell of Nazism already was sounding when Truman began his presidency. With the Red Army sweeping in from the east and Allied troops advancing from west, north, and south, Hitler four months earlier in a final desperate military gambit had ordered a twenty-four-division counteroffensive through Belgium's Ardennes Forest. The destruction of the Wehrmacht's last reserves in the Battle of the Bulge had opened the gate to the German heartland.

The Germans surrendered to General Dwight Eisenhower, Supreme Commander of the Allied Forces, on May 7, 1945, and the following day President Truman officially declared that victory over Nazi tyranny had been achieved. To celebrate the end of war in Europe, and also because it happened to be his sixty-first birthday, Truman wrote to his mother telling her of the informal telephoning that had been necessary so that Americans, British, and Soviets could make simultaneous announcements of the surrender.

Regular letters and phone calls to close family members were a routine Truman set when he first went to Washington in 1935 as the junior senator from Missouri. In fact, a few hours before Franklin Roosevelt died in Warm Springs, Georgia, Truman in Washington dictated a letter to his sister-in-law, Mrs. George Wallace. Before the letter was mailed and during the hectic four hours between the time of Roosevelt's death and the swearing-in ceremony for the new president, HST scrawled a hasty postscript: "This was dictated before the world fell in on me. But I've talked to you since and you know what a blow it was." Then in a simple sentence that revealed his attitude toward responsibility and the presidency, he added, "But I must meet it."

Truman's personal contacts with Roosevelt had been few. Even after the 1944 Democratic Convention and the subsequent election, Roosevelt, in keeping with his inclination and habit, had not felt it necessary to brief his third vice president on pending matters of state or war strategy.

It is a mistake to believe, however, that Truman came into the presidency with absolutely no preparation or expectancy of ever reaching that office. Undoubtedly, he did not expect it would be handed to him so soon after his inauguration as vice president. If he had, he would have schooled himself more fully in such matters as foreign policies, overall relations with the Soviet Union, and particularly the Yalta Conference.

At the outset, Truman had no staff of consultants or advisers to help him establish a new administration. Nor was there time to shunt critical problems aside while he chose cabinet members and aides. Most of FDR's holdovers were willing to stay on, and a few of them because of seniority and experience thought they could easily influence if not direct the thinking of the new president. He wasted no time in proving them wrong.

Truman was fond of saying that he had been elected on the Roosevelt platform and that he intended to continue FDR's programs. There is no record—no graph of the impulses in Roosevelt's mind—to tell us what his assessments of facts and problems were in regard to the Soviets, but it is clear that at first Truman hoped to follow what he thought were the ideas of his predecessor.

Yet there can be no question that the policy of unstinted cooperation with the Soviet Union—a policy nurtured by FDR—was quickly altered under the Truman administration. The goodwill generated during most of the war was soon replaced by suspicion and distrust on the parts of both East and West.

Truman had grown to maturity in a Midwestern state where isolationism still held great appeal, and even as a U.S. senator in 1941 he seemed to reflect the attitudes of many Americans when he commented upon Hitler's unexpected invasion of the Soviet Union: "If we see that Germany is winning the war, we ought to help Russia, and if Russia is winning we ought to help Germany and in that way kill as many as possible."[1]

The emergent toughening stance of the U.S. government toward the Soviet Union was not a change that could be traced to a single event or date; nor is it likely that the change was part of a carefully planned strategy. Rather it was a pragmatic policy that grew on a week-by-week basis as military urgencies lessened and new problems arose.

It is likely that President Truman's first encounter with Russian diplomats, less than two weeks after he had entered office, was more significant than he realized. A day before this encounter, Truman was briefed by Secretary of State Stettinius, Secretary of War Stimson, Major General John Dean (chief of the U.S. Military Mission in Moscow), Navy Secretary James Forrestal, Admiral Ernest J. King, General George Marshall, Admiral William Leahy, and Ambassador Averell Harriman. All, with the exception of Secretary Stimson, echoed a call for a hard line in dealing with the Soviets.

With this briefing as a backdrop, Truman met with Soviet Foreign Minister V. M. Molotov and Soviet Ambassador Andrei Gromyko late in the afternoon of April 23. Harriman and Charles Bohlen, who acted as the American interpreter, were the Americans present; Molotov and Gromyko were accompanied by their Russian interpreter, Pavlov.

On this occasion, Truman "talked tough" about alleged Soviet failures to carry out what he thought were the Yalta accords. He laid particular stress on the refusal by the Soviet-sponsored Polish government in Lublin to allow representation from the Polish government-in-exile operating out of London. Truman was blunt in telling the two Soviet diplomats that the United States was going to carry out every agreement made at Yalta and that he expected the Soviet government to do the same. Truman cut off further conversation by telling Molotov he would appreciate having that view transmitted to Stalin. Thus dismissed, Molotov and Gromyko turned and left the room.

Another incident, which gave Soviet leaders a glimpse of a president strikingly different from Franklin Roosevelt, one far less accommodating, occurred on VE Day when President Truman, accepting doubtful counsel, abruptly cut off Lend-Lease supplies to all U.S. Allies. Actually, his move hurt the British more than the Soviets, but Stalin interpreted Truman's action as an unfriendly signal from the new administration.

The suddenness of his elevation to the presidency caused Truman to make some hasty cabinet appointments. One of those was the selection of James F. Byrnes. Within hours after taking the oath of office, Truman met with Byrnes and offered him the highest appointment he could give, namely, secretary of state. The reasons for selecting Byrnes for this critical post were at least threefold: (1) Byrnes' record as senator and later "assistant president on the home front" under FDR, (2) Truman probably felt embarrassed at getting the vice-presidential nomination after having agreed to nominate Byrnes for the slot, and (3) Truman's belief that Byrnes was an insider who knew "what went on at Yalta." The last named reason would prove unwarranted, but it took time for Truman to discover his mistake.

Among legacies from Roosevelt was the expectation that leaders of the Big Three Allies—the Soviet Union, Britain, and the United States—would meet periodically to review military progress and make plans for averting future diplomatic troubles. Truman's meeting with Soviet Premier Joseph Stalin and Britain's Winston Churchill took place at Potsdam, Germany, in July 1945.

Truman relied upon Byrnes, his "able and sly" former Senate colleague, to help guide him through this important conference. On its eve, HST was given a highly secret report of the successful atomic bomb test at Alamogordo, New Mexico.

Even before leaving for Germany, he had discussed with aides what to tell the Soviets about the new weapon. A few advisers, including Secretary of War Stimson, at one point, suggested that letting the Soviets in on it might be a way of softening their postwar distrust and perhaps heading off a dangerous nuclear arms race. Others, led by Byrnes, argued that American monopoly on the bomb would make the Soviets "more manageable" in postwar diplomatic matters.

Truman decided to pursue a middle course, and on July 24, at Potsdam during a break in negotiations, he casually mentioned to Stalin that the United States had "a new weapon of unusual destructive force." According to one observer, Stalin—who, unbeknownst to Truman, already through espionage knew of the Manhattan Project and had even ordered work to begin on the Soviet Union's own atomic bomb—appeared "unimpressed."[2]

The atomic bomb was not discussed officially at Potsdam; nevertheless, its specter hovered over all the major participants. Several weeks earlier, Truman had asked Secretary Stimson to draw up a draft of a proclamation that might be issued to Japan by the United States and England. The draft should call one last time for Japanese surrender and otherwise warn of "the utter devastation of the Japanese homeland." Stimson's initial draft was refined several times, and Truman also waited until he had received approval of it from Chiang Kai-shek before July 26 when the statement was released from Potsdam.

The proclamation called for the immediate unconditional surrender of all Japanese armed forces, and it specified that Japan would be occupied until its war-making power was destroyed. "The alternative," the proclamation declared, "is prompt and utter destruction." The warning, which contained no specific reference to the atomic bomb, was signed by Truman, Churchill, and Chiang Kai-shek.

The Soviets were not told of the proclamation until after it had been released, and Byrnes attempted to smooth Molotov's indignation over this slight by pointing out that the Soviet Union was not officially at war with Japan.

Although, at Potsdam, HST continued to press for a Soviet declaration of war against Japan, the success at Alamogordo made Soviet commitment less urgent; the bomb's power—physical and psychological—provided an opportunity to end the war quickly on American terms and before, as Byrnes put it, the Soviets "could get in on the kill."[3]

Nine meetings were held at Potsdam between July 17 and July 25. The conference then was interrupted for two days while votes in the British election were being tallied. On July 28 the new British prime minister Clement Attlee arrived to replace the venerable Churchill, and the conference ended five days later on August 2, 1945.

The following decisions were reached during the negotiations: the creation of a Council of Foreign Ministers, the demilitarization of Germany, the establishment of an occupation government, war reparations, the treatment of war criminals, and the enunciation of broad principles for future governments in Austria and Poland. The most significant outcome of the meetings was never stated or realized: when compounded with subsequent Soviet-sponsored satellite governments, the Potsdam agreements froze Europe into a division that would persist for nearly five decades.

In late April 1945, after Secretary of War Stimson had briefed him on the Manhattan Project, Truman appointed a highly secret Interim Committee to advise him on the use of what Stimson said was "the most terrible weapon ever known in human history." Stimson served as chairman, and HST selected James Byrnes as the eighth member of the group. At one meeting, the group was joined by an advisory panel of four renowned physicists: Enrico Fermi, Arthur Compton, Ernest Lawrence, and J. Robert Oppenheimer.

After considerable discussion of a wide range of possibilities, the committee and panel members agreed on three conclusions:

1. The bomb should be used against Japan as soon as possible.

2. It should be used against war plants surrounded by workers' homes or other buildings susceptible to damage, in order to "make a profound psychological impression on as many inhabitants as possible." [Oppenheimer assured them the "visual effect of an atomic bombing would be tremendous."]

3. It should be used without warning.[4]

The committee and the consulting scientists considered but rejected the possibility of dropping the bomb on some target other than a city in order to demonstrate its awesome power. Scientists were unable to propose a demonstration that would produce the intended psychological effect. Besides, the thing might not work, and if it failed, the Japanese would only be encouraged in their determination to fight on. Byrnes introduced the thought, too, that if the Japanese were told in advance where the bomb was to be dropped, they might bring American prisoners of war to the area.

On Monday, August 6, Truman was aboard the *Augusta* in the Atlantic just south of Newfoundland seated with enlisted men for mess shortly before noon when he was given the message that Hiroshima had been bombed four hours earlier: "Results clear-cut successful in all respects. Visible effects greater than in any test."[5]

Declaring, "This is the greatest thing in history," Truman told Captain Graham, one of the map room officers, to show the message immediately to Byrnes at another table. An exuberant Truman then tapped on a glass for the crew's attention and announced, "We have just dropped a new bomb on Japan which has more power than twenty thousand tons of TNT. It has been an overwhelming success."[6]

Within hours, an official announcement came from Washington that a bomb had been dropped on Hiroshima. The announcement contained a second warning that, unless the Japanese surrendered immediately, more bombs would be dropped: "We shall destroy their docks, their factories, and their communications. Let there be no mistake; we shall completely destroy Japan's power to make war." Three days after the atomic bomb fell on Hiroshima, an equally devastating bomb was dropped on Nagasaki.

Of all the events occurring during Truman's presidencies none would generate as much controversy as use of the atomic bombs. With the special advantage of hindsight, critics attacked him for approving use of the bomb. Some argued that the bomb was unnecessary—Japan would have surrendered anyway. Others charged that the decision to drop the bomb was an act of "atomic diplomacy," motivated by Truman's and his advisers desire to impress the Soviets before they could get a foothold in Asia.[7]

Although Truman regretted the need to employ the terrible new weapon, he insisted that he never agonized over the matter. Nor did he ever attempt to share responsibility for the decision, assuming instead more onus than facts may have warranted.

Unquestionably, HST was sincere in his belief that he alone made the decision to drop the world's first atomic bomb. Technically, he was correct, and the belief bolstered his self-image of a forthright leader unafraid to do whatever he thought was in the best interests of his country.

In truth, Truman did not have a wide range of alternatives. Like any new weapon, the bomb had developed a momentum and constituency of its own. Indeed, Albert Einstein's letter to President Roosevelt in 1939, which provided the impetus for the Manhattan Project, had stressed the military value in that the "new phenomenon would also lead to the construction of bombs, and it is conceivable . . . that extremely powerful bombs of a new type may thus be constructed."[8]

More than a dozen years later, J. Robert Oppenheimer, the leading scientist at Los Alamos, gave short shrift to those few colleagues who questioned whether the bomb should be used.

In the summer of 1945, military reasons for using the new weapon were overwhelming. The first day of fighting on Iwo Jima exacted more American casualties than D-Day in Europe; on Okinawa, 79,000 U.S. soldiers were killed or wounded. As U.S. troops prepared to invade the main islands, Japan was deploying up to two million soldiers and additional millions of "auxiliaries" who were willing to defend their homeland to the death. General George Marshall and other military advisers told Truman that it would cost a half million or more American lives to force the enemy's surrender on his home grounds. To family members back home and to millions of men and women serving in the Pacific as well as to those in Europe getting ready for shipment to the Eastern Theater, news of the atomic bombs came as a life-saving reprieve.

All of the prestigious government leaders who were privy to plans for development of the bomb—the Manhattan Project—expected it to be used if tests were successful. The Interim Committee and its scientific advisory panel could conceive of no way in which a demonstration could be staged.

Moreover, the successful test drop in the New Mexico desert could not have remained secret much longer. Had the American public learned that a powerful new weapon, which might hasten the war's end, was in America's arsenal but was being withheld by a recalcitrant president, Truman could not have survived the outcry. This is not to imply that HST was motivated by political considerations at home; rather, it is acknowledgment that when confronted with consistent guidance from all major advisers he had little choice but to approve the long-planned project. The enterprise started by his predecessor had advanced too far to be halted by an untried president even if he had been so inclined.

In the late afternoon of August 14, the report that the Japanese had surrendered reached Truman in Washington. In just three months, he had been faced with more far-reaching decisions than any other president in history; neither Lincoln after first taking office nor FDR in the hectic domestic legislation of his first hundred days had been confronted with issues of such worldwide significance.

Truman's role in history was just beginning, however, for in the months to come other decisions would have to be made if the United States were to maintain its position as a world leader.

At first, HST tried to view Soviet leaders much as FDR had done; they were simply tough, realistic "politicians" with whom arrangements might be made through hard bargaining. He even spoke of "Old Joe" Stalin with grudging respect much like that he held for the Pendergast politicians back home in Jackson County. Actions of the Soviets in postwar Europe, particularly as they expanded their control of satellite governments, soon convinced him, however, that the Red leaders were overly ambitious and dangerously aggressive.

HST was not as yet recognized as a world spokesman on a par with Roosevelt or Churchill, but he was the leader of one of the world's two superpowers. He decided to deliver his first major address on foreign policy at a celebration of Navy Day, on October 27, 1945. In this address, which was carefully billed as a major policy statement, he stated that the United States sought no territorial expansion and was committed to the eventual return of sovereign rights to all people who had been deprived of them by force. In an oblique reference to what was happening in Central Europe, he said that all people who were prepared for self-government should be permitted to choose their own form of government without interference from any foreign source. Next he declared a significant forerunner to what would be called the Truman Doctrine:

> We shall refuse to recognize any government imposed upon any nation by the force of any foreign power. In some cases it may be impossible to prevent forceful imposition of such a government, but the United States will not recognize such government.[9]

Truman's speech on this occasion came closer to revealing the mounting tensions between the United States and the Soviet Union than any revelations hitherto given by administration spokesmen; indeed, the Navy Day talk was a harbinger of an emerging doctrine, but those who hailed the address as an announcement of a different, new policy of "firmness" were a little premature. Admittedly, there was a change from the tenor of speeches by Roosevelt, but the change was marked by implication, not by frank denunciation.

It was a foreigner who came to America who would deliver the first severe censure of Soviet actions, and he delivered it at a small private college in the heartland of America.

Franc McClure, the president of Westminster College in Fulton, Missouri, originated the idea of inviting Winston Churchill to speak there, but it was President Truman's personal message appended in ink on the engraved invitation that was most responsible for the renowned British leader's acceptance. HST urged the former prime minister to make the speech and promised to accompany him to Fulton in order to present him.

Even by the time Truman took office, the Soviet-American alliance had begun to unravel. Churchill, upset over developments in Poland, had cabled Roosevelt warning of "a great failure and an utter breakdown of what we settled in Yalta."[10] Charges and countercharges were exchanged between Roosevelt and Stalin throughout the first three months of 1946, and at the very beginning of the month in which he died, FDR cabled the Soviet dictator expressing "great concern . . . over developments of events of mutual interest since our fruitful meeting at Yalta. So far there has been a discouraging lack of progress made in the carrying out . . . of the political decisions we reached at the conferences, particularly those relating to the Polish question."[11]

At the war's end, Soviet-American relations worsened rapidly, and early in January 1946 President Truman recorded in a memorandum (unsent) to Secretary Byrnes, "I'm tired of babying the Soviets."[12]

Two months later at Fulton, on the afternoon of March 5, President Truman, clad in the American academic gown and the usual mortarboard, along with Churchill, wearing the scarlet robe of Oxford, led the procession to the stage. From there, Truman introduced his distinguished visitor and added significantly, "I know he will have something constructive to say."

Indeed, Churchill did have something to say, and in a paragraph of brilliant prose he made clear the growing schism between East and West:

A shadow has fallen across the scenes so lately lighted by the Allied victory. Nobody knows what Soviet Russia and its Communist international organization intends to do in the immediate future, or what are the limits, if any, to their expansive and proselytizing tendencies. . . . From Stettin in the Baltic to Trieste in the Adriatic, an *iron curtain* has descended across the continent.[13]

The "Iron Curtain" speech may well have been the century's greatest orator's finest effort; certainly it captured world attention and added an enduring phrase to the political lexicon. Nevertheless, some listeners beyond the immediate audience attacked Churchill for warmongering and Truman for having lent the occasion his presidential prestige.

Relations with the Soviets troubled Truman from the day he took office. In preparation for Potsdam, he had asked aides to collect information on topics that might come up, and one of those aides was George M. Elsey, who had worked in the map room for FDR. Elsey often was referred to as the "young assistant" to Clark Clifford, President Truman's first special counsel, but Elsey's contributions to Truman's presidencies were far more significant than that slightly demeaning reference might suggest.

Elsey wrote fourteen short, two-or-three-page papers briefing President Truman prior to Potsdam and accompanied him there, where he was kept busy handling the messages that flowed from the military in the Far East and the civilian staff back at the White House.

One of the most important reports Elsey prepared for Truman came after Potsdam, however, in the form of a careful one-hundred-thousand-word study entitled, "American Relations with the Soviet Union." To the extent that this study stiffened Truman's backbone the document is of considerable importance. Its purpose was to synthesize information gathered from the Departments of State, Navy, War, Justice, and other sources. Many of the points stressed in the report had been stated earlier by Churchill and others, so Elsey's document in no way was an attempt to introduce a bold new policy.

Clark Clifford submitted the report to President Truman on September 24, 1946, and his memorandum of transmittal made no mention of Elsey's pivotal role in its creation. Truman must have felt the summary was too hot for most of his staff and that public disclosure then of the seriousness of the Soviet threat would only aggravate growing tensions. The morning after receiving the report, he ordered all copies sealed, and the report did not surface until twenty years later in 1966 when Clifford gave a copy to Arthur Krock of the *New York Times*.

Krock as well as others awarded this "Russian Report" huge credit for the genesis of programs such as the Truman Doctrine, the Marshall Plan, the Berlin Airlift, and the North Atlantic Treaty Organization.[14]

The real significance of Elsey's report, however, lay in the fact that as early as the summer of 1946, six months before enunciation of the Truman Doctrine, among senior officials in the Executive branch responsible for national security there was strong consensus—consensus showing that most of Truman's advisers favored a comprehensive policy of resistance to Soviet expansionism and agreed on the posture the United States should adopt vis-à-vis the Soviet Union.

By early 1947 Great Britain no longer was able to maintain strong direction in the Eastern Mediterranean region. British leaders explained their government's retrenchment, and HST responded by delivering to Congress and the watchful world an address that openly announced the Truman Doctrine. His successful appeal—a speech which for all purposes marked the end of isolation—was for immediate economic and military aid to Greece and Turkey in order to stave off utter collapse in those two countries.

In this significant address, after describing the civil war in Greece and the Soviet threat in Turkey, HST declared, "I believe it must be the policy of the United States to support free peoples who are resisting subjugation by armed minorities or by outside pressures."

In laying the groundwork for his seminal message, HST had met three weeks earlier with key congressmen to acquaint them with the dangers and to tell them of the actions he intended to take. One of the group, the influential Republican Senator Arthur Vandenberg of Michigan, told the president that it would be necessary for him to go before Congress and "scare hell" out of the country.

That is precisely what Truman did on March 12, and his blunt warning that Communist moves were gravely and directly threatening American security resulted in bipartisan support for the doctrine that came to bear his name.

At first the Truman Doctrine seemed primarily a military enterprise aimed at containment of Soviet expansion, but later that summer its economic counterpart was added with passage of the European Recovery Act. George Marshall, former chief of the military staffs, had come out of retirement following Byrnes' dismissal in order to serve as Truman's secretary of state, and it was Marshall who announced the plan at the Harvard commencement ceremonies in June. Although others had their hands in the preparation of this monumental program, HST insisted on giving full credit to Marshall. General Marshall, HST insisted, should be the one most honored and deserved no less. Besides that, the pragmatic Missourian added, "Anything that is sent up to the Senate and House with my name on it will quiver a few times and die."[15]

Under the Marshall Plan, billions of U.S. dollars were pumped into European countries—including West Germany—in hopes that economic and political recovery would result in stable, Western-oriented governments. Churchill called the program the "most unsordid" act in the world's history.

Interestingly enough, Russia had an opportunity but declined to participate in the European Recovery Program. Former Secretary of Commerce

Henry A. Wallace, who had been dismissed in September 1946 after a brouhaha over a speech he had delivered in New York, was touring Europe the following spring and continuing to speak out against American foreign policies. Wallace gave an interesting account of one of his addresses:

> In some ways the most important talk I gave in the spring of 1947 was to about 200 members of the French Chamber of Deputies. . . .
>
> My thesis was that if Russia insisted on taking $10 billion dollars in reparations out of Germany she would make a cesspool out of Germany. Therefore, I proposed that the U.S. should make available over a period of 5 or 10 years a total of $50 billion with distribution to be made on the basis of war damage. Someone asked me how much this would mean for Russia. I said I did not know but would presume that the extent of her damage might entitle her on a pro rata basis to perhaps $10 or $20 billion worth. Naturally, this stole the headlines and no one paid any attention to the broad outline of my argument.
>
> A little later the Marshall plan was born which in the first instance followed my approach to some degree. Unfortunately, Russia turned it down. From then on it became increasingly clear that Russia wanted the cold war. Some day I suppose we shall know the full story of why the Marshall plan was turned down by Russia.[16]

By the opening of 1948, the Truman Doctrine and the Marshall Plan were in place, and an American-Soviet standoff, known as the Cold War, was entrenched as the most important reality of the postwar era. The standoff would intensify and test Truman's mettle ever further.

The more the Soviet Union tightened its hold on Eastern Europe, the more rapidly Truman and advisers advanced the policy of containment. To HST, there was no difference in totalitarian states. "I don't care what you call them," he told a reporters' conference in May 1947, "Nazi, Communist or Fascist or Franco, or anything else—they are all alike."[17]

In February the quasi-independent government of Czechoslovakia was overthrown by Communist elements, and the upheaval culminated with the suspicious death of Czech patriot Jan Masaryk. The iron curtain around the Soviet satellites was now impenetrable, while arguments over occupied zones within defeated Germany continued without letup.

An Allied Control Council had been established for the administration of the city of Berlin, which lay within the zone allocated to the Soviets, but paper agreements that each of the Allies—the United States, Britain, the Soviet Union, and France—would be granted various zones of occupation were flagrantly violated.

In late March, the Soviet military administration issued an order forbidding Allied trains from crossing the occupation border to enter Berlin unless those trains, both passenger and baggage, were checked by Soviet personnel. If unanswered, this move would have put the Soviets in full control of Berlin, contrary to the agreement that there would be equal administration and access to that war-wracked city.

HST interpreted the Soviet tactic not as a contest of legal rights but as a struggle over Germany and, in a larger sense, all of Europe. He ordered American commanders to see that essential supplies such as food, medicine, and clothing were flown into the beleaguered city. Soon the American airlift was averaging from 2,400 to 2,500 tons of supplies a day.

The Berlin crisis hung on until the spring of 1949 before Russian authorities indicated they were ready to remove the blockade. In a press conference held on April 13, Secretary of State Dean Acheson, who had replaced the venerable George Marshall when the latter requested that he be relieved from further government duty, announced that official avenues of communication were still open if Soviet officials wanted to discuss lifting the blockade and resume four-power talks on Germany.

A few weeks later, the Soviets did remove their blockade, and thus ended another of the serious international crises that occurred during Truman's first term. He used the occasion to express his satisfaction that the crisis had ended, saying he was "happy that there is a chance to take up where we left off, over ten months ago."[18]

In the meantime, Western European governments threatened by internal and external Communists met in Brussels to explore collective security measures. The resultant Brussels Pact became the foundation for the North Atlantic Treaty Organization.

This treaty gave the doctrine which bore Truman's name an obvious military tilt in June 1948 when the United States committed itself to membership in NATO. Under HST's leadership Americans were ready to put aside long-held aversions to "entangling alliances" and become the dominant partner in the emergent organization—the nation's first peacetime military alliance.

The Cold War and the Truman administration's responses set off heated debates across America, but Soviet dangers were not the only foreign problems confronting the doughty Missourian throughout his first term. The Palestine issue in some respects was his most wrenching challenge, for whatever was done in regard to this emotionally charged dilemma was certain to have far-reaching consequences. On this issue HST was subjected to enormous personal pressures.

The call to make Palestine a Jewish homeland had begun in the late nineteenth century. After World War I, Britain was given a mandate over Palestine with the understanding that independence would soon follow. That mandate continued for three decades with little interruption. In 1947 Britain announced it would withdraw from Palestine as it was doing in Greece, and the conundrum was turned over to the fledgling United Nations.

Jews everywhere clamored for partition and immediate establishment of a Jewish state; Arab countries with their numerical superiority were equally vehement in opposition. The plight of hundreds of thousands of Jews who had survived unimaginable horrors of the Holocaust exacerbated the problems.

Truman's sympathy for Holocaust victims was deep and heartfelt; in 1946 he had endorsed a plan for the admission of 100,000 Jews to Palestine. The British thought that plan entirely unworkable. American military leaders along with State Department experts told the president that Arabs would never accept the partition of Palestine—force would be necessary—and Secretary of Defense James Forrestal kept reminding Truman of the critical need for Saudi Arabian oil. Moreover, Soviet infiltration into Iran at the time was unmistakable and causing deep concern. American officials did not favor any actions that could encourage the Soviets to move farther into the Middle East under a pretext of guaranteeing peace.

Pro-Zionist mail deluged the White House, while Jewish factions relentlessly used some of HST's old friends, such as Eddie Jacobson from army days and the subsequent haberdashery business in Kansas City, to pressure him to support their cause.

HST chose not to air his position publicly but encouraged numerous aides to line up favorable votes for partition when the touchy issue came up for vote in the United Nations. In late 1947, that body voted for partition by a narrow margin, but HST's troubles with Palestine were not yet over.

Overnight, bloody clashes broke out in the Middle East as Arab populations rejected the idea of partition, and Jewish factions met violence with violence. To give both sides time to cool down, America's ambassador to the United Nations, Warren Austin, announced to the General Assembly that the United States favored abandoning the partition plan, and he then asked for a temporary UN "trusteeship" over Palestine.

Jewish groups were flabbergasted, for it was a complete, inexplicable turnaround. The contretemps stemmed from a breakdown in communications between the Executive and the State Department; Truman was in part at fault. The president had failed to inform Secretary Marshall that in yielding at last to Eddie Jacobson's persuasions he had met privately with Chaim Weizmann, the Zionists' foremost leader, and had assured him that the United States would support partition.

Truman first learned from morning newspapers of the embarrassing happening at the United Nations, and his well-known temper shot upward. That day he recorded in his diary:

> This morning I find that the State Dept. has reversed my Palestine policy. The first I know about it is what I see in the papers! Isn't that hell? I'm now in the position of a liar and a double-crosser. I never felt so in my life.[19]

The new Jewish state was declared in Jerusalem on May 14, 1948. Eleven minutes after that announcement was made in Jerusalem, Press Secretary Charles Ross in Washington released a statement from the White House that the United States was giving de facto recognition to Israel. HST's motive in helping establish the new nation had been primarily humanitarian and could be traced in part to his long-standing sympathy for human suffering. While his buddy Eddie Jacobson had not been a major carpenter, he certainly had helped drive home a finishing nail.

It will be remembered that 1948 was also an exhausting election year, and after victory at the polls that November, HST and a small group of aides, including Clark Clifford, went to the summer White House in Key West for a needed respite.

Clifford is the person commonly identified as Truman's major speech writer, and his importance in that role is indisputable. He endorsed and pushed the political strategy that enabled HST to retain his office, but by the time preparations for Truman's inaugural speech got under way, Clifford was functioning as editor and coordinator of the presidential speech staff more than as a primary writer.

While Clifford was with Truman and his coterie at Key West, his assistant, George Elsey, remained in Washington starting drafts for the inaugural address. Elsey viewed the inaugural as a unique occasion that would be followed by people throughout the world. Therefore, he believed Truman's address ought to be aimed beyond Congress and the American people; it should focus on world affairs.

Truman at first wanted his inaugural speech to emphasize domestic matters; he intended to stress foreign policy in the State of the Union message scheduled for a later delivery. It was seldom easy to change HST's mind, but in this instance, Elsey succeeded, and Truman finally sent word back from Florida for him to write the inaugural address, not the State of the Union speech, so that it concentrated on world problems.

HST's speeches were not noted for stirring slogans of the type that marked FDR's. HST's preference was for simplicity, for short and clear phrases, so the inaugural address was organized around four main ideas. In the final one, President Truman was able to declare: "We must embark on a program for making the benefits of our scientific advances and industrial programs available for the improvement and growth of undeveloped areas."

This fourth point, technical assistance to underdeveloped areas, came to eclipse all other parts of President Truman's inaugural address. Press and radio reactions were overwhelmingly favorable; even some of his rivals responded with enthusiasm.

The head of the conservative Liberty League wired, "Your inaugural address ranks with best in our history." John Foster Dulles, who within three years would become the Republican secretary of state, telegraphed, "I am deeply impressed by, and gratified for, the spiritual quality that inspired and uplifted your inaugural address." Nelson Rockefeller, later Republican vice president and potential presidential candidate, wrote, "Your inauguration speech will live as one of the great declarations of our time. It evidences a world statesmanship that will give new hope to the peoples of all lands. . . . A most significant and farsighted concept is embodied in your fourth point."[20]

Congress, at first skeptical of Truman's "bold new program," enacted the proposal into law the following June. A decade later, John F. Kennedy as a senator called for a Peace Corps to be built upon agencies (the International Cooperation Agency and the Agency for International Development) that owed their genesis to Truman's Point Four Program.

The Truman Doctrine was slightly more than three years old when its most serious challenge—the Korean War—arose. The dark event was rooted in agreements made at the end of World War II. With consent of the victorious Allies, Japanese forces north of the 38th parallel in Korea surrendered to Soviet troops; Japanese forces south of that parallel surrendered to American troops. Thus a dividing line of sorts was established.

In 1948 South Korea held elections, and Syngman Rhee was chosen as the first president of a newly named Republic of Korea. Within a month the northern part of the country set up a separate government and proclaimed itself the Democratic People's Republic of Korea.

Old hostilities simmered, and the next two years saw frequent incursions from both North and South Korea as each tried to enlarge its share of the divided country. The fragile peace was shattered in June 1950 when North Korean troops en masse crossed the 38th parallel into the southern zone.

HST had returned to Independence for a weekend at home with his family and was getting ready for bed on Saturday, June 24, when Secretary of State Dean Acheson phoned. "Mr. President," he said, "I have very serious news. The North Koreans have invaded South Korea."[21]

While in his plane winging its way back to Washington the next afternoon, HST learned that the UN Security Council had met and adopted a resolution calling for immediate withdrawal of North Korean forces and cessation of all "hostilities." The vote was nine to zero. There was no Soviet veto because their representative had walked out a year earlier when the Security Council had refused to unseat Nationalist China.

At a hastily summoned meeting on that Sunday night, HST conferred with top foreign policy advisers. There was unanimous agreement that North Korea's invasion was "Russian-sponsored," and no one dissented when General of the Armies Omar Bradley stated, "We must draw the line somewhere."[22]

HST held a second meeting the following day (June 26) in which Secretary Acheson proposed that navy and air forces give full support to South Korean troops and that such support be limited to the area south of the 38th parallel. The president endorsed the recommendation and added approval for use of the Seventh Fleet to keep Formosa from becoming involved. The recommendation included furnishing more military assistance to the Philippines and Indochina on the theory that the Communists might increase their efforts in those regions.

On June 27—just three days after the North Koreans had begun their assault—the UN Security Council met again and passed another resolution approving a proposal it had received from President Truman to the effect that "members of the United Nations furnish such assistance to the Republic of Korea as may be necessary to repel the armed attack and to restore international peace and security in the area." Thus the UN Security Council approved the "police action" already taken by the American president.[23]

Korea became the biggest single military crisis Truman faced. That conflict marked the first time the United States openly used its armed forces to halt Communist aggression. Some Republicans called it "the foreign policy blunder of the century." Averell Harriman, a staunch HST supporter, labeled it "a sour little war." Even after American casualties passed the 50,000 mark, however, Truman and major administrators kept referring to it as a "police action."

Periodically in American history there seems to arise a series of public controversies that are termed a "great debate." There were the Webster-Hayne speeches in the Senate in 1830, the Lincoln-Douglas debates of 1858, Senate debates over the League of Nations following World War I, and debates over isolationism during FDR's tenure. While debates over the Korean War never matched the eloquence in those forerunners, they equaled them in vehemence.

Joseph P. Kennedy, Democratic supporter of FDR, fired an opening shot on December 12, 1950, with an address at the law school forum at the University of Virginia, where his son Robert was president of the student senate. In the speech, Kennedy declared that in contrast to the weakness of the West, the Soviet Bloc had manpower and military strength of a type the world had never seen. The former ambassador to Britain warned:

To engage these vast armies on the European or Asian continent is foolhardy, but that is the direction towards which our policy has been tending. That policy is suicidal. It has made us no foul weather friends.[24]

When former President Herbert Hoover and Senator Robert Taft of Ohio delivered addresses that echoed Kennedy's line of argument, the press at home and abroad speculated that an orchestrated attack on HST's foreign policy was being mounted. Kennedy denied that charge and explained:

I was invited by the committee of the Law School whose duty it was to get speakers to talk on topical questions. I spent about three weeks working on the speech. I did no consultation because it covered subjects that followed my line of thinking for the last fifteen years.[25]

Two days after Kennedy spoke, Thomas Dewey, governor of New York and titular head of the Republican party, gave a rejoinder which unequivocally supported President Truman, his erstwhile rival.

Next, Truman himself took to radio and television with an address that put the blame for the Korean War squarely on Soviet Russia. Then with typical simplicity he listed four lines of policy his administration would follow:

First, we will continue to uphold, if necessary to defend with arms, the principles of the United Nations.

Second, we will continue to work with other free nations to strengthen our combined defenses.

Third, we will build up our own Army, Navy, and Air Force and make more weapons for ourselves and our Allies.

Fourth, we will expand our economy and keep it on an even keel.[26]

The bulk of public reaction was very favorable to HST's pronouncements. After a survey taken by its regional correspondents, one major newspaper concluded that citizens generally not only were ready to make the adjustments demanded by Truman's mobilization program but in some cases seemed ready to make even greater efforts.[27]

HST's speech, however, did not end the debate. Herbert Hoover gave a radio response in refutation, and five days after Hoover spoke, Taft in the Senate delivered another widely heralded rebuttal to Truman's arguments. The Ohio Republican contended that the first consideration should be to defend America, "the citadel of the free world," and that by committing troops to Korea, Truman had acted beyond his presidential authority.

For the last two years of his presidency, Korea would be Truman's unrelenting torment. Years after leaving office he would say that committing American troops to combat in that Asian peninsula had been his most difficult decision. But the world would remember he had not hesitated.

Nor was HST's case for the Korean War hurt by the dismissal of General Douglas MacArthur in April 1951.[28] When initial oratory aroused by this dramatic event had spent itself, Truman's position seemed even stronger.

At a Congressional hearing following MacArthur's dismissal, General Omar Bradley, Chairman of the Joint Chiefs of Staff, denounced MacArthur's desire to extend the war into China and insisted that such action would bring on "the wrong war, in the wrong place, at the wrong time, with the wrong enemy."[29]

On the issue of dismissal, Truman felt his position to be so right that once the step had been taken he remained aloof from the public outcry; he even defended the general's right as a private citizen to plead his case before Congress. MacArthur in turn conceded the president's authority to relieve him, so as months passed it became apparent to all that the core of the controversy was whether the president's or the field commander's strategy should prevail. Time proved to be on Truman's side.

It cannot be said that HST and members of his administration were persuasive enough to make the war in Korea a popular one; nevertheless, while Korea remained an unsettled issue, there can be little doubt that Truman was able to rally support for his decision to act in this most serious of crises.

As years passed, HST's stature rose steadily, primarily because of the foreign policies he formulated. Observers would not forget his uphill fight against the naysayers in 1948 nor his vigorous championing of civil rights long before that issue became popular with voters. But it was his decisiveness throughout the Cold War that moved him into near-greatness on a par with Franklin Roosevelt.

The fact that the United States was willing to intervene when the world was confronted with Soviet aggrandizements showed that the Truman Doctrine was more than a hollow phrase; as the nation's overriding foreign policy it may have stopped a major Communist lunge southward which, if successful, might even have engulfed Japan. Thus the Truman Doctrine marked the end of U.S. isolation and would dominate American diplomacy until August 1991, when the Soviet Union, communism's foremost bastion, finally collapsed.

Chapter 14

Personalities in Contrast

Despite many dissimilarities, Franklin Roosevelt and Harry Truman had some common bonds; most notably, they shared the same profession: both were lifelong professional politicians. True, Roosevelt had been admitted to the New York bar, but his "more or less casual" law experience lasted less than two years.

As a youth, Truman held part-time jobs as a drugstore helper, a railroad timekeeper, and a banking clerk. He became a farmer for ten years, and then, for a short time after World War I, he was a partner in an ill-fated clothing store. Even during those farming years of hard physical labor—toil that raised honest sweat and sent a man in from the fields at sunset with his overalls grimed and caked by dust, grease, and dirt—Harry Truman found time for politics.

The Populist movement was not as intense as it had been when such orators as the female firebrand from Kansas, Mary B. Lease, urged her listeners "to raise less corn and more hell," but the themes were still popular around the stove at the country store, post office, town hall, or wherever families got together. Within the Truman family, joining the Democratic party was an act of faith.

Harry was only twelve years old in 1896 when William Jennings Bryan delivered his dramatic Cross of Gold Speech to the Chicago convention and captured the party's nomination for president. Four years later, when Democrats convened in Kansas City, young Harry was a convention page and watched the party select Bryan for the second time.

While still in his twenties, Truman served for a short time as postmaster at Grandview and also as a road overseer for the county—both were political appointments made by Democrats who controlled Jackson County. Then in 1922 he ran successfully for a county judge, was defeated two years later in a bid for reelection, but returned to win successive elections for the same seat until 1934. In that year, with strong local support he won a seat in the U.S. Senate and, in a razor-thin victory, was reelected to that body six years later. Thus, Truman was an active, successful politician for nearly a quarter of a century before he stepped into the presidency.

Franklin Roosevelt's record in politics was even longer—more than three decades. FDR's entry into the field occurred in 1910 with his election to the New York Senate. He was reelected two years later but did not serve a full second term because President Woodrow Wilson appointed him assistant secretary of the navy, a political post he held for eight years.

In 1920 Democrats met in San Francisco to nominate presidential and vice-presidential candidates. FDR took a very active part in that contentious assemblage. Finally, shortly after midnight on the morning of Monday, July 6, the exhausted delegates took their forty-fourth ballot and chose James Cox, third-term governor of Ohio, as their standard-bearer. The delegates then adjourned until the next day when they nominated "up and coming" young Franklin Roosevelt for the vice presidency.

Cox and Roosevelt were defeated, but FDR captured national attention four years later with his brilliant nominating speech for Al Smith, the "happy warrior." In 1928, when Smith was nominated for the presidency, FDR replaced him as governor of the state of New York, and it was from this office that he moved into the White House for the first of his four terms—the last of which had hardly begun when death took its toll.

The most common linkage between Roosevelt and Truman, of course, was that each in his own way was a fervent Democrat. While Truman's identification with the Democratic party was inevitable given his family background, Roosevelt's affiliation was not so certain. The Roosevelt heritage pointed toward the Republican party more than the Democratic. Franklin's mother, Sara, although denigrating politicians as a class, would have been happier to see her son choose the GOP—the party to which her own father had been loyal. In addition, FDR was immensely proud of his kinship with his famous Republican cousin. As a young man, he had followed Theodore's career with eager admiration, even copying TR's pince-nez and favorite adjectives ("bully" and "dee-lighted"). During his first term at Harvard, FDR joined the Republican Club and marched through a rainstorm to support the McKinley-Roosevelt ticket, but a year later he opted to become a Democrat.

At Harvard he told friends about his personal ambitions and decided that only as a Democrat did he have any chance for a major political career. The Republican party was bulging with promising young men who had credentials as impressive as his; moreover, he was coolly pragmatic and believed that only as a Democrat from outside Sagamore Hill could anyone bearing the Roosevelt name rise to the heights he had set eyes on.[1]

Beyond politics, however, an attribute found in the makeup of both Roosevelt and Truman was a profound sense of duty for public service. In FDR's case it was noblesse oblige that came along with his patrician background and fitted in nicely with his lofty ambition. Truman, never a wealthy man but with abiding admiration for such heroic figures as Andrew Jackson and Woodrow Wilson, regarded public service as exciting while also offering more or less steady employment.

Franklin Roosevelt went to preparatory school at Groton when he was fourteen, and the training there helped shape his basic attitudes toward social problems. The headmaster at Groton was Endicott Peabody, a broad-shouldered, six-foot, square-jawed, rigid but fair disciplinarian. Peabody, a young clergyman and something of a Christian socialist, worried about the needy and underprivileged in society. There is no doubt he implanted similar concerns in the mind of young Franklin. The Groton headmaster reinforced FDR's natural optimism and became his lasting role model. In times of deep trouble, FDR liked to quote his mentor: "Things in life will not always run smoothly. Sometimes we will be rising toward the heights—then all will seem to reverse itself and start downward. The great fact to remember is that the trend of civilization is always upward."[2]

Peabody's teachings remained with FDR all his life, and near the end of his third term in the White House he explained: "As long as I live his [Dr. Peabody's] influence will mean more to me than that of any other people next to my mother and father."[3]

What stands remarkable about Franklin Roosevelt's record in the field of social justice is that it arose entirely from vicarious experiences. He came into the White House as a man who had been given everything—wealth, education, and social position—yet he understood that many of the nation's and the world's problems stemmed from lack of such social and economic rights as adequate wages and standards of living. He had never plowed a furrow, operated a factory machine, or been forced to live from paycheck to paycheck, but he was able to identify with those to whom such matters were everyday challenges.

When Harry Truman talked about wages, housing, farm prices, and equal employment opportunities he spoke from firsthand experiences. He knew what it was to roll out of bed at 5:30 on a bitterly cold morning, to bang his banjo No. 12 scoop against the corncrib and yell "whoo-eeee" to hogs a quarter mile away, to recognize the sounds of the first streams of milk rattling into a tin pail, or to coax a team of mules along a straight furrow. He liked to ride the gangplow and watch the earth curl in its black, fresh ribbon away from the shining steel moldboard. In Truman's farming years, veterinarians were scarce, so most farmers had to learn enough rudimentary surgery to ring a bull or castrate the pigs. Young Truman reputedly became so expert at the latter the neighbors joked, "When Harry sharpens his knife the pigs run for the pasture."[4]

No one who knew Harry Truman in those days considered him a hayseed. He bought a secondhand, four-cylinder Stafford automobile for about six hundred dollars at a time when owning an auto was considered a mark of affluence. Rather than being a young man come to town with mud on his boots and a wheat straw dangling from his lips, Truman dressed nattily and was seen frequently in the best entertainment and eating spots the city had to offer. Throughout his life Truman was neat and well-tailored although in informal attire he preferred colorful sports shirts—colors the more sedate Bess frequently protested.

Seen from a distance, HST, at 5 feet, 9 inches and a usual weight of about 167 pounds, did not have the imposing physical figure of FDR. In maturity, Truman's short gray hair, always combed flat and parted on the left, coupled with his high forehead, tended to give him a professorial look. In his *Memoirs*, written when he was seventy years old, Truman remembered meeting Bess Wallace when she was a little girl in Sunday School: "She had golden curls and has, to this day, the most beautiful blue eyes." Truman's eyes were also blue, but often went unnoticed because they were hidden behind thick, steel-rimmed glasses.

The closer one got to Truman the more impressive he became. His bearing was erect without stiffness; his facial expressions suggested an open, good-natured manner and an exuberance that from afar was not readily apparent. George Elsey, who served in both Roosevelt's and Truman's administrations, recalled being surprised by Truman's physical energy and mobility. "He was alert, sharp . . . he looked good, very vigorous, very strong."[5]

By the time Truman came into the presidency, American citizens were accustomed to hearing the slow, vibrant voice of FDR over the radio and seeing photographs or newsreels showing their tall, broad-shouldered president sitting comfortably behind a battery of microphones or standing majestically at a public lectern.

After polio crippled him, Roosevelt's physical movements were severely limited. Reporters and photographers covering his appearances developed a covenant among themselves not to expose the handicap, and this accord was in the main honored throughout his terms of office. There were a few exceptions, but in those years before live and competitive television had arrived, even photographers agreed that no demeaning shots would be taken of the president—photos showing him trying to walk with his heavy, cumbersome steel braces or photos that otherwise might show his crippled condition.

FDR had assets, however, that compensated for his lack of physical mobility. Among those advantages was good judgment in knowing when and where to make his appearances, a commanding presence in meetings, and an undeniable flair for the dramatic. Through practice he polished his exceptional ability to read aloud. His mobile face could reflect a wide variety of reactions and seemed to lead changes in his wide range of vocal stress and intonations. Through his voice he could portray amusement, solemnity, sarcasm, or exasperation, and he was never dull.

Both FDR and HST had political ambitions early in life. Roosevelt had so much self-confidence that he was not hesitant in telling friends of his ultimate goals; Truman shared his hopes only with the girl to whom he was engaged, and even with her he played his usual self-effacing role. Shortly after Bess agreed to their engagement, he wrote her a discursive, strangely prophetic letter:

Dear Bess:

I've been cleaning seed to show at Grandview tomorrow. . . . You'd think I was running for office if you'd see me chasing around shaking hands with people and displaying a classic cat grin . . .

You were most awful nice about the other girl but don't suppose there'll ever be one. If a fellow can pick his idol at ten and still be loyal to it at thirty, there's not much danger of his finding another. . . . How does it feel being engaged to a clodhopper who has ambitions to be Governor of Montana and Chief Executive of the U.S.? He'll do well if he gets to be a retired farmer.[6]

Below the surface, Truman had plenty of self-assurance; he just chose not to display it. If he had lacked self-confidence he could not have overcome a business failure, debt, relative obscurity, and the Pendergast stigma.

In contrast, FDR's confidence was excessive and fused with arrogance. Yet such self-assurance seemed justified considering his triumphs: overcoming a debilitating paralysis, winning approval from the common man despite a patrician background, gentle dominance in meetings, matchless political skills in disarming political opponents, and serving in the nation's highest elective office for an unprecedented period.

Courage in the face of adversities was another trait possessed by both Roosevelt and Truman. Roosevelt took control of a government near collapse and with daring optimism helped raise it from the severest economic plight in its history. Nor was he afraid to attack entrenched business and industrial powers when he felt they imperiled the general welfare. Then he led the citizenry onto a war footing when loud voices clamored against such action.

Truman's courage showed itself when, as a senator, he battled graft and corruption in the nation's defense programs. Later, as president, he brought foreign policy out of its isolationist cocoon and by forthright decisions committed the country to world leadership.

Behind the public persona of each man, however, were traits not always known to the average citizen. In FDR's case, the image was one he strove to create and was kept burnished by spin doctors like Louis Howe, speech writers, and public relations–minded aides. His image was bolstered by identifying accessories—his favorite cape, the pince-nez, the long cigarette holder—props which delighted his fans, goaded his foes, and provided daily diet for cartoonists.

The salutation, "My friends," that FDR chose to begin his fireside talks was a calculated effort to establish common ground with listeners. Similar motivation was shown in August 1944, when he met for lunch with his new vice-presidential candidate under a magnolia tree on the White House lawn. FDR suggested that he and Truman take off their jackets so that in photographs they would appear more neighborly.

Behind the facade, FDR had few, if any, intimates who could say they really knew him. Marguerite "Missy" LeHand, for example, had gotten involved in Roosevelt's run for the vice presidency in 1920, and after that election he and Eleanor, impressed with her secretarial efficiency, asked her to come to Hyde Park to help with correspondence. A year later, when FDR came down with polio and Eleanor traveled the country as his stand-in, Missy was given more responsibility for running the household.

In 1928, when FDR was elected governor of New York, Missy moved with the Roosevelt family to the governor's mansion in Albany, and by the time FDR became president she was one of the most important persons in his life—a companion who gave him needed attention, relaxation, and affection. "There's no doubt," Raymond Moley, one of FDR's brain trusters, declared, "that Missy was as close to being a wife as he ever had—or could have."[7]

White House maid Lillian Parks agreed, saying, "When Missy gave an order, we responded as if it had come from the First Lady. We knew that FDR would always back up Missy."[8]

Yet even Missy, who understood FDR's temperament as well as anyone else ever did, once confided, "He was really incapable of personal friendship with anyone."[9]

Nor did FDR exhibit loyalty to his staff or associates. He liked to operate behind the scenes and showed no reluctance in dumping Vice Presidents Garner and Henry Wallace, nor in easing out cabinet members or aides notwithstanding their past contributions. To Eleanor, her husband's callousness was something she could not understand. Joseph Lash, one of Eleanor's biographers, recorded, "She [Eleanor] could never conceive of him [*sic*] doing a reckless thing for a friend because of personal attachment. . . . President [FDR] seemed to have no bond to people. Not even his children. Completely political person."[10]

FDR enjoyed company and could be a charming host, mixing drinks, telling jokes, and sharing gossip, but he craved the center of attention. Truman, on the other hand, was gregarious and genuinely liked being an equal. It was easy for him to be one of the good old boys, to join enthusiastically in the Masons, the American Legion, Veterans of Foreign Wars, or other civic organizations. He found pleasure in camaraderie and small groups where people called him Harry and there was banter and good-natured humor. FDR preferred martinis, but bourbon was HST's choice. With Truman broad humor struck a more responsive chord than subtleties or witticisms. In private gatherings he usually listened more than dominated the conversations. To those within his inner circle, he was known to be quiet, soft spoken, modest to the point of humility, and intensely respectful of subordinates.

Truman trailed none of FDR's glory—nor any of his conceit. The day following Roosevelt's death, Truman went to the Capitol to chat with Sam Rayburn, the Speaker of the House of Representatives. The Texan told his longtime friend from Missouri that as president he was going to be surrounded by men who would flatter him and say he was the greatest man who ever lived. Rayburn added frankly, "You and I know that it just ain't so." The new president interrupted to say, "Well, I know I am not."[11]

In speech HST was straightforward, blunt, and sometimes embarrassingly honest. The hell with niceties of language; he wanted to be absolutely clear with no equivocations or attempts to mislead. From his revered mother he had developed an either-or thinking pattern: a thing was black or white, good or bad, just or unjust, desirable or undesirable. Frankness was a virtue and evasions were sinful. Such an orientation led to a style that sometimes was intransigent and more confrontational than necessary.

Roosevelt was seldom sensitive to the feelings of others—a callousness that undoubtedly was linked to his lack of close personal friends. Numerous associates of FDR commented upon his standoffishness. Henry Morgenthau, Jr., his neighbor from Hyde Park as well as his indefatigable secretary of the treasury, commented that it was impossible ever to get close to Roosevelt. Harry Hopkins, dependable aide throughout so many serious crises, noted that his chief had a side that was lacking in generosity, perhaps a form of "jealousy." According to Averell Harriman, Roosevelt seemed to enjoy other people's discomfort and was never bothered if they were unhappy.

The curmudgeonly Ickes, secretary of the interior, once told FDR that he was the most difficult man he had ever met.

"Because I get too hard at times?" FDR asked.

"No," replied Ickes, "because you won't talk frankly even with people who are loyal to you. . . . You keep your cards close up against your belly. You never put them on the table."[12]

The confrontational style of Truman was in marked contrast to Roosevelt's artful management of people and situations. Churchill noted the contrast when at Potsdam he met Truman for the first time. Lord Moran asked the British prime minister what he thought of the new American president, and Churchill replied, "He's a man of immense determination. He takes no notice of delicate ground, he just plants his foot firmly on it." Then to illustrate his statement, Churchill jumped a little off the wooden floor and brought his bare feet down with a smack.[13]

An instance of Truman's mind-set can be seen in his actions at Potsdam. In his *Memoirs*, HST wrote,

> There were many reasons for my going to Potsdam, but the most urgent, to my mind, was to get from Stalin a personal reaffirmation of Russia's entry into the war against Japan, a matter which our military chiefs were most anxious to clinch. This I was able to get from Stalin in the very first days of the conference.[14]

HST was so sure he was right that at Potsdam he went against the advice of several respected cabinet members and others within the State Department. State Department persons, with the notable exception of newly appointed Secretary Byrnes, were ambivalent or in outright disagreement with the goal of getting the Soviet Union involved in the Japanese war, but these doubters were kept off the official delegation. Secretary of War Henry Stimson had to invite himself. Stimson, full of uncertainties, had wavered in his attitude toward the Soviet Union and had advised Roosevelt not to take Soviet encroachments too seriously. He subsequently encouraged Truman to adopt a firm stance. By the time of Potsdam, Stimson was talking again about fruitful cooperation with the Soviet Union.

In ways that Roosevelt never showed, Truman could be firm when the occasion warranted. Thus when it came to dismissing members of his cabinet, major aides, or even distinguished generals, he did not hesitate to tell them so in a face-to-face encounter. Witness the cases of Henry Morgenthau, Jr., Henry Wallace, James Byrnes, Louis A. Johnson, and Douglas MacArthur.

HST showed little of FDR's willingness to compromise in order to attain immediate goals. To Truman, such goals as preserving the authority of the chief executive, protecting the "little man" from big business barons, and righting wrongs done to less fortunate people were bedrock principles not subject to bargaining for short-term gains. MacArthur was fired because he challenged the constitutional authority of the president; Taft-Hartley was unfair to laboring people; the Fair Deal aimed to redress unfair practices in civil rights, health care, education, or regional development.

FDR's principles were not so deep seated and, therefore, were more easily altered. Throughout 1940, while the president was making eloquent pleas to bolster the nation's defense efforts, there were isolated strikes by labor. Then capital, too, began to hold up production until it got favorable tax breaks. In June, Congress with FDR's strong approval raised taxes in order to meet the rising costs of the nation's conversion to defense production, but within months of that tax legislation FDR changed signals and asked for new laws that would permit companies to amortize their capital expenses within five years or less. Such permission was a tremendous boon to big corporations, for in effect it meant that they could deduct 20 percent of their capital costs before computing net income on which taxes were to be paid. Moreover, the new legislation clearly favored large corporations over small businesses.

The coterie of liberals around FDR, including his wife, were upset. Ickes thought FDR was abandoning fundamentals of the New Deal, and Treasury Secretary Morgenthau told Roosevelt it was a "lousy" bill because it sponsored "the very kinds of discrimination that the President, and the Treasury for so many years have opposed."[15]

In 1933 Roosevelt had declared the primary task was to put people to work; in 1940 the most pressing need was to convert industries of peace into industries of war, and if that meant throwing away cherished guidelines, so be it.

During his lifetime FDR was the most admired man in America; some people hated him with equal intensity. After his death, details about his private life—details carefully withheld for years—were exposed, and historians discovered numerous instances when he indulged in chicanery and deviousness.

Deeply religious, FDR found it easy to lie when it suited his purpose. In May 1937, Supreme Court Justice Willis Van Devanter, one of "Four Horsemen" on the Court hostile to many New Deal programs, announced his retirement. FDR decided to nominate Senator Hugo Black of Alabama as the replacement. Roosevelt, fearing the loss of Black's reliable vote in the Senate, remarked that he wished the new justice were twins.

FDR already had decided on the nomination but had not made it public when he invited Black to the White House. There he taunted the intended nominee by laying a Supreme Court nomination form in front of him and asking facetiously which of several names ought to go in it.

Black had been elected to the Senate in 1926—a time when the Ku Klux Klan had tremendous clout in his home state. Immediately after his confirmation by the Senate, reports of Black's involvement with the Klan appeared. At first he denied that he had ever been a member of the organization, but a persistent reporter unearthed Black's letter of resignation as well as other documentation showing that for two years he had indeed been a member, had paid his dues, and had worn the white robes.

The controversy was fueled further when Black, in a widely publicized appearance, spoke over national radio hookups and admitted his former membership. Roosevelt at the time was touring the West. To reporters who met his train or auto at every stop and clamored for a statement about Black's admission, FDR replied that he could not comment on the matter because he did not know what Black had said.

The fact was that FDR had contrived to give himself an alibi. He admitted that his son, Jimmie, had told him during the morning of October 1 that Black was going to speak at 6:30 P.M. (Pacific Coast Time), but FDR insisted he had forgotten about the event the rest of that day.

The excuse had required planning, for Roosevelt and his entourage arrived in Olympia, Washington, early in the afternoon. He made an unscheduled stop at the governor's mansion there and then rode in an open car to Tacoma. His car had to be slowed to a ten-mile-an-hour speed along the Olympia to Tacoma highway—approximately twenty miles—in order to keep him from arriving at his special train, parked on a Great Northern's siding, until more than an hour after Black's speech had ended.

Back home in Hyde Park, after the Western tour was over, he compounded the deception by saying:

After we got away from Olympia the road was wet so we slowed the procession to prevent the policemen on motorcycles from going overboard. For that reason we had a slow run and instead of being in the open car for twenty minutes I was in it for exactly two hours and ten minutes. That is the actual, simple fact.[16]

Roosevelt's artifice in this case as in others was accepted. Black's admission satisfied many critics, and after a few weeks the public controversy subsided.

Although the reading public often was told that Truman had a quick temper, Roosevelt's anger, which also lay near the surface, was kept away from public attention.

FDR did not easily forget slights, and behind the scenes he could be vindictive toward those who crossed him or threatened his programs. He reveled in racy gossip and liked to collect stories about celebrities in the same way he collected stamps or ship models. Sometimes the stories were merely for amusement in small gatherings, but one never knew when such information could be politically valuable. For instance, in 1940, Democratic insiders told him that Wendell Wilkie, his Republican challenger, kept a mistress in New York City. Roosevelt was reported as having told an aide that the scandal could prove very useful:

[We can] . . . spread it as a word-of-mouth thing, or by some people way down the line. We can't have any of our principal speakers refer to it, but the people down the line can get it out. I mean the Congress speakers, and state speakers, and so forth. They can use the raw material. . . . Now, if they want to play dirty politics in the end, we've got our own people. . . . Now you'd be amazed at how this story about the gal is spreading around the country. . . . Awful nice gal, writes for magazines and so forth and so on, a book reviewer. But nevertheless there is the fact. And one very good way of bringing it out is by calling attention to the parallel in conversation.[17]

Nor was FDR above using the taxing power of the government to go after his political enemies. In the election year of 1936, for example, several prominent Democrats bolted the party and joined the anti–New Deal Liberty League. Democrats who walked out called themselves the Peripatetics and in January met at the Mayflower Hotel in Washington to hear Al Smith unleash a barrage against the New Deal.

Few things angered Roosevelt more than criticism from former allies. He knew Smith's Mayflower speech was written by Joseph Proskauer who had contributed the "happy warrior" phrase to FDR's nominating speech for the New York governor way back in 1924. The fact that a dozen years later Proskauer was writing bitter speeches against the administration infuriated FDR.

He asked Morgenthau to direct the Secret Service, the investigative branch responsible to the secretary of the treasury, to find out the sources of Proskauer's income. If it could be shown that Proskauer was getting a $200,000 to $300,000 retainer from public utilities, that could be used to expose the reactionary forces behind Smith and his cohorts. In this instance, Morgenthau was able to convince FDR to back off and let Congress conduct the investigation.

A similar instance occurred in April 1942 when FDR sent an assistant, James Rowe, to Morgenthau and asked for a full investigation of the income taxes paid by Father Coughlin, a Detroit radio priest noted for particularly bitter attacks against the president.

On another occasion, Roosevelt requested an investigation of Hamilton Fish, the New York Republican congressman who represented Dutchess County. Morgenthau's sleuths did not find enough evidence to support an indictment, so this investigation came to naught.

FDR also wanted to use the Secret Service to investigate an unfavorable story published in the *Wall Street Journal*. This time the request drew ire from the normally supportive Morgenthau, who did not object to the practice as much as he deplored using the branch under his authority. Morgenthau declared he did not want the Secret Service assigned to such work. "I will not have the Secret Service used for this purpose," he fumed. "It's an outrageous performance. . . . If he wants that kind of thing, let him use the FBI."[18]

Indeed, FDR did use the FBI to investigate opponents or critics. In June 1940 he wrote to Director J. Edgar Hoover an effusive letter thanking him for "the many interesting and valuable reports" sent to the White House. Among the reports were summaries from information the FBI had amassed on Charles A. Lindbergh, the most idolized American of the 1920s.

Lindbergh at the time was capturing headlines by urging isolation and asserting that Britain had no chance against Hitler's military might.

In addition to files on Lindbergh, the FBI by the summer of 1940 had conducted background checks on 131 critics of the president, including Senators Burton K. Wheeler of Montana and Gerald Nye of North Dakota. Before the presidential campaign of that year ended, the number swelled to more than two hundred full or partial investigations. One of them became public knowledge and cost FDR support of the country's most influential labor leader.

In October, John L. Lewis, head of the United Mine Workers, went to the White House to complain that the FBI was investigating him, tapping his phone lines, and doing so on direct orders from the president. When Roosevelt denied the charges, Lewis stormed out the door.

A few days later, Lewis went on the air to level his wiretapping charge. J. Edgar Hoover from the FBI denied the allegation, saying that "the Bureau never has and is not now making an investigation of John L. Lewis." The director's reply was carefully phrased and technically correct because the FBI was not actually conducting a full investigation of Lewis. However, it was investigating his daughter who lived with him and worked in his office. Moreover, the FBI also was investigating the Congress of Industrial Organizations, another group headed by Lewis. Thus in these two related surveillances the Bureau in actuality was monitoring all of the labor's leader's telephone calls.[19]

The underhandedness of FDR did not fit the mold in which HST was cast. Capable of stubborn enmity or unflinching loyalty, Truman was a man whose emotions often surfaced and who could be a tough adversary to political foes, but he owned a simple, old-fashioned sense of honor.

Once, after a meeting President Truman held with congressional leaders in the Cabinet Room, an aide picked up a manila envelope left behind in error. It was clear from the annotations on the face that it not only belonged to a Republican senator but that the contents dealt with Republican congressional strategy. The envelope was promptly carried into the Oval Office. Did the president want to see it? The response was as emphatic as Henry Stimson's had been when, as Herbert Hoover's secretary of state, he had closed down the department's cryptographic unit with the statement, "Gentlemen do not read other men's mail." Truman's sentiments were the same, more earthily expressed, and the envelope was returned unread to the Capitol by messenger.[20]

Although HST on occasion might lash out against an individual opponent, he seldom held grudges very long and eventually forgave nearly all his enemies. He made up with nearly everyone with whom he quarreled: John L. Lewis, Dwight Eisenhower, Harold Ickes, and in part with Richard Nixon, to name a few.

Within weeks of taking office in April 1945, Truman invited former president Herbert Hoover to the White House. Hoover, the anathema of the Depression and favorite whipping boy for the Democratic party, had become a political pariah and had not set foot in the White House since Roosevelt's first inauguration. HST asked Hoover to serve as Honorary Chairman of the Famine Emergency Committee—a post which Hoover accepted at once and fulfilled with distinction. The regard the two presidents developed for one another matured into a friendship that would last the rest of their lives.

A more dramatic if less consequential example of Truman's forgiving spirit can be seen in his relationship with the music critic Paul Hume of the *Washington Post*.

In 1950, Margaret Truman, HST's twenty-six-year-old daughter and only child, aspired toward an operatic career, and because she was the president's daughter her public appearances attracted great attention. At a concert given in Constitution Hall during early December 1950, President and Mrs. Truman and their guests, British Prime Minister Clement Attlee, British Ambassador Sir Oliver Franks, and Lady Franks, were among those in the audience. Hume's review the next day was unfavorable, stating that while Margaret was "extremely attractive" on stage her singing "is flat a good deal of the time—more last night than at any time we have heard her in past years."[21]

Hume's review detonated HST's anger through his shortest fuse, protection of his family. Hurrying to the Oval Office, he penned an intemperate letter to Hume and then summoned a messenger to deliver it. In his letter the angry president fulminated:

> I have just read your lousy review buried in the back pages. You sound like a frustrated old man who never made a success, an eight-ulcer man on a four-ulcer job, and all four ulcers working.
>
> I never met you, but if I do you'll need a new nose and plenty of beefsteak and perhaps a supporter below. Westbrook Pegler, a guttersnipe, is a gentleman compared to you. You can take that more of an insult than as a reflection on your ancestry.[22]

The fires kindled by this outburst burned for several weeks, but as the years passed, the strong feelings aroused by the incident began to weaken and had completely evaporated by 1953–1954. In those years Hume, who really had great respect for Truman and rated him the most musical of all United States presidents, wrote to Truman in Independence asking about his favorite music. (As Hume suspected, the "Missouri Waltz" was not on the list.) Truman graciously replied, and more correspondence followed. Then in 1959 Hume went to Independence where a very cordial ex-president greeted him and took him on an extended tour of the Truman Library.

That night, at a concert in Kansas City, Hume saw President and Mrs. Truman sitting across the aisle from him. Hume thanked Truman for being so generous toward him earlier that day, and HST, turning to his wife, said, "Oh, Bess, this is Paul Hume. I told you he was in the office today." According to Hume, Mrs. Truman was "as gracious as always."[23]

A few months later, when HST and Bess visited Washington, the former president invited Hume and his wife to their suite at the Mayflower Hotel for cocktails and a small private reception. As in the case of Hoover, friendship and respect had replaced the anger of an earlier decade.

There were two notable exceptions to HST's forgiveness: Clare Boothe Luce and Adam Clayton Powell. Both had hit Truman in his tenderest spot, namely, love and respect for the women in his family. Luce once made a sneering remark about Mrs. Truman having worked on Truman's senatorial payroll, and Powell had charged that Mrs. Truman, steeped in Southern tradition and prejudice, ought to be called not the First Lady but the "last lady" of the land. Those remarks HST would not forgive, and he vowed that neither Luce nor Powell would ever be invited to the White House while he was there, and they were not.

In sharp contrast with Roosevelt, Truman in public was very much like he was in private, and as a result much would be written about his personal habits, particularly his language. HST's overriding goal in all communications—be it written or oral—was clarity. He actually possessed a broad vocabulary because of his extensive reading, but this fact usually went unnoticed because of his fondness for terseness.

HST's vocabulary reflected his interests and culture. He liked to use vernacular expressions, and frequently his words were common but pungent. So much has been publicized about his use of profanity that he sometimes was pictured as an uncouth, vulgar person. The picture could hardly be more distorted.

Considering his life experiences, HST's occasional bursts of profanity should not be surprising; what was surprising though was that he made no attempt to polish his habitual language. On the contrary, he seemed to take puckish delight in criticisms of his expressions.

In truth, Truman was far less profane than most presidents before him, and certainly far less so than several who succeeded him. If judged on a scale of profanity frequency, HST would rank well below Eisenhower, who could and did swear like the trooper he had been. John F. Kennedy's private conversations were larded with vulgarities filtered out by careful White House public relations experts. Lyndon Johnson swore often and at times seemed obsessed with scatological terms. In his debates with Kennedy in 1960, Richard Nixon vowed that if he got into the White House the schoolchildren of America would never hear him use the kind of language Truman had employed. (Nixon was almost right on this score, for it was not until the Watergate tapes were played that his penchant for vulgarities was exposed.)

Most of the profanities Truman used were pretty mild if measured by later standards. The word "damn," for instance, is pretty tame unless it is uttered by an American president. One such circumstance arose in September 1947, when King Carol of Romania was presented to Truman. Carol asked the president if he spoke French, and Truman, who did not care for Carol mainly because of his womanizing, answered abruptly, "No, and damn little English!"

One of Truman's favorite vulgarities was "son-of-a-bitch." He used it carelessly, sometimes as pure name-calling and at other times in a friendly vein similar to Owen Wister's Virginian—"When you call me that, smile!"

HST nearly always avoided profanity if there were women present. Early in life he had put them on a pedestal, and there they remained. He believed it was a gentleman's duty to shelter ladies from the seamier sides of life, including coarseness of language. His sensitivity on this score can be seen in an incident involving Beth Short, his correspondence secretary. Following a press conference during which he had used the word "damn," HST encountered Mrs. Short in the elevator and offered an apology: "Beth, I didn't know you were present. If I had known you were there, I would not have used that word."[24]

FDR was more circumspect than HST was about language, and he enjoyed its subtleties in a manner Truman could not appreciate. When everything was going well, FDR liked to relax with correspondents and was not above indulging in horseplay with them. Obviously a showman, he relished repartee and private jokes.

Two months after his first inauguration, several correspondents joined with Appointments Secretary Marvin McIntyre on the portico of the White House, where they harmonized in "Home on the Range." The following night, FDR had the group appear at the White House again for a "command performance." The National Broadcasting Company persuaded them to sing over the airwaves; the president listened in, called the studio, disguising his voice, and offered them a contract. When the NBC spokesman asked who was calling, FDR answered by saying he was "the advertising manager for Cascarets [a famous laxative]." He thought so well of the joke that at his next press conference he announced that the group would resign because "they had a very handsome offer to sing on the Cascaret Hour."[25]

FDR's humor surfaced at another time when a news conference had to be canceled because he was laid up in bed with a bad cold. The *Washington Post* ran an item explaining the cancellation but had an egregious typographical error in the caption, which read, "FDR in Bed with Coed." Hardly had that early edition reached the White House than a *Post* reporter picked up the phone to hear that unmistakable voice say, "This is Frank Roosevelt. I'd like 100 copies of that first edition of the POST. I want to send it to all my friends." The circulation department, however, had learned of the error and had sent runners scurrying out to recover all the papers from street corner vendors. The offending papers were destroyed, and FDR never got his copies.[26]

Such humor undoubtedly helped FDR cope with the burdens he carried. Critics might claim he was all veneer and no substance, but the famous smile and easy jokes masked an iron will not to succumb to despair or defeat. How else can one explain his gaiety and optimism despite frequent illnesses and a lasting paralysis? Beneath the surface levity was unshakable determination—ruthless at times—to get what he wanted.

FDR's genius lay in originating great plans and concepts, not in executing them. Given his inattention to detail, it is understandable that as an administrator he often was disorganized and unpredictable. Programs overlapped, fell short of intended purposes, or were woefully remiss in day-by-day practice, yet his great serenity and faith in himself served the country well throughout extremely critical times.

Undeniably, he lifted America from the depth of its Great Depression and followed that triumph with an uncanny sensitivity to public opinion— a sensitivity that enabled him to lead the people one step at a time from isolation to mobilization. Then his eloquence galvanized the citizenry to an extraordinary level of unity during four years of war. Such a record can never be forgotten.

When it came to administrative talents, Truman by comparison with Roosevelt was very organized and methodical. He studied issues and wanted mountains of facts, plain and unvarnished, before making a decision. Then having made the decision, he insisted on details and assurances as to how it was being administered. His work habits rubbed off on people around him, and his White House staff became noted for its daily efficiency. Not without personal prejudices, Truman tried hard to be president of all the people and to strengthen the office which he held in such high regard.

HST's domestic appeals arose from his advocacy of broad programs, including public works, social security, full employment, labor legislation, fair employment of blacks, and integration of the armed forces. But it was resolution in the conduct of America's foreign policy that earned him his niche in the hall of near-greatness.

It was Truman's determination and persistence in the Cold War that established the Berlin airlift, the Truman Doctrine, the Marshall Plan, and NATO. His support was fundamental to the creation of the State of Israel, and he met the confrontation in Korea with instant action, showing that, under his leadership, America would not shirk its responsibilities.

The genuine accomplishments of Franklin Roosevelt and Harry Truman are indelible; there is no need to paint either in colors brighter than life. Each can be shown to have had human failings upon occasion, but these lapses should not obscure the valid reasons for their statures. Indeed, we must be careful in examining their personal shortcomings lest we ignore the wisdom of an old Persian proverb: "When the blacksmith came to shoe the horse, the louse lifted its leg!"

PART III

SIXTH AND SEVENTH AGES

Chapter 15

Slipper'd Pantaloons

The sixth age shifts
Into the lean and slipper'd pantaloon . . .
—William Shakespeare, *As You Like It*,
II, vii, 157–58.

For Franklin Roosevelt there would be no "lean and slipper'd pantaloon" age; he died in office just two and a half months after his sixty-third birthday. Harry Truman was more than five years older, approaching his sixty-ninth birthday, when he left the White House.

"What was the first thing you did when you got back to Independence?" an inquisitive reporter asked the former president.

"Carried the suitcases up to the attic," came HST's unpretentious reply.

The Constitutional amendment limiting a president to two terms was ratified in 1951 but specifically exempted Truman. However, in March 1952, at a Jefferson-Jackson Day Dinner he announced that he would not be a candidate for reelection. Despite shouts of protest from fervent supporters he declared that his decision was final; he would "not accept a renomination."

At the time HST made his announcement, the winds of politics had gathered and were blowing with mounting force toward an Eisenhower candidacy. The ardor with which both parties courted the general was not surprising, for he was a genuine war hero and a man with enormous personal appeal. Eisenhower supported the Truman Doctrine, particularly in regard to Europe. Furthermore, uncertainty about Eisenhower's party affiliation, as well as his ambiguity on domestic issues, rather than being liabilities seemed to enhance his candidacy.

When at last Eisenhower allied himself with their party, Republican hopes shot upward. Party stalwarts chortled over the chance to recapture the White House for the first time in twenty years, and they adopted communism, Korea, and corruption as battle cries. The party's hopes were raised even farther by Truman's precipitous slide in public opinion polls.

In Truman's second term, and particularly throughout 1952, charges of wrongdoing were lodged against several lesser figures in his administration. While the "mess in Washington" as alleged by Republicans was exaggerated far beyond its actual proportions, there were some undeniable instances.

Presidential aide George Elsey gave HST a memorandum warning that signs of corruption were spreading rapidly. Elsey's memo and other evidence caused Truman to move swiftly and forcefully to clean house, especially in the tax division which seemed to show the most instances of naivete at best or malfeasance at worst.

The president ordered Attorney General J. Howard McGrath to investigate allegations of wrongdoings within the Internal Revenue Service, and when McGrath failed to do that job satisfactorily HST promptly fired him. Later he sacked T. Lamar Caudle, assistant attorney general in charge of the Tax Division, as soon as he learned of Caudle's misdeeds. Several other lesser figures resigned under pressure from the Oval Office.

Charges and countercharges made headlines, which in turn raised doubts and contributed to Truman's declining popularity. Indeed, public opinion polls reveal an extraordinarily changeable public image of him. Shortly after taking office, following FDR's death, he benefited from a wave of sympathy and registered an 87 percent approval rating. By the fall of 1946, the rating had dropped to 32 percent, but largely because of his strong stand in international matters it climbed back to 60 percent in the following year.

The extensive, hard-hitting, whistle-stop campaign in 1948 greatly enhanced Truman's reputation, and by January 1949 he was riding a crest of 69 percent approval. Then the yo-yo pattern of public ratings resumed as the polls started downward. By 1950 he was below 50 percent, and during 1951 and 1952 his standing ranged from a high of 37 percent to a low of 23 percent.[1]

With an approval rating of only 23 percent, HST's rating was at its lowest point—a nadir unequaled until Richard Nixon's fall from grace twenty-two years later.

In 1952 it was no great surprise, therefore, when Eisenhower won the presidency. Notwithstanding the oratory of his Democratic opponent, Governor Adlai E. Stevenson of Illinois, it was Eisenhower who amassed popular appeal and won most of the newspaper endorsements. He collected 80.2 percent of daily newspaper circulation, while Stevenson could muster only 10.8 percent. In later assessments of that 1952 campaign, most observers agreed that no Democrat could have beaten Ike.

On Inauguration Day, January 20, 1953, Truman, sitting in front of Herbert Hoover, the nation's other ex-president, listened intently as Eisenhower delivered his inaugural address. The actual transfer of power from Truman to Eisenhower took less than a minute and required a mere thirty-five words.

An hour later, the man who had been driven to the Capitol as President of the United States, possessed of all the rights and powers of that office, became a private citizen who with his wife, Bess, was driven through the streets of Washington almost unnoticed. The ex-president and former first lady went to the Georgetown home of Dean Acheson for a quick lunch.

The crowd assembled in front of Acheson's home kept shouting, "We want Harry," but HST only grinned and replied, "I'm just a private citizen now."[2]

To close friends on that occasion he emphasized his changed status. "Two hours ago I could have said five words and been quoted in 15 minutes in every capital of the world. Now I could talk for two hours and nobody would give a damn."

After lunch with the Achesons a small motorcade, unrecognized in the hubbub of Washington traffic, took the Trumans to Union Station where they boarded a train and headed for home in Independence.

When the train pulled into the station at Independence on that January 21, 1953, about 8,500 cheering persons were waiting. Another 1,500 were gathered at the Truman home.

"I was completely unprepared for what was to happen when we arrived back in Independence," HST later wrote in his book, *Mr. Citizen.* "I expected that there would probably be a reception of some kind, perhaps a hundred or so."[3] Of the enthusiastic turnout, he made a diary note: "It was the payoff for 30 years of hell and hard work."

The Truman home in Independence was built in 1865 by Bess Truman's maternal grandfather, George Porterfield Gates, and for years the house and grounds at 219 North Delaware Street was known as the Gates Mansion. When Harry and Bess married in 1919 they moved into the home then owned and occupied by Bess' mother, Madge (Gates) Wallace. Mrs.

Wallace continued to live with her daughter and son-in-law wherever they were, including the White House, until her death on December 5, 1952.

As Truman rose in public recognition, the Independence home became accepted as his residence and was regarded as the Summer White House throughout his presidency. The home was impressive then and stands today as a major attraction for visitors to Independence. The buildings are surrounded by stately maples and elms, and the house is distinguished by its many gables, its several porches, and its stained glass windows. Inside its rambling, clapboard Victorian structure are an old-fashioned parlor, a music room, a large dining room, kitchen, and seven bedrooms. There are three fireplaces with marbled mantels, and outside in the rear is a former coach house now serving as a multicar garage. After the home became famous and souvenir hunters started chipping off bits of the structures, a high iron fence was erected to enclose the entire lot.

At the time he returned to Independence, Truman enjoyed excellent physical health; his doctor said he had the heart and muscles of a man twenty years younger. Vigorous walking was always an important part of his life. As a young man living in the countryside, he often walked the one mile between the family farm and Grandview, and in World War I he frequently found himself on foot with his men during difficult forced marches.

The army taught Truman the brisk pace of 120 steps a minute, and he tried to maintain this rate as he grew older. As president, his early morning routine included walks, flanked by Secret Service men and often accompanied by reporters attempting to ask questions and take notes on the run. The rapid walks became his trademark, and he continued them during most years of his retirement.

While the private, neighborly life in a Midwestern community was a welcome relief from tumultuous Washington, retirement did not come easily for him. Inactivity was not a part of the Truman nature. Nor could he reasonably expect to withdraw entirely from public life. Party leaders and government officials continued to seek his assistance.

The mail he received in his first months out of office was unbelievable. In the first two weeks, more than 70,000 letters poured in, and characteristically HST felt he had to answer them. He rented a sizable office in nearby Kansas City where his public papers, numbering some 3.5 million documents, filled cabinets, boxes, and more than a dozen filing cabinets.[4]

In addition to tidying up details from his presidency, HST had several personal enterprises into which he threw himself wholeheartedly. The first was the writing of his memoirs.

Truman left the White House empty-handed, and in retirement he refused to take any job or titular position that would trade on his presidency. Several of his predecessors had died in financial straits, including the penniless Ulysses S. Grant, who had tried to provide for his family by toiling over memoirs while dying of throat cancer. Not poverty-stricken, Truman was far from being a rich man, and he came home without a presidential pension or allowance of any kind. Thus he had no financial help for research and compilation of his autobiography. It was afterward that the Former Presidents Act of 1958 sought to rectify such instances of national neglect and established a $25,000 annual pension and $50,000 a year for office and staff.

Truman's memoirs were published in two volumes: Volume 1, *Year of Decisions*, 1955; and Volume 2, *Years of Trial and Hope*, 1956. The first volume offers a brief look at his background, his astonishment at finding himself suddenly thrust into the presidency, the ending of the war, and conversion to a peacetime economy.

Somewhat like their author, the books fairly bristle with activity; the writer strides through the great events of 1945 in a fast-paced manner that is chatty and vigorous. Like most memoirs, there are few elements of self-doubts or hints of possible mistakes. The writing reflects a typical HST characteristic: everything is black or white, and from that perception came his decisiveness.

HST's style as an author is terse and pungent with little exploration of the complexity and nuances of the issues he faced. The *Memoirs* reveal him as a leader with strengths as well as weaknesses and with generous as well as petty qualities.

A lack of subtlety and imagination in the larger sense keep his *Memoirs* from being first rate; nevertheless, they are invaluable in showing how he grappled with seemingly insurmountable problems, including a dubious foreign policy legacy from the Roosevelt administration.

In contrast with Roosevelt, Truman was unlikely to change course once he set out on it. His resolution to confront Russian expansion was unshakable, but he was equally firm in his determination not to extend the area of conflict, hence his showdown with General MacArthur. The outcome of that episode meant that HST had preserved the supremacy of civil authority and the unchallengeable right of the president to shape overall military and foreign policy. Indeed, the *Memoirs* show how deeply Truman revered the office of the presidency, guarded its role, and protected it from encroachments by Congress, military leaders, or foreign powers.

Truman's *Memoirs* did not go unchallenged. One of the attacks came from his former secretary of state, James Byrnes. In a prepared statement given to United Press, Byrnes offered his version of the rift between him and President Truman:

> My previous writing makes clear that I always had the impression, while I was Secretary of State, that Mr. Truman had unreserved confidence in me. . . . Had Mr. Truman read to me in January 1946, the "lecture" he now reports I certainly would have resigned immediately. . . . Those relations [ones between Byrnes and Truman] remained cordial until I made an address at Washington and Lee University in June 1949 . . . in which I was critical of the degree of government spending in the domestic field. Mr. Truman did not like that speech and wrote me a note in which he said: "Since your Washington and Lee speech I know how Caesar felt when he said, 'Et tu, brute.' "
>
> In my reply to this note I wrote to him that in my speech there was no mention of him and that my criticism was of the trend of both political parties. In concluding, I said: "I hope you are not going to think of me as a Brutus because I am no Brutus. I hope you are not going to think of yourself as a Caesar, because you are no Caesar."[5]

With advancing age, Truman's feistiness was easily triggered, and this unkind cut from Byrnes was not one he would forget. Truman was simmering over it two years later when he sat down and composed a handwritten letter to Dean Acheson about the Potsdam Conference. HST kept the letter around for awhile and then in April 1957 again wrote to Acheson, saying, "I wrote you a longhand letter after I had talked to you about the Potsdam papers, but I haven't made up my mind to send it." The original letter, in which HST vented his anger against Byrnes, was never sent but was found among Truman's papers and in part read,

March 15, 1957

Dear Dean:

It was certainly a pleasure to talk with you about Potsdam . . .

I hardly ever look back for the purpose of contemplating "what might have been." Potsdam brings to mind "what might have been" had you been there instead of the Congressman, Senator, Supreme Court Justice, Presidential Assistant, Secretary of State, Governor of Secession South Carolina the Honorable James F. Byrnes.

At that time I trusted him implicitly—and he was then conniving to run the Presidency over my head! . . .

What a show that was! But a large number of agreements were reached in spite of the setup—only to be broken as soon as the unconscionable Russian Dictator returned to Moscow! And I liked the little son of a bitch.[6]

Retirement gave Truman the opportunity to do more than scratch old political wounds, however; leisure years also brought the chance to indulge his passion for histories and biographies. Known to be an avid reader, after he entered the presidency, it seemed the most natural gift an admirer could send was something for him to read. As a result, while he was in the White House and during the almost twenty years he lived afterward, HST accumulated a sizable personal library. At the time of his death there were approximately 1,000 volumes in his personal office at the Truman Library, and another 4,000 books that had been sent to him were stored in other rooms there.

During his retirement years, HST was literally surrounded by books. The best indication that he had at least partially read a particular book were annotations he often made in the margins. Sometimes these annotations extended across the top and bottom of several pages.

Nearly all of the books sent him have inscriptions in them. A note from Karl Menninger of the Menninger Clinic in Topeka accompanies his book, *The Crime of Punishment*, and reads, "For President Harry S. Truman, who once assured me that marrying a Missourian was the best thing I ever did. From two admirers, that Missourian and her husband."

In his book, *A Democrat Looks at His Party*, Dean Acheson wrote, "To Harry S. Truman, the first of living Democrats who will rank with the greatest of them all." In 1961, comedian Harpo Marx sent Truman his book called *Harpo Speaks*, and in it is inscribed, "From the man who says nothing to the man who always says the right thing. Respectfully, Harpo." Irish dramatist Brendan Behan sent his book *Brendan Behan's Island* together with a complimentary inscription about the style of writing in Truman's *Memoirs* and then added a gratuitous, obscene comment about the quality of Churchill's writing.[7]

For thirteen years of his retirement—from 1953 to 1966—HST remained very active. In those years, presidents and other men who sought the office, heads of state, the glittering and the famous came calling. He went to his office six days a week, wrote his *Memoirs*, kept up a heavy volume of correspondence, lunched with old friends, and took his daily walks. He also traveled across the country making speeches on government and political parties.

In those first thirteen years of retirement he found time to visit Hawaii and to make two pleasure trips to Europe. He had received several invitations from Oxford University to accept an honorary degree but had declined them either because of other commitments or, as happened in 1954, because an "obstreperous gall bladder" had to be removed. Then in early summer of 1956 Harry and Bess, accompanied by Mr. and Mrs. Stanley Woodward, visited England, France, Italy, and Greece. Woodward had been chief of protocol during Truman's presidencies and was thoroughly knowledgeable of the proprieties linked with visits by a former president of the United States. As was his custom, HST kept kinfolk back home regularly informed of what he and his wife did on this relaxing journey.

The Trumans made a second trip to Europe in 1958, this time accompanied by Mr. and Mrs. Sam Rosenman. Rosenman, veteran speech writer for FDR, also wrote important speeches during the first years of Truman's presidencies. This second trip was very private compared with the earlier one; there were no degrees to accept, less mail to answer, few cables or press conferences, and no syndicated accounts of their touring. The former president had no official duties and repeatedly said that he and his wife were simply Mr. and Mrs. Truman of Independence, Missouri, come to see the Continent during a quiet summer.

Pleasant European trips were not the chief concern of Truman during those years, however. As early as 1951 he had begun thinking of a library where his public and private papers might be stored. One morning in that year, while sitting at the breakfast table aboard the presidential yacht, the U.S.S. *Williamsburg*, he drew a map of a piece of property that he thought would be an ideal location for a library.

The eventual library was not built on the spot Truman originally picked—a "fine grove of trees" on the old Grandview farm—but on 13.6 acres that had been part of Slover Park and other land donated by the city of Independence along U.S. Route 24.

At the outset, HST's vision for the Truman Library was its use as a research center where students from all levels could study the presidency and government of the United States. Accordingly, in July 1954, a board of trustees for the Harry S. Truman Library, Inc., was created. Ground was broken a year later on May 8, 1955, the former president's seventy-first birthday, and in 1957 the Truman Library along with its accompanying museum was officially dedicated.

Most persons who tour the museum are unaware that much of the history of the post–World War II era is stored in endless rows of cardboard boxes in a humidity-controlled room. The library has served the scholarly community as one of the indispensable repositories for records that hold the key to decisions made by President Truman and his staff during those critical eight years following World War II.

To millions of persons who do not use the library's research collections but come to Independence to experience the nature of the man, his presidency, and the community he called home, the library and museum provide a link to the significance of the Truman years.

Many of President Truman's closest aides, confidants, and cabinet members have donated their personal papers thus providing additional insights and documentations. The archives contain more than 13 million pages and take up 6,600 linear feet. There are also more than 80,000 still photographs, documentary films and recordings, along with 18,000 museum objects, including priceless gifts from heads of state and hokey, handmade presents sent to the president.[8]

In retirement Mr. Truman worked out of a private office at the library from its opening until 1966, granting interviews, conducting personal business, writing articles, and greeting visiting dignitaries. He often talked with researchers and gave civic lectures in the small museum auditorium, usually emphasizing the importance of studying history.

HST took pains to make clear the library's purpose. It was not to be anything like the monuments to Washington or Lincoln in the nation's capital; rather it was to be a research place that might be expanded into a presidential and regional history center for the Midwest. He asked that the library's purpose be chiseled in Indiana limestone on the building's entrance: "The papers of the Presidents are among the most valuable sources of material for history. They ought to be preserved and they ought to be used."

HST returned to the library on only two occasions after 1966, for by that time age and illnesses were beginning to take their tolls. In 1961 he visited the White House for the first time since he had left it in 1953. Two years later when President John Kennedy was assassinated, the seventy-nine-year-old former president was so shocked he had to go to bed.

His once indefatigable energy was fading, and by 1964 Mr. Truman was slowing down so much that he declined to attend the Democratic Convention, explaining, "I am having to budget very carefully what time may yet be left to me to do the things that still remain undone."

In October of that year, he was badly shaken by a fall in his bathtub, breaking two ribs and cutting the skin above his right eye. HST never fully recovered from that accident and began to lose weight. His hearing deteriorated; his false teeth did not fit properly; and his mind began to be episodic. He still read a lot and occasionally received visitors, but he no longer went to his office in the library. Mr. Truman's last public appearances were made in 1969, when he was eighty-five and in rapidly failing health.

Chapter 16

Last Scenes

Last scene of all,
That ends this strange eventful history . . .
　　　　　　　　　　—William Shakespeare, *As You Like It*,
　　　　　　　　　　　　　　　　　II, vii, 163–64.

In the last week of March 1945, President Franklin Roosevelt went to Hyde Park for a few days. He returned to Washington on March 28, and the following day the ill and exhausted president left for a period of rest at Warm Springs, Georgia.

On April 9, Lucy Rutherfurd arrived from Aiken, South Carolina, with her friend, the society portraitist Elizabeth Shoumatoff, whom she had commissioned to paint a portrait of the president.

Thursday, April 12, the painter was in the fourth day of her work, and President Roosevelt sat in a big leather chair facing the fireplace in the living room of the cottage while Lucy sat on a nearby couch. Laura Delano, Franklin's cousin nicknamed Aunt Polly, was in and out of the room as she arranged flowers and other decorations. It was shortly before noon, and Roosevelt was getting tired of holding his position for the demanding artist.

Lunch was almost ready when the president shakily pressed his left hand against his forehead and said softly, "I have a terrific headache." His eyes half closed as he slumped in his chair.

At 5:45 P.M. (Eastern War Time), the Columbia Broadcasting System in New York was airing a serial drama, "Wilderness Road," based on the life of Daniel Boone. In the newsroom the first teletype that came through simply read, "F.D.R. DEAD." John Daly, CBS news correspondent standing nearby preparing for his evening broadcast to begin in half an hour, ran into the main news studio and asked for a "live" mike. Within minutes (5:49:00 P.M.) Daly announced:

> We interrupt this program to bring you a special news bulletin from CBS World News. A press association has just announced that President Roosevelt is dead. There are no further details as yet, but CBS World News will return to the air in just a few moments with more information as it is received in our New York headquarters.[1]

It was the passing of only one man at a time when hundreds of others were dying among the hedgerows of Europe or the caves of Okinawa. Yet it was more than that, for FDR had been a soldier of a different sort—a soldier who in his own way had fought battles against personal illness as well as perils for the country he served. His death meant there would be no more fireside chats, no more Hundred Days, no more New Deal, no more third and fourth terms.

The stone, once dropped, spread its ripples around the world. In Amsterdam, the controlling German News Agency (DNB) interrupted a musical program to announce FDR's death; two minutes later, an announcer in London over the British Broadcasting Company intoned: "It is with deep regret that we report the death of President Franklin Roosevelt." At about the same time, a Mercedes with a bulletproof windshield crept through the rubble in the streets of Berlin and delivered Joseph Goebbels to his Berlin office, darkened by round-the-clock RAF and American bombings. A grinning secretary came in to inform the Nazi propaganda minister that Roosevelt was dead.

"Bring out the best champagne," Goebbels ordered, "and get the Fuehrer on the phone." To Hitler, Goebbels shouted, "My Fuehrer, I congratulate you. Roosevelt is dead. It is written in the stars that the second half of April will be the turning point for us. This is almost Friday, April thirteenth. It is the turning point."[2]

In America, citizens were stunned. Slowly, the shock was replaced by a sense of the enormity of their loss. The U.S. Congress is usually a very political body, but on April 13, the day after FDR's death, it could not have been described better than two sentences that appeared in an editorial of the *Omaha World-Herald*: "There are no Republicans in America today, no Democrats, no New Dealers or anti-New Dealers. There are only Americans, united in a sense of national bereavement."[3]

Meanwhile, in Washington, arrangements were made for the state funeral. The body of the fallen commander in chief arrived from Warm Springs on April 14. Hundreds of thousands standing along the route from Union Station to the White House watched the flag-draped casket drawn by six white horses with a seventh for guide wend slowly through the streets of Washington.

Men and women of the armed forces marched in slow, measured cadence ahead of the catafalque, and service bands played the dirge for a commander fallen in war. Overhead, bombers and fighter planes roared back and forth, symbol of the armed might Roosevelt had worked hard to build. Many watchers wept unashamedly as a black army caisson carrying the casket made its way slowly toward the Executive Mansion.

That afternoon, Saturday, April 14, a brief funeral service according to FDR's own instructions written several years earlier was held in the East Room of the White House. At 4:00 P.M. President Harry Truman entered and sat across the aisle from Mrs. Roosevelt and members of the Roosevelt family. At Mrs. Roosevelt's request, the ceremony began with "Faith of Our Fathers," a hymn her husband had loved. In the flower-decked room, the casket stood on a small oriental rug before an altar, and on the other side of the room was a vacant wheelchair—mute symbol of the malady that had struck Roosevelt in his prime but had not kept him down.

The rites lasted only twenty-three minutes. An Episcopal bishop repeated the words of Roosevelt's first inaugural: "The only thing we have to fear is fear itself." Mrs. Roosevelt sat stoically dry-eyed through the prayers and hymns, but many of the distinguished visitors were unable to keep from tears and other signs of unmistakable grief.

The next day a special train carried the body for internment in the garden of the Roosevelt estate at Hyde Park. After the graveside rites there were completed, Mrs. Roosevelt, wearing a simple black dress on which she had pinned the small pearl-decorated fleur-de-lis Franklin had given her as a wedding present, walked alone back to the house. Later, to reporters who attempted to question her, she gave a simple reply. "The story," she said, "is over."

The story for Harry Truman, however, was far from over. The next eight years would be epochal ones for him and the nation. When Truman left the presidency in 1953 he enjoyed relatively good health and continued to do so until the mid-1960s. Gall bladder surgery in 1954 had laid him low for a short time, but he bounced back to his usual strenuous activities until his bathtub fall in 1964. There was speculation that the fall may have been caused by increasing episodes of vertigo, which had forced him to give up the customary morning walks. Arthritis in his knees and hips further limited his mobility.

As HST slowed down, Bess seldom left his side. For several years in the latter stages of his life she was the family chauffeur, a post she relinquished only when arthritis began to trouble her, too. "We've been in love since we were 5 and 6 years old, and we still are," Truman said in 1969. "She was my sweetheart from the first day I saw her."

In the summer of 1972 HST was hospitalized for two weeks because of gastrointestinal problems. He rallied from that attack and returned home, but six months later on the afternoon of December 5 he was taken near collapse by ambulance to the Research Hospital in nearby Kansas City. There he was diagnosed as suffering from lung congestion, and his condition was listed as "critical."

America watched and listened to daily reports as doctors tried to unclog blockages in his lungs and vascular system. Mrs. Truman, eighty-seven years old and relying heavily on a metal cane, was at the hospital with him daily. Margaret came from New York, and HST put up a brave front for both of them, smiling and saying he was "all right." But that was not true.

The lung congestion worsened and was complicated by heart irregularity, kidney blockages, and a failing digestive system. Compound illnesses were inexorably overcoming his will and stamina.

The Christmas season approached as HST lay hospitalized and battling death. Family and nurses put tiny decorations around his room, and as long as he could talk he tried to rally everyone's spirits, but he was sinking fast. On Sunday morning, December 24, Mrs. Walter Killilae, the night duty nurse, leaned over to tell him she was to have that night off because it was Christmas Eve. She said she wanted him there when she got back. "He squeezed my hand," she later said, "which leads me to believe his mind was still responsive."[4]

The next day he fell into a deep coma, and a hospital spokesman told reporters that his chances were "very, very small." Margaret again was summoned from New York and arrived on Christmas Day to see her father for one last time. Mother and daughter, facing the inevitable, returned to their Independence home late on Christmas Day but were called early the next morning and told the distressing news. The eighty-eight-year-old husband and father had passed away, breathing his last at 7:50 A.M. on Tuesday, December 26, 1972.

Mother and daughter viewed the body at a nearby funeral home. Buried with President Truman would be several mementos he treasured—his Masonic pin and apron and 33rd-degree Scottish Rite ring. And he would be dressed in his favorite dark blue pin-striped suit, white shirt, and black tie. The flag-draped light mahogany casket then was permanently sealed.

The casket was taken by motorcade the fifteen blocks from the funeral home to the Truman Library where it lay in state in the main lobby until noon on Thursday. President Richard Nixon and his wife flew in from Washington to lay a wreath at the library and to pay their respects to Mrs. Truman and other members of the family. The only other living former president, Lyndon B. Johnson, who would himself die three weeks later, came with Mrs. Johnson to honor the "man from Independence." Neither the Nixons nor the Johnsons remained for Thursday's private funeral, but thousands of mourners, common people and world leaders, walked slowly through the crescent-shaped library to pay a final tribute. An estimated 75,000 people had filed past the bier in the lobby of the library, all night, with few breaks in the line until the doors were closed at 11 A.M.

The Truman funeral rites were short and simple, just as he had requested—designed more as a farewell to an old and good friend than a ceremonial send-off to a former president of the United States.

During the final services, the immediate family sat behind a curtain at the back of the stage. The rites were held in the 251-seat auditorium of the library, and then Mr. Truman was buried with no pomp and very little pageantry in the library's courtyard—a spot he had selected.

"I would like to be buried out there," he once had said, pointing from the window of his office in the library. "I want to be out there so I can get up and walk into my office if I want to."[5]

Mrs. Truman never lost her composure throughout the ordeal except at one point during the graveside prayer when she accepted a white handkerchief from her daughter to wipe away tears for beloved Harry.

A blanket of red carnations on the coffin went into the grave with President Truman. Red carnations were his favorite flower, and these were a gift from the family. Bess requested that anyone wishing to send flowers should contribute instead to the scholarship fund at the Truman Library or to a favorite charity. Gestures of that sort would be just what the former president would have wanted. Thus, even in death, the common touch of Harry Truman—a touch that had won the hearts of so many of his countrymen—was preserved.

Notes

So much has been published about Franklin Roosevelt and Harry Truman that I have avoided extensive documentation, especially in Part I. Readers who want to delve further into the lives of these two principals should consult any of several excellent biographies listed in the bibliography. For Roosevelt, works by James MacGregor Burns, Kenneth S. Davis, Frank Freidel, Joseph P. Lash, or Geoffrey C. Ward are recommended. One will find comparable detail about Truman in books by Robert J. Donovan, Robert H. Ferrell, David McCullough, or Robert Underhill.

Abbreviations used in Notes: FDRL (Franklin D. Roosevelt Library, Hyde Park, New York), PPF (President's Personal File, FDRL), PSF (President's Secretary File, FDRL), FDR Papers (The Public Papers and Addresses of Franklin D. Roosevelt), HSTL (Harry S. Truman Library, Independence, Missouri), PSF (President's Speech File, HSTL), and HST Papers (Public Papers of the United States Presidents: Harry S. Truman).

CHAPTER 1. ENTRANCES

1. Frank Freidel, *Franklin D. Roosevelt: The Apprenticeship* (Boston: Little, Brown, 1952), p. 13.

2. Sara Roosevelt, *My Boy Franklin* (New York: Ray Long and Richard R. Smith, 1933), pp. 12–13.

3. Margaret Truman reported: "Dad owed the middle initial in his name to both grandparents. To placate their touchy elders, his parents added an S, but studiously refrained from deciding whether it stood for Solomon or Shippe." Margaret Truman, *Harry S. Truman* (New York: William Morrow, 1973), p. 46.

CHAPTER 2. SCHOOL BOYS

1. Elliott Roosevelt (ed.), *FDR: His Personal Letters: Early Years* (New York: Duell, Sloan, and Pearce, 1948), vol. 1, p. 16.

2. William D. Hassett, *Off the Record with FDR 1942–1945* (New Brunswick, New Jersey: Rutgers University Press, 1958), p. 9.

3. Margaret Truman, *Harry S. Truman*, p. 49.

4. Charles F. Horne (ed.), *Great Men and Famous Women* (New York: Selmar Hess, 1894).

CHAPTER 3. YOUNG LOVERS

1. FDR Diary, 1901–03, Franklin Delano Roosevelt Library. Hereinafter referred to as FDRL.

2. Ibid.

3. For a more extended discussion of Franklin and Alice Sohier at this time, see Ted Morgan, *FDR: A Biography* (New York: Simon and Schuster, 1985), pp. 82–83.

4. Ibid.

5. Richard Harrity and Ralph G. Martin, *Eleanor Roosevelt: Her Life in Pictures* (New York: Duell, Sloan, and Pearce, 1958), p. 17.

6. Joseph P. Lash, *Eleanor and Franklin* (New York: W. W. Norton, 1971), pp. 309–11.

7. Merle Miller reported without documentation that President Truman expressed this opinion to him while the two were in Truman's office at the Truman Library in Independence in 1962. See Merle Miller, *Plain Speaking: An Oral Biography of Harry S. Truman* (New York: Berkley Publishing, 1974), pp. 384–85.

8. Harry S. Truman, *Memoirs by Harry Truman: Year of Decisions* (Garden City, New York: Doubleday, 1955), vol. 1, p. 116. Hereinafter referred to as Truman Memoirs.

9. This anecdote is told in several biographies. See, for example, Bert Cochran, *Harry Truman and the Crisis Presidency* (New York: Funk and Wagnalls, 1973), p. 41.

10. Dean Acheson, *Present at the Creation* (New York: W. W. Norton, 1969), p. 150.

11. Quoted by Marianne Means, *The Woman in the White House* (New York: Random House, 1963), p. 219.

CHAPTER 4. SOLDIERS

1. Josephus Daniels, *The Wilson Era: Years of Peace, 1910–1917* (Chapel Hill: University of North Carolina Press, 1944), p. 253.

2. Michael R. Beschloss, *Kennedy and Roosevelt: The Uneasy Alliance* (New York: W. W. Norton, 1980), p. 230.

3. Elliott Roosevelt, *FDR: His Personal Letters*, vol. 1, pp. 442–71. Also see Eleanor Roosevelt's account of this trip in her travel diary, FDRL.

4. As quoted by Jonathan Daniels, *The Man of Independence* (Port Washington, New York: Kennikat Press, 1950), p. 58.

5. *Whistle Stop*, Harry S. Truman Library Newsletter, vol. 15, no. 1, 1987.

6. Letter to Bess, November 23, 1918. Papers of Harry S. Truman, Pre-Presidential Files, Harry S. Truman Library. Hereinafter referred to as HSTL.

7. Quoted by Alonzo Hamby, "The Great Drive Has Taken Place and I Had a Part in It," *Whistle Stop*, Harry S. Truman Library Newsletter, vol. 15, no. 4, 1987.

8. Vere Leigh, *Oral History Transcript*, HSTL.

CHAPTER 5. PRELUDES

1. Grenville Clark, *Harvard Alumni Bulletin*, No. 47 (April 28, 1945), p. 452.

2. John Keller and Joe Boldt, "Franklin's on His Own Now: Last Days of Louis McHenry Howe," *Saturday Evening Post* (October 1940), p. 42.

3. As quoted by Josephus Daniels, *The Wilson Era: Years of Peace*, p. 124.

4. Readers who wish further details about FDR's record as assistant secretary of the navy should consult any or all of the following books: Geoffrey C. Ward, *A First-Class Temperament: The Emergence of Franklin Roosevelt* (New York: Harper and Row, 1989); Freidel, *Franklin D. Roosevelt*; Kenneth S. Davis, *FDR: The Beckoning of Destiny 1882–1928* (New York: G. P. Putnam's Sons, 1971).

5. *Independence Examiner*, November 5, 1924.

6. Harry S. Truman, Autobiography, p. 35, HSTL.

7. Ibid., pp. 49–50. In this handwritten autobiography the date is clearly 1940, but President Truman must have been mistaken and meant to write 1944.

CHAPTER 6. THE HUSTINGS

1. Walter Lippmann, *New York Herald Tribune*, January 8, 1932. Also, see Walter Lippmann, *Interpretations, 1931–1932* (New York: Macmillan, 1932), pp. 259–62.

2. Samuel I. Rosenman (ed.), *The Public Papers and Addresses of Franklin D. Roosevelt* (New York: Random House, 1938), vol. 1, p. 659. Hereinafter referred to as FDR Papers.

3. Oral History Transcript of interview with Franklin D. Roosevelt, Jr., FDRL, p. 66. Also quoted by John H. Sharon, "The Psychology of the Fireside Chat" (master's thesis, Princeton University, 1949), FDRL.

4. Persons wanting more details on FDR's career as a public speaker should see "Franklin Delano Roosevelt," a scholarly essay by Earnest Brandenburg and

Waldo W. Braden in *History and Criticism of American Public Address*, vol. 3, edited by Marie Hochmuth Nichols (New York: Longmans, Green, 1955), pp. 458–530.

5. Lew Sarett and William Trufant Foster, *Basic Principles of Speech* (New York: Houghton Mifflin, 1936), pp. 193–94.

6. For examples, see Edgar Hinde, Oral History Transcript, p. 19; Edward D. McKim, Oral History Transcript, p. 22; Charles T. Curry, Oral History Transcript, p. 2; all in HSTL.

7. Truman, *Autobiography*, pp. 25–26, President's Speech File (hereinafter referred to as PSF), HSTL.

8. Edward D. McKim, Oral History Transcript, pp. 22–23, HSTL.

9. *St. Louis Dispatch*, November 4, 1934, pp. 1a and 2h.

10. Typewritten draft of manuscript, Papers of Harry S. Truman, Senatorial File, Box 163, Folder 2, HSTL.

11. Ibid.

12. John Daly, as recorded by Edward R. Murrow and Fred W. Friendly, "I Can Hear It Now—1933–1945," Columbia Masterworks Records ML 4905.

13. For these and other similar responses, see Jack Redding's *Inside the Democratic Party* (Indianapolis: Bobbs-Merrill, 1958), pp. 178–81.

14. For a more detailed narrative of this campaign, see Irwin Ross, *The Loneliest Campaign: The Truman Victory of 1948* (Westport, Connecticut: Greenwood Press, 1968).

CHAPTER 7. FDR: ECONOMICS

1. *Des Moines Register*, March 3, 1933.

2. Otil L. Graham and Meghan Robinson Wander (eds.), *Franklin D. Roosevelt: His Life and His Times* (Boston: G. K. Hall, 1985), p. 415.

3. Robert E. Sherwood, *Roosevelt and Hopkins: An Intimate History* (New York: Harper and Bros., 1948), p. 52.

4. Graham and Wander, *Franklin D. Roosevelt*, p. 185.

5. Harvard Sitkoff (ed.), *Fifty Years Later: The New Deal Evaluated* (New York: Oxford University Press, 1978), p. 230.

CHAPTER 8. HST: ECONOMICS

1. Truman, *Memoirs*, vol. 1, p. 21.

2. Walter Mills (ed.), *The Forrestal Diaries* (New York: Viking Press, 1951), p. 113.

3. Samuel Irving Rosenman, Oral History Transcript, p. 51, HSTL.

4. Richard E. Neustadt, "Extending the Horizons of Democratic Liberalism," in *The Truman Years*, edited by J. Joseph Huthmacher (Hinsdale, Illinois: Dryden Press, 1972), p. 82.

5. John Morton Blum, *From the Morgenthau Diaries*, Vol. 2, *Years of Urgency* (Boston: Houghton Mifflin, 1965), p. 292.

6. President Truman's handwritten draft of this intended speech can be found in Box 28, Papers of Clark Clifford, PSF, HSTL.

7. *Public Papers of the United States President: Harry S. Truman* (Washington, D.C.: U.S. Government Printing Office, 1961), pp. 298–301. Hereinafter referred to as HST Papers.

CHAPTER 9. FDR: POLITICIAN

1. James MacGregor Burns, *Roosevelt: The Lion and the Fox* (New York: Harcourt, Brace & World, 1956), p. 35.

2. Raymond Moley, *After Seven Years* (New York: Harper and Bros., 1939), pp. 121–22.

3. Joseph P. Lash, *Eleanor Roosevelt and Her Friends* (Garden City, New York: Doubleday, 1982), p. 278.

4. Harold L. Ickes, *The Secret Diary of Harold L. Ickes: The First Thousand Days, 1933–1936* (New York: Simon and Schuster, 1953), p. 640.

5. Quoted by Morgan, *FDR: A Biography*, pp. 363–64.

6. Sherwood, *Roosevelt and Hopkins*, pp. 51–52.

7. Charles A. Beard and Mary R. Beard, *America in Mid-Passage*, Vol. 2 (New York: Macmillan, 1939), pp. 947–49.

8. PPF, Box 200, FDRL.

9. John Morton Blum, *Roosevelt and Morgenthau* (Boston: Houghton Mifflin, 1970), p. 127.

10. Brandeis was eighty; Van Devanter, seventy-seven; McReynolds, seventy-five; Sutherland, seventy-four; Hughes, seventy-four; Butler, seventy; Cardozo, sixty-six; Stone, sixty-five; and Roberts, sixty-one.

CHAPTER 10. HST: POLITICIAN

1. *Kansas City Journal Post*, September 12, 1935.

2. *Congressional Record*, 7th Congress, 3d sess., pp. 1932–34.

3. *St. Louis Post Dispatch*, February 16, 17, 1938.

4. *Kansas City Star*, January 31, 1938.

5. Truman, Autobiography, pp. 43–44, HSTL.

6. Roger Edward Wilson, "The Truman Committee" (Ph.D. diss., Harvard University), p. 456, HSTL.

7. Margaret Truman, *Harry S. Truman*, p. 185.

8. Ibid., pp. 185–86.

9. Edward D. McKim, Oral History Transcript, HSTL.

10. One of FDR's most careful biographers offered the following explanatory note: "Since the President's death, medical articles have appeared which asserted

that FDR sustained three cerebral strokes while in office. There is no competent evidence to support this. In 1972 Dr.Howard Bruenn assured me that he, as the President's personal physician, observed nothing to support the contention. He does not doubt that FDR had a generalized arteriosclerosis. Reduced nourishment to the brain limits the ability to think out complex problems. Narrowing arteries, with increased strain on the heart, would make Roosevelt less competent—an old man at sixty-three." Jim Bishop, *FDR's Last Year* (New York: Pocket Books, 1975), p. 95.

11. *Chicago Daily Tribune*, October 17, 1944.

12. Truman, *Memoirs*, vol. 1, p. 2.

13. Will Lissner, *New York Times*, October 28, 1945.

14. James E. Pollard, "Truman and the Press," *Journalism Quarterly* 28 (Fall 1951): 458.

15. Douglass Cater, *The Fourth Branch of Government* (Boston: Houghton Mifflin, 1959), p. 42.

16. George M. Elsey, in foreword to Robert Underhill's *The Truman Persuasions* (Ames: Iowa State University Press, 1981), p. vii.

17. William Shakespeare, *Julius Caesar, III, ii, 222* in *The Complete Works of Shakespeare*, edited by Hardin Craig (Greenview, Illinois: Scott, Foresman, 1961), p. 788.

18. It is not the purpose of this book to give a detailed account of the 1948 campaign. Readers who want further information on it should consult one or more of the following: Jules Abels, *Out of the Jaws of Victory* (New York: Henry Holt, 1959); David McCullough, *Truman* (New York: Simon and Schuster, 1992), Ross, *The Loneliest Campaign*; and Underhill, *The Truman Persuasions*.

CHAPTER 11.　FDR: FOREIGN POLICIES (1933–1936)

1. FDR Papers, vol. 2, p. 4.

2. Father Edmund A. Walsh, in a lecture to Air Force officers at the Institute of Languages and Linguistics, Washington, D.C., February 1952.

3. John C. Fitzpatrick (ed.), *The Writings of George Washington from the Original Manuscript Sources 1745–1799* (Washington, D.C.: U.S. Government Printing Office, 1940), vol. 35, pp. 233–34.

4. Moley, *After Seven Years*, pp. 215–16.

5. Burns, *The Lion and the Fox*, p. 178.

6. Ickes, *Secret Diary*, pp. 422–23.

7. Haile Selassie's mobilization order can be found in several sources. For examples, see William E. Kinsella, Jr., *Leadership in Isolation: FDR and World War II* (Boston: G. K. Hall, 1978), p. 74; Robert Dallek, *Franklin D. Roosevelt and American Foreign Policy, 1932–1945* (New York: Oxford University Press, 1979), p. 112.

8. Lawrence S. Wittner, *The Rebels Against War: The American Peace Movement, 1933–1984* (Philadelphia: Temple University Press, 1984), pp. 2–3.

9. Donald F. Drummond, *The Passing of American Neutrality, 1937–1941* (Ann Arbor: University of Michigan Press, 1955), pp. 42–43.

10. FDR Papers, August 14, 1936.

11. According to Samuel Rosenman, this address was prepared by William C. Bullitt, ambassador to the Soviet Union (1933–1936) and later ambassador to France (1936–1941). Bullitt told Rosenman that the phrase "I hate war" was one he remembered from President Woodrow Wilson. Rosenman gave the following account: "During a private talk with President Wilson soon after the declaration of war by the United States, Wilson, with tears in his eyes, had dramatically seized Bullitt's hand and, in great emotion, had used that phrase." See Samuel I. Rosenman, *Working with Roosevelt* (New York: Da Capo Press, 1972), p. 108.

12. *New York Times*, October 6, 1937.

13. Harold L. Ickes, "My Twelve Years with FDR," *Saturday Evening Post* 221 (July 17, 1948), p. 97.

14. Rosenman, *Working with Roosevelt*, p. 167.

CHAPTER 12.   FDR: FOREIGN POLICIES (1937–1945)

1. Winston S. Churchill, *The Gathering Storm* (Boston: Houghton Mifflin, 1948), p. 355.

2. Kenneth S. Davis, *FDR: Into the Storm 1937–1940* (New York: Random House, 1993), p. 437.

3. Ibid., pp. 437–38.

4. Ibid., p. 440.

5. Samuel E. Morison, *The Oxford History of the American People* (New York: Oxford University Press, 1965), p. 992.

6. Dallek, *Franklin D. Roosevelt and American Foreign Policy*, p. 187.

7. Richard M. Ketchum, *The Borrowed Years 1938–1941* (New York: Random House, 1989), p. 180.

8. FDR Papers, vol. 8, p. 455.

9. Ibid., p, 463.

10. Warren F. Kimball (ed.), *Churchill and Roosevelt: The Complete Correspondence* (Princeton, New Jersey: Princeton University Press, 1984), p. 24.

11. Morgenthau Diaries, entry for December 8, 1937.

12. Beschloss, *Kennedy and Roosevelt*, pp. 199–200.

13. Joseph C. Grew, *Turbulent Era: A Diplomatic Record of Forty Years, 1904–1945* (Boston: Houghton Mifflin, 1952), p. 1233.

14. FDR Papers, vol. 9, pp. 607–8.

15. *Washington Post*, December 30, 1940.

16. Ibid.

17. Rosenman, *Working with Roosevelt*, pp. 260–61.

18. Winston S. Churchill, *The Grand Alliance* (Boston: Houghton Mifflin, 1950), p. 128.

19. U.S. Department of Defense, "The 'Magic' Background of Pearl Harbor," p. 66. National Archives.

20. As quoted by James MacGregor Burns, *Roosevelt: Soldier of Freedom 1940–1945* (New York: Harcourt Brace Jovanovich, 1970), p. 323.

21. T. Harry Williams, Richard N. Current, and Frank Freidel, *A History of the United States [since 1865]*, 2nd ed. (New York: Alfred A. Knopf, 1966), p. 639.

22. Lord Moran (Sir Charles Wilson), *Churchill: Taken from Diaries of Lord Moran* (Boston: Houghton Mifflin, 1966), p. 242.

23. Sherwood, *Roosevelt and Hopkins*, p. 870.

24. Burns, *Soldier of Freedom*, p. 572.

CHAPTER 13. HST: FOREIGN POLICIES

1. As quoted in *New York Times*, June 24, 1941.

2. Gregg Herken, "Atomic and Hydrogen Bombs," in *The Harry S. Truman Encyclopedia*, edited by Richard S. Kirkendall (Boston: G. K. Hall, 1989), pp. 13–14.

3. James F. Byrnes, *Speaking Frankly* (New York: Harper and Bros., 1947), pp. 208–13. Also, see Robert L. Messer, *The End of an American Alliance* (Chapel Hill: University of North Carolina Press, 1982), pp. 163–64.

4. Martin J. Sherwin, *A World Destroyed: Hiroshima and the Origins of the Arms Race* (New York: Vintage Press, 1987), p. 208.

5. White House Map Room Message, August 6, 1945, Box 88, National Defense—Atomic Energy, Elsey Papers, HSTL. See also, Rosenman Papers, Box 2, 1945, Potsdam Conference, HSTL.

6. Margaret Truman, *Harry S. Truman*, p. 282.

7. For examples of such criticisms, see Gar Alperovitz, *Atomic Diplomacy: Hiroshima and Potsdam* (New York: Simon and Schuster, 1965); Barton J. Bernstein (ed.), *The Atomic Bomb: The Critical Issues* (Boston: Little, Brown, 1976).

8. Albert Einstein's letter to Roosevelt, dated August 2, 1939, "America since Hoover" Collection, FDRL.

9. HST Papers, 1945, p. 434.

10. Winston S. Churchill, *Triumph and Tragedy* (Boston: Houghton Mifflin, 1953), p. 426.

11. Robert J. Donovan, *Conflict and Crisis: The Presidency of Harry S. Truman, 1945–1948* (New York: W. W. Norton, 1977), pp. 11–12. Also, see Roosevelt's cable to Stalin, April 1, 1945. *Foreign Relations of the United States, Diplomatic Papers* (Washington, D.C.: U.S. Government Printing Office, 1970), pp. 194–96.

12. Robert H. Ferrell (ed.), *Off the Record: The Private Papers of Harry S. Truman* (New York: Harper & Row), pp. 79–80.

13. For a more detailed account and analysis of the Iron Curtain speech, see this author's article, "Fulton's Finest Hour," *Quarterly Journal of Speech* (April 1966): 155–63.

14. Arthur Krock, *Memoirs: Sixty Years on the Firing Line* (New York: Funk and Wagnalls, 1968), p. 224.

15. Quoted by David McCullough from an interview with Clark Clifford. McCullough, *Truman*, p. 564.

16. Henry A. Wallace in a personal letter to this author dated August 31, 1954.

17. HST Papers, 1947, p. 238.

18. HST Papers, 1949, p. 214.

19. Ferrell, *Off the Record*, p. 127.

20. PPF, Speeches, January 5, 1949, to February 22, 1949, Folder 1, Inaugural Address, HSTL.

21. McCullough, *Truman*, p. 775.

22. Omar N. Bradley and Clay Bair, *A General's Life: An Autobiography* (New York: Simon and Schuster, 1983), pp. 534–35.

23. *Korea*, vol. 7 of *Foreign Relations of the United States, 1950* (Washington, D.C.: U.S. Government Printing Office, 1976), p. 211.

24. *Vital Speeches*, vol. 17, January 1951, p. 171.

25. Joseph P. Kennedy in a personal letter to this author dated January 3, 1954.

26. *New York Times*, December 16, 1950.

27. *New York Times*, December 17, 1950.

28. The MacArthur episode is treated in biographies of Truman and MacArthur, in most general histories of the period, and in many special books or articles dealing with the event. Discussions of the controversy and its outcome can be found in each of the following books: Francis H. Heller (ed.), *The Korean War* (Lawrence: Regents Press of Kansas, 1977); Acheson, *Present at the Creation* (New York: W. W. Norton, 1969); Joseph C. Goulden, *Korea: The Untold Story* (New York: Times Books, 1982); Douglas MacArthur, *Reminiscences and the Korean War* (Cambridge, Massachusetts: Harvard University Press, 1959); and Charles A. Willoughby, *MacArthur 1941–1951* (New York: McGraw-Hill, 1954).

29. Richard P. Stebbins (ed.), *The United States in World Affairs 1951* (New York: Harper and Bros., 1952), p. 108.

CHAPTER 14. PERSONALITIES IN CONTRAST

1. "Franklin eagerly explained his reasoning to Alice Sohier during one of their evenings together that year (1901). Her father was a lifelong Republican; so would she be, and, at least in retrospect, she thought Franklin's straightforward explanation 'the most calculating, unprincipled thing she'd ever heard.'" Re-

ported by Geoffrey Ward from a personal interview with Emily Shaw, Alice Sohier's granddaughter. See Ward, *A First-Class Temperament*, p. 93.

2. "Notes and News," *School and Society* 60 (1944): 346.

3. Ibid.

4. Quoted by Frank McNaughton and Walter Hehmeyer, *This Man Truman* (New York: McGraw-Hill, 1945), p. 29.

5. Quoted by David McCullough from an interview with Elsey. McCullough, *Truman*, p. 364.

6. Ferrell, *Off the Record*, p. 142–43.

7. Raymond Moley, *The First New Deal* (New York: Harcourt, Brace and World, 1966), pp. 273–75.

8. Lillian Rogers Parks, *The Roosevelts: A Family in Turmoil* (Englewood, New Jersey: Fleet, 1981), p. 177.

9. See, Fulton Oursler, *Behold This Dreamer* (Boston: Little, Brown, 1964), pp. 424–25.

10. Joseph Lash Diary, January 1, 1942, Lash Papers, FDRL.

11. From a filmed interview with Speaker Sam Rayburn by Martin Agronsky (NBC), April 1945. Also, quoted by David McCullough, *Truman*, p. 357.

12. Ketchum, *The Borrowed Years*, p. 399.

13. Lord Moran, *Diaries*, p. 293.

14. Truman, *Memoirs*, vol. 1, p. 411.

15. Doris Kearns Goodwin, *No Ordinary Time* (New York: Simon and Schuster, 1994), pp. 156–57.

16. FDR Papers, vol. 5, 1937, p. 414.

17. Morgan, *FDR: A Biography*, p. 534.

18. Ibid., p. 554.

19. Curt Gentry, *J. Edgar Hoover: The Man and His Secrets* (New York: W. W. Norton, 1991), pp. 237–38.

20. George Elsey in the foreword to Underhill, *The Truman Persuasions*, p. viii.

21. *Washington Post*, December 6, 1950, p. 12b.

22. *Washington Post*, December 9, 1950, p. 1.

23. "The Music Critic and the President: Second Time Around," *Whistle Stop*, vol. 16, no. 2, 1988.

24. Incident described by Beth Campbell Short, correspondence secretary to the president (September 1952–January 1953), at HSTL Conference on the Administration of the Presidency under Harry S. Truman, May 1977.

25. *Franklin Roosevelt's Complete Press Conferences*, May 16, 1933, vol. 1, p. 264, FDRL.

26. Chalmers Roberts, "Franklin Delano Roosevelt," in *Ten Presidents and the Press*, Kenneth W. Thompson, ed. (Washington, D.C.: University Press of America, 1983), pp. 24–25.

CHAPTER 15. SLIPPER'D PANTALOONS

1. Summary taken from Alonzo L. Hamby's entry under "Biographers and Public Reputations," in *The Harry S. Truman Encyclopedia*, edited by Kirkendall, pp. 27–28.

2. McCullough, *Truman*, p. 922.

3. Harry S. Truman, *Mr. Citizen* (New York: Geis and Associates, 1953), p. 23.

4. Margaret Truman, *Harry S. Truman*, pp. 561–62.

5. Reported by *Des Moines Register*, November 30, 1955.

6. Ferrell, *Off the Record*, pp. 348–49.

7. *Whistle Stop*, vol. 7, Spring 1979, HSTL.

8. "Library a Window on Truman Presidency," *Kansas City Star*, May 6, 1984.

CHAPTER 16. LAST SCENES

1. *Franklin Delano Roosevelt: A Memorial* (New York: Pocket Books, 1945), pp. 1–2.

2. Bishop, *FDR's Last Year*, pp. 816–17.

3. *Omaha World-Herald*, April 13, 1945.

4. McCullough, *Truman*, pp. 987–88.

5. *Chicago Sun-Times*, December 28, 1972.

Bibliography

BOOKS

Abels, Jules. *Out of the Jaws of Victory*. New York: Henry Holt, 1959.

Acheson, Dean. *Present at the Creation*. New York: W. W. Norton, 1969.

Alperovitz, Gar. *Atomic Diplomacy: Hiroshima and Potsdam*. New York: Simon and Schuster, 1965.

Alsop, Joseph. *FDR—A Centenary Remembrance, 1882–1945*. New York: Viking Press, 1982.

Asbell, Bernard. *When F.D.R. Died*. New York: Holt, Rhinehart and Winston, 1961.

Beard, Charles A., and Mary R. Beard. *America in Mid-Passage*, vol. 2. New York: Macmillan, 1939.

Bernstein, Barton J., ed. *The Atomic Bomb: The Critical Issues*. Boston: Little, Brown, 1976.

Beschloss, Michael R. *Kennedy and Roosevelt: The Uneasy Alliance*. New York: W. W. Norton, 1980.

Bishop, Jim. *FDR's Last Year—April 1944–April 1945*. New York: Pocket Books, 1975.

Blum, John Morton. *From the Morgenthau Diaries*. Boston: Houghton Mifflin. Volume 1, *Years of Crisis, 1928–1938* (1959); Volume 2, *Years of Urgency, 1938–1941* (1965); Volume 3, *Years of War, 1941–1945* (1967).

———. *Roosevelt and Morgenthau*. Boston: Houghton Mifflin, 1970.

Bradley, Omar N., and Clay Bair. *A General's Life: An Autobiography*. New York: Simon and Schuster, 1983.

Buhite, Russell D., and David W. Levy, eds. *FDR's Fireside Chats*. Norman: University of Oklahoma Press, 1992.

Burns, James MacGregor. *Roosevelt: The Lion and the Fox*. New York: Harcourt, Brace and World, 1956.

————. *Roosevelt: Soldier of Freedom 1940–1945*. New York: Harcourt Brace Jovanovich, 1970.

Byrnes, James F. *Speaking Frankly*. New York: Harper and Bros., 1947.

Cater, Douglass. *The Fourth Branch of Government*. Boston: Houghton Mifflin, 1959.

Churchill, Winston S. *The Gathering Storm*. Boston: Houghton Mifflin, 1948.

————. *The Grand Alliance*. Boston: Houghton Mifflin, 1950.

Clay, Lucius D. *Decision in Germany*. New York: Doubleday, 1950.

Cochran, Bert. *Harry Truman and the Crisis Presidency*. New York: Funk and Wagnalls, 1973.

Cole, Wayne S. *Roosevelt and the Isolationists 1932–1945*. Lincoln: University of Nebraska Press, 1983.

Collier, Peter, with David Horowitz. *The Roosevelts: An American Saga*. New York: Simon and Schuster, 1994.

Cook, Blanche Wiesen. *Eleanor Roosevelt*, Volume 1, *1884–1933*. New York: Viking Press, 1992.

Dallek, Robert. *Franklin D. Roosevelt and American Foreign Policy, 1932–1945*. New York: Oxford University Press, 1979.

Daniels, Jonathan. *The Man of Independence*. Port Washington, New York: Kennikat Press, 1950.

Daniels, Josephus. *The Wilson Era: Years of Peace, 1910–1917*. Chapel Hill: University of North Carolina Press, 1944.

————. *The Wilson Era: Years of War and After, 1917–1923*. Chapel Hill: University of North Carolina Press, 1946.

Davis, Kenneth S. *FDR: The Beckoning of Destiny 1882–1928*. New York: G. P. Putnam's Sons, 1971.

————. *FDR: The New York Years 1928–1933*. New York: Random House, 1979.

————. *FDR: Into the Storm 1937–1940*. New York: Random House, 1993.

Donovan, Robert J. *Conflict and Crisis: The Presidency of Harry S. Truman, 1945–1948*. New York: W. W. Norton, 1977.

————. *Tumultuous Years: The Presidency of Harry S. Truman, 1949–1953*. New York: W. W. Norton, 1982.

Drummond, Donald F. *The Passing of American Neutrality, 1937–1941*. Ann Arbor: University of Michigan Press, 1955.

Eisenhower, David. *Eisenhower at War 1943–1945*. New York: Random House, 1986.

Ferrell, Robert H., ed. *Off the Record: The Private Papers of Harry S. Truman*. New York: Harper & Row, 1980.

————. *Dear Bess: The Letters from Harry to Bess Truman, 1910–1959*. New York: W. W. Norton, 1983.

Franklin Delano Roosevelt: A Memorial. New York: Pocket Books, 1945.

Fish, Hamilton. *FDR: The Other Side of the Coin*. New York: Vantage Press, 1976.

Fitzpatrick, John C., ed. *The Writings of George Washington from the Original Manuscript Sources 1745–1799*, vol. 35. Washington, D.C.: U.S. Government Printing Office, 1940.

Freidel, Frank. *Franklin D. Roosevelt: The Apprenticeship*. Boston: Little, Brown, 1952.

Gaddis, John Lewis. *The United States and the Origins of the Cold War 1941–1947*. New York: Columbia University Press, 1972.

Gentry, Curt. *J. Edgar Hoover: The Man and His Secrets*. New York: W. W. Norton, 1991.

Goldberg, Richard Thayer. *The Making of Franklin D. Roosevelt: Triumph over Disability*. Cambridge, Massachusetts: Abt Books, 1981.

Goodwin, Doris Kearns. *No Ordinary Time*. New York: Simon and Schuster, 1994.

Goulden, Joseph C. *Korea: The Untold Story*. New York: Times Books, 1982.

Graham, Otil L., and Meghan Robinson Wander, eds. *Franklin D. Roosevelt: His Life and His Times*. Boston: G. K. Hall, 1985.

Greer, Thomas H. *What Roosevelt Thought: The Social and Political Ideas of Franklin D. Roosevelt*. East Lansing: Michigan University Press, 1958.

Grew, Joseph C. *Turbulent Era: A Diplomatic Record of Forty Years, 1904–1945*. Boston: Houghton Mifflin, 1952.

Gunther, John. *Roosevelt in Retrospect*. London: The Non-Fiction Book Club, 1950.

Hallgren, Mauritz A. *The Gay Reformer: Profits before Plenty under Franklin D. Roosevelt*. New York, 1935.

Harris, Bill. *Homes of the Presidents*. New York: Crescent Books, 1987.

Harrity, Richard, and Ralph G. Martin. *Eleanor Roosevelt: Her Life in Pictures*. New York: Duell, Sloan, and Pearce, 1958.

Hassett, William D. *Off the Record with FDR 1942–1945*. New Brunswick, New Jersey: Rutgers University Press, 1958.

Heller, Francis H., ed. *The Korean War*. Lawrence: Regents Press of Kansas, 1977.

Herzstein, Robert E. *Roosevelt & Hitler: Prelude to War*. New York: Paragon House, 1989.

Horne, Charles F., ed. *Great Men and Famous Women*. New York: Selmar Hess, 1894.

Huthmacher, J. Joseph, ed. *The Truman Years*. Hinsdale, Illinois: Dryden Press, 1972.

Ickes, Harold L. *The Secret Diary of Harold L. Ickes: The First Thousand Days, 1933–1936*. New York: Simon and Schuster, 1953.

Ketchum, Richard M. *The Borrowed Years 1938–1941*. New York: Random House, 1989.

Kimball, Warren F., ed. *Churchill and Roosevelt: The Complete Correspondence*. Princeton, New Jersey: Princeton University Press, 1984.

Kinsella, William E., Jr. *Leadership in Isolation: FDR and World War II*. Boston: G. K. Hall, 1978.

Kirkendall, Richard S., ed. *The Harry S. Truman Encyclopedia*. Boston: G. K. Hall, 1989.

Krock, Arthur. *Memoirs: Sixty Years on the Firing Line*. New York: Funk and Wagnalls, 1968.

Lash, Joseph P. *Eleanor and Franklin*. New York: W. W. Norton, 1971.

————. *Eleanor Roosevelt and Her Friends*. Garden City, New York: Doubleday, 1982.

Leahy, William D. *I Was There*. New York: Whittlesey House, McGraw-Hill, 1950.

Leuchtenberg, William E. *In the Shadow of the FDR: From Harry Truman to Ronald Reagan*. Ithaca, New York: Cornell University Press, 1983.

Lilienthal, David E. *The Atomic Energy Years 1945–1950*. New York: Harper and Row, 1964.

Lippmann, Walter. *Interpretations, 1931–1932*. New York: Macmillan, 1932.

Loewenheim, Francis L., Harold D. Langley, and Manfred Jones, eds. *Roosevelt and Churchill: Their Secret Wartime Correspondence*. New York: Saturday Review Press, 1975.

Lord Moran (Sir Charles Wilson). *Churchill: Taken from Diaries of Lord Moran*. Boston: Houghton Mifflin, 1966.

Ludwig, Emil. *Roosevelt: A Study in Fortune and Power*. New York: Viking Press, 1938.

MacArthur, Douglas. *Reminiscences and the Korean War*. Cambridge, Massachusetts: Harvard University Press, 1959.

McCullough, David. *Truman*. New York: Simon and Schuster, 1992.

McNaughton, Frank, and Walter Hehmeyer. *This Man Truman*. New York: McGraw-Hill, 1945.

Means, Marianne. *The Woman in the White House*. New York: Random House, 1963.

Mee, Charles L., Jr. *Meeting at Potsdam*. New York: M. Evans, 1975.

Messer, Robert L. *The End of an American Alliance*. Chapel Hill: University of North Carolina Press, 1982.

Miller, Merle. *Plain Speaking: An Oral Biography of Harry S. Truman*. New York: Berkley Publishing, 1974.

Miller, Nathan. *FDR: An Intimate History*. New York: Doubleday, 1983.

Miller, Richard. *Truman: The Rise to Power*. New York: McGraw-Hill, 1986.

Mills, Walter, ed. *The Forrestal Diaries*. New York: Viking Press, 1951.

Moley, Raymond. *After Seven Years*. New York: Harper and Bros., 1939.

————. *The First New Deal*. New York: Harcourt, Brace and World, 1966.

Morgan, Ted. *FDR: A Biography*. New York: Simon and Schuster, 1985.

Morison, Samuel E. *The Oxford History of the American People*. New York: Oxford University Press, 1965.

Nichols, Marie Hochmuth. *History and Criticism of American Public Address*, vol. 3. New York: Longmans, Green, 1955.

Oursler, Fulton. *Beyond This Dreamer*. Boston: Little, Brown, 1964.

Parks, Lillian Rogers. *The Roosevelts: A Family in Turmoil*. Englewood, New Jersey: Fleet, 1981.

Parmet, Herbert S., and Marie B. Hecht. *Never Again: A President Runs for a Third Term*. New York: Macmillan, 1968.

Perkins, Dexter. *The New Age of Franklin Roosevelt 1932–1945*. Chicago: University of Chicago Press, 1957.

Perkins, Frances. *The Roosevelt I Knew*. New York: Viking Press, 1946.

Phillips, Cabell. *The Truman Presidency*. Toronto, Ontario: Macmillan, 1966.

Public Papers of the United States Presidents: Harry S. Truman. 8 vols. Washington, D.C.: U.S. Government Printing Office, 1961.

Redding, Jack. *Inside the Democratic Party*. Indianapolis: Bobbs-Merrill, 1958.

Roosevelt, Eleanor. *The Autobiography of Eleanor Roosevelt*. Boston: G. K. Hall, 1984.

Roosevelt, Elliott, ed. *FDR: His Personal Letters*, 3 vols. New York: Duell, Sloan and Pearce, 1948.

Roosevelt, Sara (as told to Isabel Leighton and Gabrielle Forbush). *My Boy Franklin*. New York: Ray Long and Richard R. Smith, 1933.

Rosenman, Samuel I., ed. *The Public Papers and Addresses of Franklin D. Roosevelt*. 13 vols. New York: Random House, 1938.

———. *Working with Roosevelt*. New York: Da Capo Press, 1972.

Ross, Irwin. *The Loneliest Campaign: The Truman Victory of 1948*. Westport, Connecticut: Greenwood Press, 1968.

Russell, Francis. *The Shadow of Blooming Grove: Warren G. Harding and His Times*. New York: McGraw-Hill, 1968.

Sarett, Lew, and William Trufant Foster. *Basic Principles of Speech*. New York: Houghton Mifflin, 1936.

Schlesinger, Arthur M., Jr. *The Crisis of the Old Order, 1919–1933*. Boston: Houghton Mifflin, 1957.

———. *The Coming of the New Deal*. Boston: Houghton Mifflin, 1958.

———. *The Politics of Upheaval: The Age of Roosevelt*. Boston: Houghton Mifflin, 1960.

Sherwin, Martin J. *A World Destroyed: Hiroshima and the Origins of the Arms Race*. New York: Vintage Press, 1987.

Sherwood, Robert E. *Roosevelt and Hopkins: An Intimate History*. New York: Harper and Bros., 1948.

Sitkoff, Harvard, ed. *Fifty Years Later: The New Deal Evaluated*. New York: Oxford University Press, 1978.

Smith, Tim, ed. *Merriman Smith's Book of Presidents: A White House Memoir.* New York: W. W. Norton, 1972.

Stebbins, Richard P., ed. *The United States in World Affairs 1951.* New York: Harper and Bros., 1952.

Thompson, Kenneth W., ed. *Ten Presidents and the Press.* Washington, D.C.: University Press of America, 1983.

Thompson, Robert Smith. *A Time for War.* New York: Prentice Hall, 1991.

Truman, Harry S. *Mr. Citizen.* New York: Geis and Associates, 1953.

———. *Memoirs by Harry Truman,* Volume 1, *Year of Decisions.* Garden City, New York: Doubleday, 1955.

———. *Memoirs by Harry Truman,* Volume 2, *Years of Trial and Hope.* Garden City, New York: Doubleday, 1956.

Truman, Margaret. *Harry S. Truman.* New York: William Morrow, 1973.

Tugwell, Rexford G. *The Democratic Roosevelt.* Baltimore: Penguin Books, 1957.

Underhill, Robert. *The Truman Persuasions.* Ames: Iowa State University Press, 1981.

———. *The Bully Pulpit.* New York: Vantage Press, 1988.

Walker, Martin. *The Cold War.* New York: Henry Holt, 1994.

Ward, Geoffrey C. *Before the Trumpet: Young Franklin Roosevelt, 1882–1905.* New York: Harper and Row, 1985.

———. *A First-Class Temperament: The Emergence of Franklin Roosevelt.* New York: Harper and Row, 1989.

Wecter, Dixon. *The Age of the Great Depression, 1929–1941.* New York: Macmillan, 1948.

Willoughby, Charles A. *MacArthur 1941–1951.* New York: McGraw-Hill, 1954.

Wittner, Lawrence S. *The Rebels against War: The American Peace Movement, 1933–1984.* Philadelphia: Temple University Press, 1984.

Zevin, Ben D., ed. *Franklin D. Roosevelt: Nothing to Fear.* Boston: Houghton Mifflin, 1946.

JOURNALS, MAGAZINES, AND NEWSPAPERS

Atlantic Monthly
Bulletin of the Atomic Scientists
Chicago Daily Tribune
Chicago Sun-Times
Des Moines Register
Harvard Alumni Bulletin (Cambridge, Massachusetts: Shenandoah Valley Press)
Independence Examiner (Independence, Missouri)
Journalism Quarterly
Kansas City Journal Post
Kansas City Star
New Republic

New York Herald Tribune
New York Times
Omaha World-Herald
Public Opinion Quarterly
Quarterly Journal of Speech
St. Louis Post Dispatch
St. Louis Star
Saturday Evening Post
School and Society
U.S. News and World Report
Vital Speeches
Washington Post (Washington, D.C.)
Whistle Stop (Independence, Missouri: Harry S. Truman Library Newsletter)

ORAL HISTORIES AND OTHER SOURCES

Charles S. Murphy, Oral History Transcript, HSTL.
Charles T. Curry, Oral History Transcript, HSTL.
Clark Clifford, Papers, HSTL.
Columbia Masterworks Records ML 4905. Edward R. Murrow and Fred W. Friendly, "I Can Hear It Now—1933–1945."
Congressional Record.
David E. Bell, Oral History Transcript, HSTL.
Eban Ayers, Diary, HSTL.
Edgar Hinde, Oral History Transcript, HSTL.
Edward D. McKim, Oral History Transcript, HSTL.
Foreign Relations of the United States, Diplomatic Papers.
Franklin D. Roosevelt, Jr., Oral History, FDRL.
George Elsey, Papers, HSTL.
Harry S. Truman, Autobiography, HSTL.
Harry Vaughan, Papers, HSTL.
Invitational Conference, Truman Library Institute, May 5, 6, 7, 1977.
Jonathan Daniels, interview with Harry S. Truman, November 12, 1949, HSTL.
Joseph Lash, Papers, FDRL.
Martin Agronsky, filmed interview with Sam Rayburn, NBC.
Nuremberg Documents.
Personal letters to author.
Samuel Irving Rosenman, Oral History Transcript, HSTL.
Thomas Heed, "Prelude to Whistlestop: Harry S. Truman the Apprentice Campaigner" (Ph.D. diss., Columbia University, 1975), HSTL.
Vere Leigh, Oral History Transcript, HSTL.

Index

ROBERT UNDERHILL is Professor Emeritus of English and Speech at Iowa State University. His two earlier books on American presidents are *The Truman Persuasions* (1981) and *The Bully Pulpit* (1989).

ISBN 0-275-95420-X

90000>

EAN

9 780275 954208

HARDCOVER BAR CODE

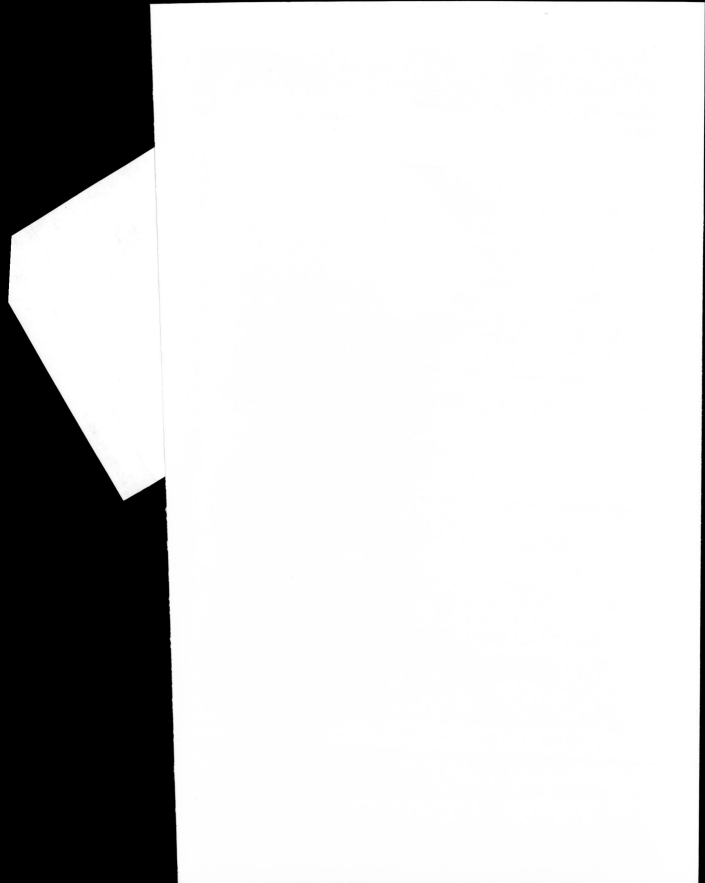

DATE DUE

AF

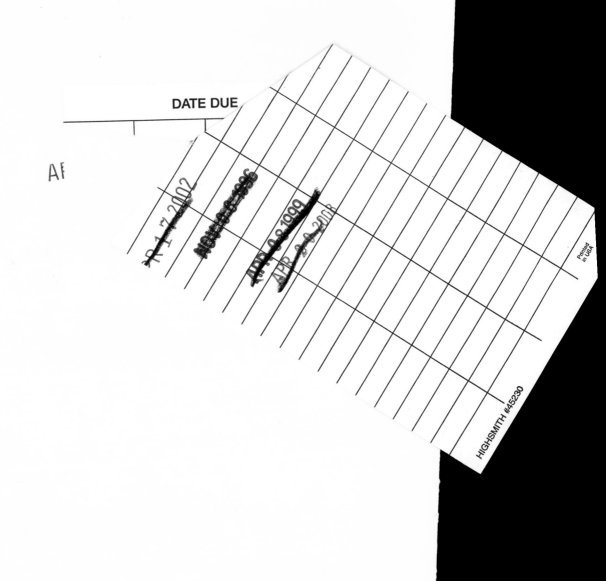

MAR 17 2002

NOV 06 1998

APR 09 1999

APR 26 2008

HIGHSMITH #45230

Printed
in USA